THE ART AND TECHNIQUE OF SOARING

THE ART AND TECHNIQUE OF SOARING

RICHARD A. WOLTERS

DRAWINGS BY EDWARD HANKE

McGRAW-HILL BOOK COMPANY
NEW YORK ST. LOUIS SAN FRANCISCO
DUSSELDORF LONDON MEXICO SYDNEY TORONTO

Library of Congress Catalog Card Number: 78-168460

6789 KPKP 7987

07-071560-2

Designed by Robert Aulicino

By the same author:

ONCE UPON A THERMAL

about dogs

CITY DOG

GUN DOG

FAMILY DOG

WATER DOG

INSTANT DOG

BEAU

LIVING ON WHEELS

DEDICATION

To Olive, my 115-pound crew chief and first mate

. . . who swings a 100-pound wing

. . . who swabs a sailplane down in nothing flat

. . . who checks the ship over like a mother hen

. . . who stays calm when I get uptight before a cross-country flight

. . . who faithfully remembers everything including shoving gum into my mouth the moment before take-off

. . . who pulls a 30-foot trailer over all kinds of countryside, using road maps and aircraft charts to follow me

. . . who stays glued to the car's aircraft radio awaiting my every command

. . . who sweats me out if contact is lost

. . . who figures out my position anyway

. . . who can and does flash me a smile when we meet hours later in some farmer's field.

ACKNOWLEDGMENTS

... Thanks to Ted Hanke, the artist who said when I approached him with this project, "The thought brings tears of joy to my eyes."

... Thanks to Ron Appelbe, aircraft photo specialist, for his technical help and keen photographic eyes.

... To Eddie Wilkinson, who rides the back seat and watches every move of his students, a thanks for looking over my shoulder too.

... Thanks to Ed Malsberg, who only flies a commuter train, but read every word to be sure the non-flier would understand it.

... Thanks to Paul Schweizer, America's leading sailplane manufacturer, for checking me out technically.

... Thanks also to a host of others: Art Hurst, Gordon Lamb, Margaret Kvaka, Bob Buck, Gleb Derujinsky, Cathy Branca, and every pilot I have flown with ... something from all of them is in this book.

TABLE OF CONTENTS

WHY THIS BOOK

When I decided to sail, I had an outboard motor on my boat. It gave me so much trouble that one day I threw it overboard, was freed, and became a purist. When I decided to fly, I decided to soar. After the first flight with my instructor he gave me a book to read, saying it was the best he had. The first chapter was on motors, carburetors, and things like that. It received the same treatment as the outboard.

During that first sailplane flight I fell in love with this spark-plugless sport, but I soon found out that there was very little written on the level I needed. Either the material was too simple, written with drawings for a twelve-year-old, or it was too advanced, written for an engineer who obviously could understand motors.

This book is written in words, not mathematical formulas. It's written for you to learn to soar, and for learning in the United States—not Great Britain or New Zealand. It's written for a whole new sector of our sporting population who are becoming infatuated with the idea of soaring like a bird and who do not know where to start. This book is for the beginner, the person starting from the nest.

There is plenty of literature singing the praises and glories of soaring. The challenge, excitement, and magnificence of this sport make for excellent prose, but they won't help you learn to fly. We don't spend much time on the history of gliding. Sure, it's fascinating, but it won't help you much at 3,000 feet. I'm assuming you have already seen the light, have been smitten by the idea, and want to taste its thrills yourself. The purpose of this book is information, to teach you to soar.

The book is not meant to be read like a novel. Going from cover to cover, you might become discouraged and feel you could never retain all this information. By rereading the appropriate chapters as you progress through your first year, you'll come to understand my approach. This is the material I wish I'd had when I started.

I've tried to write this book honestly without glossing over the hazards. Paul Schweizer, vice president of the Schweizer Aircraft Corporation, the largest manufacturer of sailplanes in the U.S., has said that the beginner should be advised of the hazards of soaring, just as he should if he were taking up skiing or scuba diving, but he should also be advised that the hazards are readily mastered with the proper training and procedure. I agree, and if you understand the problems they won't be problems.

Can all this be learned without previous flight training? Hundreds have done it that way. I did, and I'm still here, as this book proves.

R. A. W.

1 YOU SHOULD KNOW

Soaring evokes more curiosity and questions than any other sport. It seems to spark the imagination even of those who will never try it. Information about this game is scanty, and the poor soaring pilot is badgered with questions. Go to any gliderport on a pleasant summer day and watch a pilot start to prepare for the day's flight. Ten to one, some stranger will sidle up to watch, then start asking the questions.

It's understandable for those who are genuinely interested in learning to soar that they should have questions. If they don't, they'd better think twice about plunging into this game. Any kind of flying is only for the responsible person, and intelligent questions are an integral part of learning.

The first question that is asked, and should be asked, is:

HOW SAFE IS SOARING?

Soaring today *is* a safe sport, as the records will show. The uninitiated can be heard saying, "You wouldn't get me up in one of those things without a motor for a million dollars." Of course, they do not know what keeps a sailplane up for hours at a time, or that a motor with its volatile fuel is the most dangerous part of the power plane.

Soaring is no longer a self-taught art. The beginner is taken step by step through a rigorous training with an instructor. The Federal Aviation Agency regulates all soaring activity. It's interesting to note that it considers the sport safe enough to allow a fourteen-year-old to fly solo, whereas a youngster can't get a beginner's driving permit for a car until he's sixteen in most states.

Sailplanes are not flimsy affairs; they are built to withstand greater stresses than most light power planes.

The examination of the number of deaths in soaring and the cause of accidents is revealing. In the last three years, two deaths occurred when a pilot and passenger died doing acrobatics in an old plane that was not rated for acrobatics, and they were specifically warned about it beforehand. Five deaths were due to improper handling on landing. To prevent this sort of accident in soaring, the cardinal rule is to keep adequate flying speed near the ground. This is drilled into every student. It can be concluded that all the deaths were due to poor judgment, not being familiar with the equipment, and avoidable. Robert Buck, senior pilot for TWA and an avid soaring pilot, has concluded from all the FAA statistics that soaring is as safe as flying in a commercial airliner.

WHAT KEEPS A SAILPLANE UP WITHOUT A MOTOR?

The propeller forces air over the wings and the control surfaces of an airplane. The air that passes over and under the wings produces the lift. When it passes over the control surfaces, the airplane can maneuver. A sailplane flies by the same principle, except there is no propeller to force air over its surfaces. To accomplish this, a sailplane points its nose down and gravity produces the speed necessary to allow the flow of air to do exactly what it does for the airplane. That means the sailplane is always in a descending attitude. Of course, it can stay up for hours by flying in large masses of air that are ascending. In other words, a sailplane is always going down in air that is going up. When the updrafts ascend at a faster rate than the sailplane descends, the result will be a climb.

Some people have the impression that once aloft a sailplane floats around aimlessly until it comes down. They are amazed to learn it can climb. A sailplane has the same controls as an airplane, and it has ultimate controllability. In one important way power is an advantage; when a sailplane pilot starts his landing pattern he's committed to land. A sailplane does not have ability to fly around and attempt the landing again. It's got to be right the first time.

HOW MUCH CONTROL DO YOU HAVE FLYING A SAILPLANE?

The controls are basically the same as for an airplane; there are three. The ailerons turn the plane by banking it. The elevator controls the up and down attitude or speed, and the rudder helps the plane turn. The dive brakes and spoilers are an added control. They make a sailplane descend.

HOW MANY DIFFERENT CONTROLS DO SAILPLANES HAVE?

Nothing. The sailplane would fly itself. Often a pilot will do just that to rest for short periods of time.

WHAT WOULD HAPPEN IF YOU TOOK YOUR HANDS AND FEET OFF THE CONTROLS WHILE FLYING?

A sailplane is predictable, and in this respect is just like an airplane; to get it out of control the pilot has to be doing something awfully, awfully wrong.

CAN YOU BE SURE A SAILPLANE IS GOING TO GLIDE DOWN SAFELY AND NOT SUDDENLY SPIN OUT OF CONTROL?

HOW ARE SAILPLANES CONSTRUCTED?

This question usually implies that since there is no motor, sailplanes are more like kits and have to be light and therefore flimsy affairs. This is wrong on both counts. Sailplanes aren't light; they don't float on the air. Many competition planes even carry water tanks in their wings for added ballast. All sailplanes are built to withstand greater stress factors than most small power planes. A wide variety of materials is utilized, and new ones are being added to the list constantly. Today's glues are stronger than the materials they are bonding; a fabric-covered wooden ship is very strong. Many sailplanes are all aluminum and built like battleships. The latest material is fiberglass. Exact shapes can be molded without the bulk of supporting members and still have the necessary strength.

Whether flying a wooden, metal, or fiberglass plane, today's pilot can be unconcerned about structural failure in fully approved, licensed sailplanes when they are operated properly within design limitations.

On the production line at the Schweizer Aircraft Corp. sailplanes are manufactured with the same methods and materials as modern jets and engineered to sustain more stress than most powered craft.

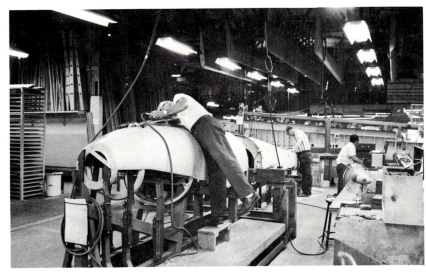

IS IT NECESSARY TO WEAR A PARACHUTE?

No, a chute is only required while doing acrobatics and for competition flying. Seats in a sailplane are designed so that chutes can be worn. Without them the pilot would be uncomfortable, and a pillow the size of the parachute would be necessary, so a chute is worn for comfort and assurance, just in case.

WHEN WOULD YOU USE A PARACHUTE?

Most pilots would answer "Never." The prospects of a licensed sailplane breaking up in flight due to structural failure are so remote that this wouldn't be considered a reason for wearing one. Midair collision would be the main reason; it's possible but not probable. Very few power pilots wear chutes. It is more difficult to get out of a small power plane. All sailplanes have quick-release canopies that jettison off, but most glider pilots agree that if possible they'd ride the plane down since there is no power to drive them into the ground or fuel to burn.

WHAT DOES IT COST TO START?

Soaring is within the means of almost any budget. For the person starting with no previous flight experience, it will cost about $500 at a commercial flying school to obtain a private pilot's license with glider rating. This cost can be cut substantially by joining a club that offers flight training.

Once the pilot has proved his proficiency, he will be able to rent a sailplane. The average cost of renting is $9 to $10 an hour, plus the cost of the tow.

WHAT IS THE TOW?

The early gliders were run down a hill into the wind, shoved off cliffs, or shot into the air as if by a slingshot. This latter method, called bungee launch, became the most efficient and commonly used. The tail of the plane was staked to the ground, the nose of the craft hooked to a heavy rubber rope, or bungee cord. Five to a dozen men on each end of the bungee would run forward. When they got "to the end of their rope," the stake cord was cut and the plane would be flung into the air.

The bungee launch. A pilot needs friends.

Today there are three accepted methods for launching. Auto tow is accomplished on a runway by pulling the sailplane like a kite with a long rope. A flexible single-strand wire is used in the second method. A motor-driven winch pulls the plane into the air. In both of these methods, once the plane has gathered speed, the pilot points it up and releases at the top of the arc. A good launch by these methods will produce up to 1,500 feet. Winch and auto tow are used more in Europe because they are relatively inexpensive. Practically all launching in this country is done by airplane. It's by far the safest method, and any desired altitude can be reached. The cost of air tow is about $6 to 3,000 feet, or $2 per 1,000 feet to any altitude.

Air tow is formation flying on a 200-foot line.

The sailplane pilot has a knob that he pulls which opens the hook. The tow pilot has a similar hook on the tail of the airplane. He can release the sailplane if something goes wrong with the sailplane's hook.

HOW DO YOU RELEASE FROM THE ROPE?

That's what the book is about. Popular belief is that it's the wind. Wind is the horizontal flow of air. Sailplanes climb on updrafts, or vertical movement of air. There are four updraft conditions operating in conjunction with the earth's surface that we know a good bit about today: ridge lift, thermals, sea breeze front, and mountain or lee wave. Two conditions, wind sheer and cold fronts,

ONCE THE SAILPLANE IS FREE, WHAT KEEPS IT UP?

Ridge lift

are not usually utilized by the beginner. We're just learning about the jet stream; when it is conquered, soaring flight may be extended even further.

Ridge lift is produced by a strong wind blowing against the face of an obstruction, such as a mountain ridge, so that air is deflected upward. The sailplane flies on the cushion of air that's deflected vertically.

Thermal flying is actually powered by the sun, and can take place during daylight hours any place on the globe. The sun heats the earth at different rates according to the makeup of the surface. A field of dark soil, for example, will heat up more than a wooded area. The heat of the sun does not heat the air. The air is warmed from ground heat, and since the ground is of different temperatures according to its makeup, the air above it will be heated unevenly. It will rise over the warmest areas. The rising air goes up like a bubble and can have tremendous power. The sailplane flies one of these bubbles, or thermals, by staying within its confines as it goes up.

A sea breeze front is caused by the air over the land being warmed more than the air over the water. The warm air rises, and the cool air moves in from the sea and acts like a small cold front. The cool air moves in under the warm air and lifts it up. It is the rising air in this area of convergence that keeps the sailplane up.

The lee wave is produced because air, like water, is a fluid. Under certain conditions they both make waves. Visualize an ocean wave: it goes up, forms a crest, then goes down. The sailplane flies on the up side of the air wave.

HOW HIGH WILL A SAILPLANE GO?

It's almost unbelievable to think that a powerless plane can achieve heights in a mountain wave that are beyond the flights of our commercial jet liners. Flights of almost 50,000 feet have been made in such air waves. This is the limit of man's capability on oxygen alone; beyond it a pressure system is necessary. When that happens, what heights will be reached? Waves are known to go up 100,000 feet.

HOW FAR WILL A SAILPLANE FLY ON THERMALS?

By repeatedly climbing in a thermal and then flying on to the next thermal, cross-country flights of over 700 miles have been made. Flights of several hundred miles are commonplace. The power of a good thermal updraft can enable a plane to climb from 500 to 1,500 feet a minute.

HOW LONG CAN YOU STAY UP?

Ridge soaring is the easiest way to stay aloft. At one phase of the progress in soaring history, duration flights were the ultimate goal. This soon proved to be fruitless. Ridge-flying flights of over 60 hours were made. Such records were discontinued after a few pilots fell asleep and killed themselves. These flights proved two things: that man could stay awake a long time and that a wind could blow steadily and interminably in a direction perpendicular to a ridge.

We'll discuss later how to find the place. If you already know where there is a gliderport, the first thing you should do is take a flight in a two-seater, a trainer ship. The flight will be safer than the car trip you made to the gliderport. It will cost about $10, including the tow. The flight will last about a half hour, and once aloft the pilot will allow you to try your hand at the controls if you wish. They're dual, so he'll be able to take over at any point. If you display interest, he'll explain everything he's doing. If you have any doubt about flying with a stranger, relax; he's required to have his commercial pilot rating, so he's approved by the FAA to fly for hire.

HOW DO YOU GET STARTED?

Yes. All flying is under the jurisdiction of the FAA. A student license is required before soloing. Any licensed instructor can initiate the application. There is no cost involved. The student must be fourteen years old before he can pilot the sailplane, but he may take instruction before that. There is no upper age limit. It's required that an applicant read, speak, and understand English, and it must be certified that there is no known physical defect making him unable to pilot a glider. No physical examination is necessary. The student license is good for two years and is renewable. Student pilots may not carry passengers, nor may they operate the sailplane in solo flight outside a designated area without the instructor's permission. There are many restrictions on the student pilot, but the safety record justifies these precautions.

IS A LICENSE REQUIRED?

The student must be sixteen years old, and all other requirements are the same as for a student license. He also must pass a written test given by the FAA. There are only a few schools that give the ground course for the glider rating examination. Some of the clubs offer it, but most students study for the written exam on their own. The test covers regulations, traffic rules, cross-country flying, meteorology, evaluation of weather reports, flight problems, and safety. The FAA will furnish a list of the study materials needed. The examination is not difficult, yet it is tricky. Not only do the examiners want to see if a student knows the facts; they also want him to demonstrate that he can think.

WHAT'S REQUIRED FOR A PRIVATE PILOT'S LICENSE WITH GLIDER RATING?

Practically all the students in this country take their training using aero tow. They will need at least 30 flights and 10 hours of flying time. The regulations do not specify how much of the time must be dual with an instructor, but the average student will require a little more than the 10-hour minimum.

After the student takes and passes the written examination, has logged the required amount of flight time, and demonstrates satisfactorily to his instructor that he is going to make a qualified pilot, he'll be signed out for a flight test with an FAA examiner. On passing the flight test he'll receive his license.

Naturally it depends on the individual, and in some ways the weather. It's possible to take a concentrated course at a soaring school and get the rating in two weeks. The weekend flyer can do it

HOW LONG WILL IT TAKE TO GET A LICENSE?

in three to four months if he works at it. Once a student starts, he should plan to take lessons on a regular schedule. Progress will be faster if there aren't long time lapses between lessons, since there seems to be a rhythm to the learning pattern.

WILL POWER FLIGHT EXPERIENCE HELP?

Yes, but it's not necessary. The advantage of power experience is that time spent in the air can be built up fast; even a lot of passenger time in a small plane will help. Learning to fly is not only learning the mechanics of driving the machine but also learning to operate in a new environment. Many instructors like to teach the basic controls in a power plane since they are the same as in a glider, and they can stay in the air until the lessons are learned. But it can work both ways. The soaring pilot who takes up power flying will fly "cleaner" and with more precision. The power pilot learns to let the engine "drag" him through the maneuvers; a soaring pilot must fly by carefully coordinating the controls. In cross-country soaring, previous navigation experience would be valuable, but this can be learned by navigating with aeronautical charts as a passenger in a small plane.

HOW DO YOU NAVIGATE IN A SAILPLANE?

Sailplanes are flown in what are known as VFR conditions (visual flight rules). Cloud flying is forbidden unless the pilot is instrument-rated, the ship equipped for blind flying, a flight plan filed, and clearance given by Air Traffic Control. But this all becomes academic, since soaring requires fair weather, and cross-country flights can't be made and shouldn't be attempted in poor conditions. Therefore, ground visibility is always going to be at least adequate.

It should be obvious that a straight course between two points is an improbability in a sailplane, so sophisticated navigational equipment is useless. To get from point A to point B, one has to fly where the lift is. This means you will fly in the general direction of point B. A direct compass course can't be used, but it will provide a general heading to follow. This leaves one alternative, and it's a rather simple one, to follow your progress on an aeronautical chart. It's the road map of the air, and its symbols show all the major features on the ground that you'll see from the air. Simple pilotage can be practiced around the home base; it doesn't take long to get the hang of it. The compass gives you a general direction. Your chart tells you where you are. Your actual flight might be a zigzag along a course, and you'll continually change compass heading and fly for landmarks ahead that will constantly bring you back on course. For example, if you climb in a thermal and the whole air mass drifts you 5 miles off course, you'll want to glide back onto course to find your next thermal. To fly from A to B you may have to fly to a dozen intermediate points, but you'll always know approximately where you are. There is enough information on the charts to pinpoint your exact location if you wish.

No, and for that reason cross-country flying should not be tried until the pilot has had sufficient landing experience. He'll practice short field and spot landings at his home field until he has perfect control.

CAN YOU ALWAYS REACH YOUR DESTINATION?

A clearing, a farmer's field, a golf course, and in some parts of the country roads are used for landing. A 150-yard landing field is more than ample space. A pilot learns to "read" the terrain to pick a likely spot, and once he touches down he only needs 50 yards or less to stop the roll-out.

WHERE DO YOU LAND IF YOU DON'T REACH AN AIRPORT?

A pilot never lets himself get into that situation. He'll never leave an area where there are landing areas if he doesn't have enough height to get onto the next landing spot.

WHAT HAPPENS IF THERE IS NO PLACE TO LAND?

They're so fascinated about the motorless craft that if the pilot is polite the farmer will give him a hand with his plane. Rarely does one hear of a farmer who gives a pilot a hard time. The pilot will try to pick a field that has just been harvested or plowed so there will be no crop damage. If crop damage is sustained, the pilot should offer to pay.

WHAT DOES A FARMER SAY ABOUT THAT?

He should have liability insurance for his own protection. Most pilots carry fire, theft, and nonflying accident coverage. Hull or in-flight insurance is available but expensive.

DOES A PILOT CARRY INSURANCE?

In some cases you could call for a tow plane to come and tow you back into the air, but the usual procedure is for the pilot to radio or phone for his crew to bring the plane's trailer. The sailplane is dismantled and loaded and trailered home.

IF YOU LAND IN A FARMER'S FIELD, HOW DO YOU RETRIEVE THE PLANE?

IS THAT A BIG JOB?

Most modern plane manufacturers claim the job can be done in three minutes. Actually it's a 10-minute job for two people. Older planes will require three people and a little longer time, but it's a very simple job. The ease of dismantling is an important part of the design; manufacturers will supply a trailer for the glider, or it can be home-built.

DO SAILPLANES HAVE RADIOS?

Most do, especially when cross-country flying is to be attempted. The pilot's ground crew is usually equipped with very high frequency (VHF) radio so it can stay in communication from the ground. Two aircraft channels are set aside for training and glider operations, 123.3 and 123.5 megacycles.

WHAT OTHER INSTRUMENTS DO SAILPLANES HAVE?

A compass, air speed indicator, and altimeter are required for licensing. The variometer is a fast-acting rate-of-climb indicator and is extremely important. It tells if the sailplane is in a rising or sinking mass of air. A stop watch or clock with a sweep second hand is very useful. The rest depend on your pocketbook.

WHAT DOES A SAILPLANE COST?

Because of the limited market, no manufacturer has attempted to mass-produce sailplanes, so the price is high. The range is from $5,000 to $10,000. The most popular sailplane in this country is the 1-26 single-seater manufactured by the Schweizer Aircraft Corporation; it costs about $5,500 and is available in kits for $3,500.

Sailplanes are a very good investment because the demand for secondhand ships is high. Unlike automobiles, sailplanes hold their value because there is nothing to wear out and the sport is growing faster than the supply of planes.

Added to the cost of the plane is the trailer. A good, fitted, covered trailer of fiberglass or aluminum will cost $1,000 to $1,500. Many pilots make their own at a cost of a few hundred dollars.

Instruments will cost from $200 for the bare minimum to $2,000. Selection depends on the pocketbook.

The initial investment is high!

HOW MUCH IS THE UPKEEP?

This is the best part of the costs of soaring. Hangar space at a commercial gliderport is about $20 a month. It costs about $25 to get the plane inspected each year. The only other expenses are insurance and the cost of the tows. Minor repairs are made by the pilot.

DO YOU HAVE TO OWN YOUR OWN PLANE?

Partnerships are very common in soaring. Two or more pilots will get together and jointly own and split the expenses. It's like any other game, they've got to get along. Soaring is a sport in which teamwork plays a very important role. Even if you are an individual owner there is a lot of groundwork to the sport. You've got to help the other guy get into the air, and in return he'll help you.

WHAT ABOUT CLUBS?

A club operation is a very satisfactory way to fly for those who don't want to make the initial investment or feel they won't fly enough to justify the expenditure. Most clubs operate and own the basic equipment—tow plane, two-place trainers, and intermediate single-place sailplanes for local flying. The cost varies; some sell stock and some have an initiation fee of a few hundred dollars. Current operating costs are usually handled by monthly dues. Some clubs are highly organized, and some are loose-knit affairs.

HOW DO YOU FIND OUT ABOUT CLUBS?

The Soaring Society of America keeps a current list of both the commercial establishments and the clubs that are operating in the country. Some clubs require that your initial training be taken at a commercial school, and others will start a student from scratch. Although the clubs are strictly for flying, you'll find they are social as well.

WHAT IS THE SOARING SOCIETY OF AMERICA?

Like any organization, it's many things to many people. If you are a beginner and want to find out where to fly in your area, the SSA can tell you. If you are a competition pilot and want to know how to qualify for the national championships, the SAA can tell you.

The society was started in 1932 when a group of pilots got together to organize that year's national competition. Today it has much to offer the individual pilot. *Soaring* alone, its monthly magazine, is worth the yearly dues. It also publishes a directory listing its membership, places to soar, commercial establishments, clubs, records, awards, flying regulations, and much miscellaneous information about the sport.

The SAA is our representative to the Federation Aeronautique Internationale, with headquarters in Paris. The FAI is the international organization recognized as the governing body in charge of aviation records, championships, and achievement awards.

The society conducts a continual national safety program, represents the soaring pilot with the federal regulatory agencies, has research and development programs, and in general assists local groups in organizing. One of its main functions is to sanction regional contests, run the national championships, and sponsor teams for international competition.

WHAT KIND OF COMPETITION DOES SOARING OFFER?

There is every level of competition, so the answer is not a simple one. The learning itself is one form. You will soon discover that you are always out to beat your own record, and for those who like this kind of competition, soaring offers a formal program.

It originated in the early days in Germany and was soon adopted by all countries affiliated with the FAI. The qualifications for each of the awards are set forth in the Sporting Code of the Federation Aeronautique Internationale. In those early years they were the A, B, and C badges. A was for a 30-second solo flight, and C, the highest award, was for a five-minute flight above the point of release. This doesn't sound like much of an accomplishment today. The requirements for the awards have changed to keep pace with the progress of the sport, and today there is the Silver Badge, the Gold Badge, and the Gold with Diamonds.

The SSA has been delegated the authority to administer the awards in this country for the FAI. Each country has its own association responsible to the world organization. So although you are competing against yourself for the badges, the same rules and proof of completion apply, no matter where in the world you are flying. A pilot in Russia, South Africa, New Zealand, or 60 miles from New York City must accomplish the same tasks to be awarded the lapel pin. The pin, three white gulls on a blue background, is surrounded by a wreath. The badges are truly an international common language, each having the country's designated aircraft identification letter, and they are numbered consecutively.

Three accomplishments are necessary for the Silver Badge with silver wreath: an altitude gain of 3,280 feet above a low point in a flight, a single flight of five hours duration, and a cross-country flight of 32.2 miles.

The Gold Badge requires an altitude gain of 9,700 feet and a cross-country flight of 186 miles, plus the five hour duration, which does not have to be repeated if it was already accomplished in winning the silver award.

A diamond can be added to the gold wreath for each of the following achievements: an altitude gain of 16,400 feet, a flight of 186 miles to a preannounced goal, and a distance flight of 312 miles.

Official observers, cameras, and barographs are used as proof, and the wearer of any pin can be quite proud of his accomplishment.

DO SAILPLANES COMPETE AGAINST EACH OTHER?

Yes, in the mildest to the most grueling kinds of meets. Open-house or picnic meets make pleasant weekend fun where the whole family joins in. In such meets, eating is as important as the flying. Tasks are simple and usually set so all contestants will arrive back at the gliderport in time for the food. "Little Guys" meets are springing up all over the country. They are low-pressure competitions primarily to teach cross-country flying in ships of low performance.

In this country we have a one-design-class competition. The Schweizer 1-26 owners have sufficient numbers so that they have a national organization. They run 1-26 regattas which again are fun meets, and they run regional and national championships. In these meets food is secondary; some of the best pilots in the country fly in these competitions.

The SSA regulates sanctioned regional competitions. Besides the trophies, the pilots of the regionals are competing for a place in the national event held yearly. The winners of the nationals are fighting for a place on the U.S. team to fly in the biannual World Championship.

A Silver Badge is a requirement for the five-day regional event, and the Gold is necessary for the nationals. These events are usually grueling affairs. Close teamwork is needed between a retrieving crew and pilot. Flights of 300 miles are common, and even 500-mile flights are accomplished. Ten days of this in a national or international event calls for stamina and cool nerves. The pilot and plane are only as good as his crew and its trailer. A simple thing such as a car or a trailer breakdown can put the pilot out of the contest.

The interesting thing about regional competitions is that inexperienced pilots are eligible to fly. That's how one learns to become a competitive pilot. The "big boys" go out of their way to bring a new pilot along. Soaring is one of the few sports where this is so.

Speed and distance tasks. A pilot flies through a "starting gate," then goes off on course. The usual flight is an out and return, a flight around a triangle, or just free flight in any direction. The flight is in a prescribed direction, around turn points which are photographed. Some tasks call for free flight after the triangle is completed, or free flight within a prescribed area. The task is set up by the committee according to the weather conditions for the day.

WHAT ARE THE TASKS IN A COMPETITION?

A final glide over a finish line at 150 mph is not uncommon.

HOW FAST WILL A COMPETITION PLANE FLY?

The design of each plane determines its optimum gliding speed; it's usually 15 to 20 mph above the stall speed. The range can vary for planes of different performance from 45 to 60 mph.

WHAT'S THE AVERAGE FLYING SPEED?

There is confusion about the word "stall"; most people associate it with an engine. A sailplane like an airplane has to have enough speed so its wings will support its weight. If the flying speed is too slow, it will not fly; that's the stall. Some sailplanes stall at as low as 28 mph, others at as high as 45.

A SAILPLANE DOESN'T HAVE AN ENGINE. HOW CAN IT HAVE A STALL SPEED?

There are high-performance and low-performance planes. Students and beginners fly the low-performance planes. They are "forgiving" and easy to fly. Performance is usually expressed as L/D, which means lift over drag. This measurement is made gliding in still air; for every foot the plane drops it will go forward a certain distance. A low-performance trainer could have an L/D of 17 to 1

WHAT IS MEANT BY SAILPLANES OF DIFFERENT PERFORMANCE?

(1) A contest day starts with a pilots' meeting. A weather briefing is given, the cross-country task for the day is announced and the pilots choose their take-off time. (2) Planes are assembled and checked in preparation for starting line-up on the runway. (3) Every two minutes a plane is towed aloft. (4) The trailers are readied for the word from the pilot that he will go through the start gate and off on course. (5) The crew follows on main highways or back roads in order to stay under their pilot, if possible. (6) Aircraft radio in the car and plane makes it possible to keep in contact. In a contest, a smart crew is as important as a smart pilot. (7) A downed pilot is retrieved by his crew. The trailer will be brought into the field for disassembly of the sailplane. It'll be loaded on the trailer and returned to the airport.

(17 feet forward for every foot of altitude lost). Open-class competition ships have an L/D of almost 50 to 1. The break point in this definition is about 30. Ships of low performance, below 30 to 1, are good in very weak conditions because they are floaters. High-performance planes can penetrate against the wind and can fly at high speeds without losing altitude fast.

WHAT ARE OPEN-CLASS SHIPS?

Sailplanes are divided into two classes, open and standard. The specifications of the standard class are set down by an international committee. The aim is to limit the size and features to keep the costs within bounds. For example, a standard ship may not have a wing span more than 15 meters, almost 50 feet. Anything goes in the open class; they're being made with wing spans of over 67 feet, and the cost is proportional. Standard planes won't have the performance of the open class, but their smaller size is in many ways an advantage, especially on the ground.

WHAT SEASONS OF THE YEAR DO YOU FLY?

Sailplanes are flown in good weather in all seasons. It depends on the location of the airport and whether it has snow removal equipment. If it does, winter makes no difference. Of course, sailplanes don't have heaters, so warm clothes and electric socks might be necessary.

IF YOU GOT INTO A STRONG UPDRAFT, COULD YOU COME DOWN?

The dive brakes and spoilers are designed to kill the lift over a portion of the wings and will allow you to descend at any desired rate of speed. Many sailplanes have what are known as terminal velocity brakes: the plane can be headed straight down, zooming toward the earth, and with the brakes extended the ship will never exceed the speed that will cause structural damage.

DO PILOTS USE OXYGEN?

Yes, some ships are equipped to carry oxygen. It should be used above 10,000 feet.

SOARING SOUNDS EXCITING. IS IT FUN?

Yes, it is, but it's work. Many popular-magazine writers get carried away when writing about the sport. A pilot is busy making decisions, continually searching for "fuel," and calculating the effect of the constantly changing conditions on his flight. Floating like a bird? Lord of the skies? Possibly so, but the human computer is a closer analogy.

WHAT SPECIAL TALENTS ARE NEEDED?

If you can handle a car well, make quick decisions, and are safe behind a wheel, you'll be able to fly a sailplane. Any kind of flying requires planning, then executing the plan step by step. Good body coordination is essential. Decision making, keeping cool, and sticking to a procedure will keep a pilot out of trouble. More to the point, the special talent would be self-confidence. This is what the instructor instills in a student.

IS SOARING SCARY?

Fear only comes from things you don't understand. The training will be so complete that you'll understand what the game is all about. No, it's not a scary sport, but that isn't the same as saying you'll never be scared. No pilot can claim that.

WHERE DOES ONE SOAR?

Naturally it should be as close to home as possible so that as much time as possible can be spent in the air. This is not the kind of sport one participates in only while vacationing. The Soaring Society publishes a complete listing of gliderport operations. Some are better than others, and generally you'll be stuck with the one nearest to you.

Practically every state in the Union has active soaring facilities.

WHERE ELSE DOES ONE SOAR?

If you own your own ship, the possibilities are limitless. If not, you will be restricted to commercial operations, but the best locations usually have planes for rent. You will be required to present your log book or your license and take a check ride with an instructor before you may rent equipment. Hertz should do the same thing; it's expensive to be second best.

Soaring, the SSA's monthly magazine, features a monthly calendar. It lists not only the sanctioned competitions but also the weekend events. Practically all long holiday weekends give soaring enthusiasts the excuse to have an event. You will be welcome and have a good time even if it rains.

The fun of the game is to explore different areas. This can be done inexpensively by hooking the sailplane and trailer behind the family car and with the camping gear aboard make the rounds of the different weekend events. Camping seems to go hand in hand with soaring.

WHAT ABOUT SOARING VACATIONS?

Ski areas provide excellent soaring conditions, so it's only natural that many of these areas are putting in glider operations as an off-season attraction. Accommodations can be whatever you want, from primitive camping to luxury hotels. *Soaring* carries ads for many of the facilities that cater to the vacationer. Great vacations can be had from Hawaii to the Virgin Islands, from Sugarbush, Vermont, to Tehachapi, California. Spectacular mountain flying and vacationing can be had at such places as Colorado Springs and Bishop, California. In the East, Harris Hill at Elmira, New York, caters to the soaring buff.

There are almost 300 listed locations in the country and the number is growing, yet the sport has a character about it that makes it more like a fraternal organization. There is very little snobbishness around a soaring site. It's a cooperative sport, so nice people are always welcome.

WHAT KIND OF A SPORT IS SOARING?

Soaring is unique; it cannot be compared with any team games, since one man must be quarterback, pitcher, goal keeper, batsman, manager, captain, and even back-up substitute. In some ways it's like golf. There the opponent is the ball, or is it yourself? Skiing possibly comes closer; you can't overextend in golf, but the skier is often called upon to plow new paths at high speed under uncertain conditions. Fast decisions must be made, and body coordination is essential. Is the soaring pilot like the bird hunter who is always safety-conscious? When his judgment is off and coordination lacking, he misses the bird and only gets an empty pot and a sneer from his dog. Part of soaring has the thrill of car racing; it, too, requires cool nerves, absolute understanding of the machine, concentration, and split-second planning. Sailing might even be closer; it's man against the elements. His knowledge, self-confidence, and even the boat are pitted against all the forces the weather or sea can throw at him. The potential of danger heightens the excitement of sailing. Navigation is essential in sailing and soaring and is an extremely gratifying skill. There are many technical similarities between the two-dimensional world of sailing and the three dimensions of soaring.

In our society today there is very little opportunity to express a pioneering spirit. Here is a sport that accommodates this need. Exploration, achievement, and competition play basic roles in sport. Soaring has all three.

Take a little piece of all of these sports, add the motivations for them, put them in the cockpit of a sailplane, and you'll have a soaring enthusiast. His bag won't be the mountain goat or the salmon; the hawk is his nearest kindred spirit.

IT'S GOING TO BE LIKE THIS

Once the canopy is closed you're pretty much committed to the flight. If you like it, you have said, you might go on and take your student training. They've put you in the front seat of the trainer, and although you wouldn't dare say so, the seat belt and shoulder harness are comforting. Later you'll chuckle at this first ambivalence, but for now you might as well go through the motions of these thoughts and get them out of the way. The sailplane, so graceful in flight, is clumsy, lopsided, and out of its element on the ground. Sitting in it, waiting for takeoff, you feel awkward. You've prepared yourself the best you can for the new experience, but even now, before it starts, something seems wrong. The world's already cockeyed, but you don't realize why until the lowered wing is lifted off the ground and held level by the wing boy . . . a signal to start the flight. Your instructor is at the controls behind you. Takeoff speed is not as fast as driving your car, but some giggle or tend to grab on because they're above the ground, flying . . . flying parallel to it. When the tow plane gathers its speed and is off, that's when things change . . . fast. Why does the new pilot tend to look down? Is it because he's breaking his earthly ties, for the first time? Is it because he's seeing old familiar things from a new perspective and they are strange and exciting? Weren't trees to be seen from the trunks up? Now, houses seen from the roofs down? Roads seen from all the way around their curves? Cars get smaller and smaller and move slower and slower. Leaves no longer exist, they're blobs of color, so are the fields. Things seem unreal . . . you're detached. People and their emotions are down there only because you know it. When you break with below, there is a whole new vista, out and away . . . mountains . . . sky . . . rivers . . . towns. That spectrum, it's rewarding in the silence.

2

THE PAST

SOARING: WHENCE IT CAME

If you're an adventurous person who has been jaded by the less exciting sports, then soaring may be the answer for you. What man hasn't followed the flight of a soaring bird with envy and admiration, envy for the freedom from earthly ties and admiration for the skill and effortless beauty of flight? All men have had an atavistic desire to fly.

The story goes that while the sorcerer Simon Magnus was flying around ancient Rome he was shot down by Saint Peter with some well-aimed prayers. This may have had a dampening effect on the art of flying. A thousand years later, in Constantinople, a Saracen stood on the tower facing the Hippodrome. He stuffed his flowing white robe with willow branches and, at the urging of the waiting crowd below, flapped down. They blotted him up with a prayer rug. The word hadn't been passed to John Damien, fifteenth-century court physician to King James III of Scotland. Poor John was buried on the spot, below the tower. The monk Oliver of Malmesbury, "causet to mak ane pair of wingis" and crossly announced after breaking both his legs that he had forgotten to fit a tail to his hinder parts. Is it possible that King Lear was mad because his father was killed practicing the necromantic arts by flying over the ancient site of London?

The great minds of our Western world—Leonardo, Albertus Magnus, Roger Bacon—all dabbled with the theory of flight but made very little real contribution to the art. Dante, the mathematician of Perugia, has been credited with several faltering gliding flights over Lake Trasimeno about 1490. He returned to his mathematics, and lived.

Flight has always been part of man's folklore and his art. He probably always dreamed of flying, and to satisfy his frustration adorned his gods with wings. Eight centuries before Christ the Chinese god of thunder had wings of a bat. Ahura Mazda, the Persian god of gods, was a winged disk guarded by winged lions with human heads. The Egyptian goddess Isis appears with outstretched wings on the sarcophagus of Ramses III. "Winged Victory," the magnificent statue from the isle of Samothrace, was only one of the crowd of Greek gods to have wings. Hermes later reappeared as the Roman god Mercury. When Christianity replaced paganism in the West, wings were incorporated with renewed emphasis in the art and literature of the new religion. Throughout the Renaissance wings were associated with the good things of life, such as love and religion. Death was made attractive by them. Even today, what prisoner hasn't dreamed of wings? They symbolize freedom.

Flight has never been far removed from man's thoughts. Perhaps his innate fascination stems from his early migrations across the earth; possibly he lightened the drudgery of his travels by wishful fantasies as he watched the birds flying gracefully over obstacles while he toiled arduously on the earth.

Through the centuries man slowly conquered much of his environment, and now has even reached the moon, but it was only 160-odd years ago that the first effective theories were advanced about manned flight. Sir George Cayley's articles published in 1809 on aerial navigation stood for a hundred years as the best material on the subject.

Historians can now trace a direct line of successful contributions from Cayley's research to the flights of the Wright brothers. Although Captain LeBris, a Frenchman, isn't in the mainstream of the progress, his story should be told. He was only one of hundreds who tried their hand at flying. Like most sailors, the captain was infatuated by the albatross, which explains much of his success. He built an "artificial bird" that weighed 92 pounds, had a 50-foot wing span, and looked like an albatross. He set the whole creature in a cart, hired a driver, and headed both contraptions into a 10-mile-an-hour wind. LeBris stood erect in the boat-like body and by an arrangement of levers varied the inclination of the wings. His flight was a success. At the propitious moment, with the horse at full gait, he released the ropes that secured the rig to the cart. There is only one hitch to the flight: the rope accidentally encompassed the waist of the cart driver. The bird soared up 300 feet carrying the cheering, triumphant sailor as the screaming, terrified peasant dangled below to become the first nonpaying passenger in history.

The problems of flight remained an unsolved mystery to the world until Otto Lilienthal, an engineer from Berlin, put the Cayley theories into practice. He is rightly regarded as the apostle of gliding

flight. He made hundreds of steady glides from an artificial hill. His 44-pound plane carried him over a distance of 300 feet; Lilienthal was the first to understand and use gravity as his motor power and stability in flight control.

Lilienthal's method of maintaining balance in the air was by shifting his weight. In 1896, on the first flight where he decided to change this method for a more advanced system, he met his death.

THE EARLY AMERICAN SCENE

Late in life Octave Chanute, a railroad engineer, devoted his interests to gliding. He was already knowledgeable about the dynamics of flight and familiar with Lilienthal's gliding experiments. His flights were conducted on the shore of Lake Michigan.

Chanute was the first to predict that motor power would not be necessary for long flights. "The machine," he wrote, "would be so constructed that the position of the center of gravity would give the apparatus a downward inclination. With such a machine one would circle like a bird, rise spirally like a bird and soar in any direction."

Professor J. J. Montgomery, whose experiments were of a singular nature, might be forgotten if it weren't for the spectacular flights of Daniel Maloney flying in the professor's craft. At Santa Clara, California, Maloney was lifted by a hot air balloon to a height of 4,000 feet and cut loose.

"In the course of the descent," a newspaper account stated, "the most extraordinary and complex maneuvers were accomplished—spirals and circling turns were executed with ease and grace almost beyond description, level flight with and against the wind, figure-eight evolutions performed without difficulty, and hair-raising dives with speeds, as estimated by eye-witnesses, of over sixty-eight miles an hour, and yet after a flight of approximately eight miles in twenty minutes the machine was brought to rest upon a previously designated spot, three-quarters of a mile from where the balloon had been released, so lightly that the aviator was not even jarred, despite the fact that he was compelled to land on his feet, not on a special alighting gear."

Chanute characterized that flight as "the most daring fete [sic] ever attempted." Even today the flight of that kite-like contraption would seem spectacular, but such events didn't prepare the public for the Wright brothers. Few were ready to dare believe that man could fly, and Maloney's death on a subsequent flight reinforced their belief.

THE BROTHERS WRIGHT

Soaring flight rather than motor flight was the ultimate goal of the brothers. Their success in both areas can be attributed to their recognition that much of the available information was wrong.

Wilbur wrote, "We had taken up aeronautics merely as a sport. We reluctantly entered upon the scientific side of it."

Every schoolboy knows the rest of their story. Their gliding experiments were so successful that it was merely a matter of adding their 12-horsepower motor to their best glider to attain flight.

The country was not ready for their success. The advent of powered flight excited nothing more than curiosity in this country. Europe acclaimed the Wright brothers before their achievement was accepted in America. Finally Teddy Roosevelt instructed the Army to investigate this new gadget to estimate its worth. Ironically, soaring—without which powered flight was impossible—was relegated to the shadows.

World War I gave power flying a premature impetus. After the war flying languished, and there was very little commercial outlet for the machine or its pilot. War stories gave the whole industry a daredevil aura. In this country it was powered flight that attracted the few who were interested in aviation.

A gliding renaissance was forced on Germany by the terms of the Versailles Treaty. The Rhone Gliding Meet of 1912 was reinstated in 1920. The results of that and the next year's meet showed that there was no substantial improvement in the art. Shortly after the 1921 competition the first breakthrough came. Herr Klemperer flew a monoplane glider for 13 minutes, and a few weeks later Herr Harth flew for 21 minutes. Orville Wright's record was broken, but no one in this country seemed to care.

At best, the renaissance was short-lived. Improvements were slow, and gliding did not capture the fancy of the general public. A stagnation also became evident in general aviation. Flying was for the daredevils and barnstormers. The aeroplane payloads were small, with little commercial value. Flying for the flapper society was a joy ride, and in this country they were doing most of their flying on bathtub gin.

Late in 1927 the world made an about-face; it found a hero. Lucky Lindy captured the hearts and admiration of all men. The public could relate to this shy, retiring, good-looking kid. Everyone became aviation-conscious.

A less spectacular event occurred in soaring a year later. The variometer was invented by Lippisch and Kronfeld. This instrument was to become the breakthrough to soaring; it would allow even the inexperienced pilot to find and stay within the confines of a thermal. The glider would become a sailplane and be able to both ascend and descend. The sport of motorless flight received an impetus from a newly discovered energy source. In 1929 Kronfeld flew to 6,000 feet and traveled 90 miles cross-country in a storm cloud.

THE DOLDRUM YEARS

ELMIRA, AMERICA'S CAPITAL

During the early 1930s in this country, there was a small group of dedicated purists who continued in search of true soaring flight. Elmira, New York, was the center of their activity, and even today that city advertises itself as the "Gliding Capital of America." The broad valleys and high ridges there, much like the Rhone Valley, offered excellent ridge-soaring conditions. It was there in 1930 that Wolf Hirth, a visitor from Germany, flew the first blue-sky thermal flight. Prior to this it was believed that thermals were only associated with storm clouds.

Eyewitnesses claim that they thought Hirth had gone out of his mind. After the takeoff, instead of following the ridge, he flew straight out over the valley. He started to circle, and up he went.

A picture from the S.S.A. Historical Museum at Elmira of a launch from Harris Hill

By flying to Appalachin, New York, about 40 miles, Hirth made the first cross-country flight in the U.S.

Who was the first American to break away from the ridge in a soaring thermal flight? The answer is challengeable, but Emil Lehecka, one of the pioneers, claims it was Richard DuPont. "We didn't use only one site at Elmira for launch, we had many. It all depended on the direction of the prevailing wind. We had learned to stay up for hours on end if the wind held out. We were flying from site number four, and Richard decided it was time to go home. Instead of taking the plane apart and trailering it down the mountain he decided to glide down into the valley. He was launched off the ridge and flew straight away. There were no clouds, but he started to circle and up he went. He hit dry thermals and flew for over an hour."

Who was first is really not important. The important thing about those early flights at Elmira was that they were soaring flights and understood as such. The thermal as a new source of energy was discovered. It not only supported a plane but propelled it upward. Historically, this becomes notable because utilizing the thermal establishes a new phase in motorless flight; gliding flight became soaring flight. The pilot and his machine were finally unleashed from the confines of gliding on a cushion of air above a ridge. This meant that from a low point in flight altitude could be regained, and true cross-country flying could be accomplished.

Except for the soaring pilot, not much attention was paid to this source of energy because it didn't seem to have any other practical or commercial application. So it took the small group of dedicated pilots a long time to develop the sophisticated sailplanes as we know them today.

It's not the purpose of this book to trace the history of the modern achievements in the sport, it's only important for you to know that you come along at a time when much is known about the art of soaring, and it's a magnificent sport.

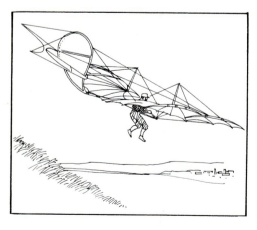

A typical panel of a modern sailplane shows how sophisticated the art of soaring has become. Two cameras mounted on the left are for photographing competition turn points. The stop watch, below, for timing the climbs in thermals. Behind the clock (out of view) is the oxygen regulator; the mask is on the seat of the parachute. From left to right on the panel, the compass is the farthest to the left. Above, combination air speed indicator and variometer, used to calculate the best flying speed between thermals. Below, the accelerometer gives a direct G-load reading. Top center, the air speed indicator. Center, the altimeter. Bottom, the radio. Right top, electric variometer with scales for the weakest up to the strongest conditions. Below, turn and bank indicator. Right, clock with lapse time setting. Below the clock, the audio volume controls for the variometer. You can hear as well as see what the instrument is doing. Dial below the right side of the panel, electric accumulator for a direct read-out, averaging the variometer fluctuations over a 90-second period. Handle to the right is for retracting the landing gear.

IT'S GOING TO BE LIKE THIS

Flight number 10 will be the next entered in your log book. You're 2,000 feet over the field. You've been off tow for an indeterminable length of time . . . four hours, or maybe four minutes. A hot flash travels from the base of the neck up behind the ears. You can't see the instructor sitting behind you, but from the tone of his voice you can visualize him either wiping his brow or snugging-up his harness. "What might you consider that maneuver?" he questions in a voice that is soft but filled with irony. No answer. You go about your work, steep 360-degree turns to the left and then to the right. You had doped it out so well after the last flight. It was going to be duck soup this time. You'd even thought it out in bed . . . left foot, coordinate left hand . . . in the living room . . . right foot, right hand . . . at your desk . . . left foot, left hand . . . on the subway . . . right foot, right hand. "Oops! Excuse me, ma'm." "It's not a bulldozer you're driving," comes the voice from the rear. "Try it again. Be gentle. Coordinate it. Know what I mean?" He only makes $6 an hour sitting back there, and may only work three hours a day, but he's the most important person in the world. The harder you try to prove you're his best student, the faster things turn sour. "Well, OK. Let's go on to something else. Give me slow flight, shallow left turn and after a 180 break into a turn stall." Let's see, did he say shallow turn, slow flight, and a stall after 90? . . . "Watch for other traffic. You started that turn without even looking to clear the air." And so it goes. He takes it in for the landing, not suggesting this time that you even ride the controls down with him. . . . Utter incompetence. . . . Why does one ever get involved with such a sport? Things were going so well . . . maybe golf. . . . "Don't be so dejected," he laughs when the flight is over. "It happens to everybody. The learning curve and all that sort of thing. You were doing great, then things fell apart on this flight. Best thing that could happen to you . . . takes the cockiness out of you. A humble pilot's a good pilot."

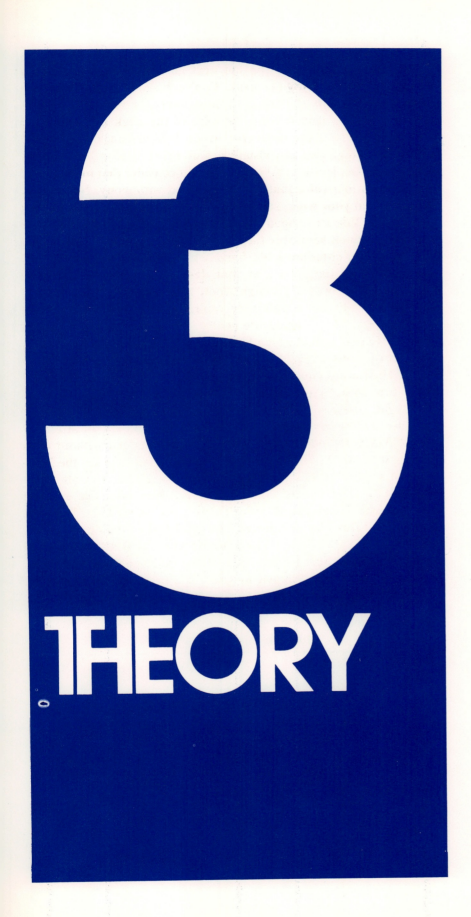

3

THEORY

There are two approaches to the theory of flying: one is for the engineer and one is for the pilot. We're going to narrow it down for the soaring pilot.

Drag and weight are easy to understand; lift is another story.

THE FORCES

Let's start at the beginning. Although motorless flight came first, we're oriented toward the power plane. The airplane has four forces acting on it. It might be easiest to think of them in pairs; two of them help it fly, and two of them inhibit flight. The theory for sustaining level flight calls for a canceling effect so that there will be an equilibrium among all four forces. Forward *thrust* provided by the motor cancels out *drag,* and the pull of *gravity* as a downward force is offset by the *lift* of the wings. Put all of these into balance and you'll have successful level flight.

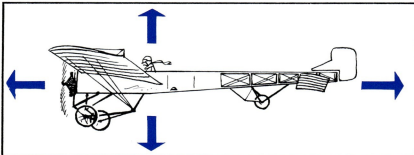

Let's eliminate the thrust, the motor from the airplane, and the three forces that remain will be utilized in soaring. Thus, with a few changes, mainly in wing design, a sailplane emerges, but it will be unable to sustain level flight because there is no motor to provide thrust.

The three remaining forces are the same as in the airplane. Drag is the wind resistance or retarding force of the plane itself as it passes through the air. Weight, or gravity, is the downward force that will now be converted into thrust. In the airplane gravity, or weight, was considered a useless force that had to be overcome. In the sailplane we're going to utilize this force as thrust. Lift, which sustains flight, is produced by the wings.

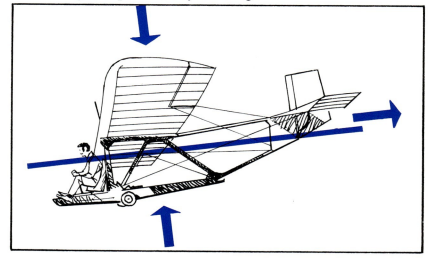

Put your hand out the window of a moving car and you'll know what drag is. Drop a hammer on your foot and you'll understand gravity. There is no simple experiment like these to explain how the wing does its work.

It's interesting to muse with the thought that for centuries flying was within the reach of man. It might have happened hundreds of years ago if he had only turned his attention to the soaring birds instead of the wing-flapping kind. Boats became man's major means of transportation. As he developed this sailing skill, he actually discovered the theory of flight without even knowing it.

The old square-riggers were inefficient beauties. Their principle was to fill their royal sails as you fill a bag. Higher pressure developed on the upwind side of the sail than on the lee. The sail moved from the high-pressure area toward the low and carried the boat with it. In effect the wind pushed the boat. One thing the old royal sails did have in common with a sailplane's wing: movement was from the high-pressure area to the low. With the sail this motion was forward; with the wing the direction of movement is up, and is called lift.

The major disadvantage of the square-rigger was its inability to sail close into the wind. The Marconi rig replaced the square rigs because it could sail close into the wind. The belly of the sail is not only held in its bag-like shape by the pressure of the wind, it's held in its curved shape by the differential of pressures on the two sides of the cloth. If you could observe the wind from a position directly above the mast, you would see that it strikes the sail much as the air strikes a plane's wing. And you would note that the aerodynamic shape of the sail as seen from above is similar to the cross section of a wing seen from its tip. The motion of the wing produced by air flowing over this airfoil shape is called lift. The motion of the sail is called headway. The difference between the square-rig sail and the Marconi can be stated simply: the former is pushed forward, and the latter is sucked forward. To understand this, we have to look at a phenomenon in physics known as Bernoulli's principle.

This principle states that the pressure of a liquid or gas decreases at points where the speed of either fluid increases. It's really simple to understand if you will think of a fire hose. The pumps push the water through the hose at high pressure. As the water reaches the nozzle and squeezes through it, its velocity increases, but at that point the pressure is decreased.

Here's how the principle is applied to a wing as it flies through the air. As air is forced past the wing it is broken into two segments: part goes over the wing, and part passes under it. The top of the wing is curved, and we'll assume for this discussion that the bottom is flat. The air starts its flow at the leading edge of the wing, splits, and meets again at the trailing edge. Because of the curve on top of the wing, the air that goes over it has to travel a greater distance than the air that goes along the flat surface underneath. Since the top air has to go a greater distance, it has to go faster to catch up

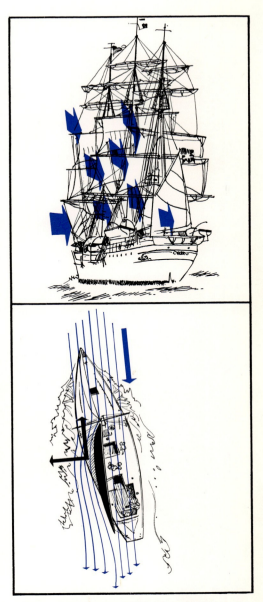

BERNOULLI'S PRINCIPLE

with its counterpart underneath. Remember the principle; as the speed of a fluid increases the pressure decreases. The faster air on top sustains a decrease of pressure. You might think of the topside air as thinning out as it races to cover the longer distance in the same period of time; thinned air is less dense. The pressure under the wing hasn't changed. Now the wing will act like the square-rig sail. The direction of the motion will be from high pressure toward the low. Instead of a forward motion it's an upward motion. Lift is created.

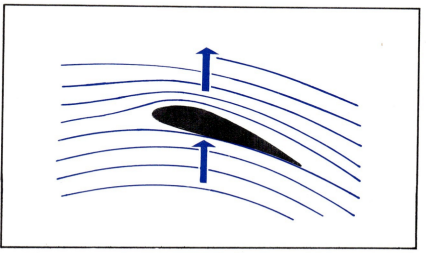

The same principle works on the Marconi-rigged sail. The air has to travel a greater distance because of the lee-side belly in the sail. It's interesting to note that the air in the "bag" of the sail is calm. The wind on the upwind side travels a shorter distance; therefore the pressure is higher on this upwind side.

Now that wasn't so bad, and we explained Bernoulli without even referring to relative wind, Joukowski's theory, Reynolds' number, Raplace's equation, laminar flow, and books and reams of formulas that every self-respecting engineer can spew by rote. And that's just the point. As simple as we have made it, this stuff is for the engineer, not the pilot. It won't do you a bit of good to be able to count molecules of air above and below your wing when you're staring out of your cockpit into the ground. A theory should be a working tool to accomplish a job, not a means of showing off at a cocktail party.

We are not saying that the Bernoulli principle as applied to a wing does not work. What we are saying is that this principle is built into the design of the wing or, for that matter, the sail. Scientists call this a constant. No matter what controls the pilot uses, he can't change the design that makes the Bernoulli principle work. What we're going to look for is the variable. That's the part of flying the pilot should understand.

Sooner or later every student is going to ask his instructor to explain the mystery of lift. That's when Bernoulli gets into the act. But it's overused as the theory of flight; it's not the whole story.

HOW IMPORTANT IS BERNOULLI?

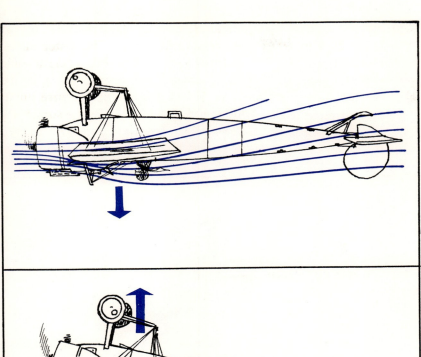

How does an airplane fly upside-down? If we examine the Bernoulli principle, we can actually prove that upside-down flight is impossible, since the principle states that the direction of movement or lift is toward the surface of the wing that has the least pressure exerted against it. As the drawing shows, in the case of the upside-down plane the direction of lift is downward, since the thinner air is now on the bottom surface. Yet every school boy has seen them fly upside down at the county fair. There must be more than this principle working on the wing. Bernoulli is not the whole act . . .

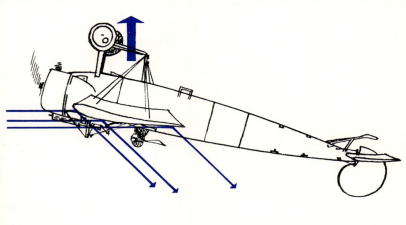

. . . Note the angle the plane flies to make upside-down flight possible. The line of flight is more acute. At this angle there is an action we can call a planing force that produces lift. The plane's wing meets the air at a higher angle and washes the air down to produce lift . . .

. . . Any school boy carrying a board in a high wind can tell you about this kind of lift.

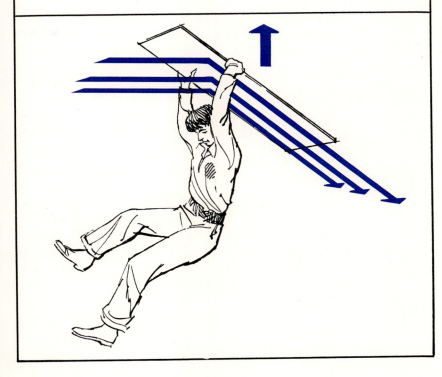

The angle of incidence is the angle at which the wing is attached to the fuselage. If an imaginary line is extended lengthwise through the fuselage from nose to tail, the angle the wing makes with this line (angle of incidence) is determined by the airfoil design. This angle is fixed and can't be changed by the pilot. ⟶

Angle of incidence is often confused with Angle of Attack. The drawing below shows the flow of air over the wing at various Angles of Attack. As the angle is increased both lift and drag increase. There comes a point, at about 18 degrees, where the air can't get over the top of the wing. A swirl or burbling starts. This increases the pressure on top of the wing. It causes a sudden and large loss of lift.

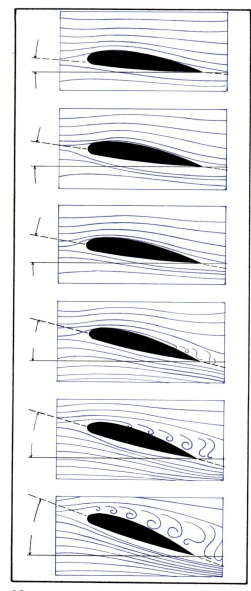

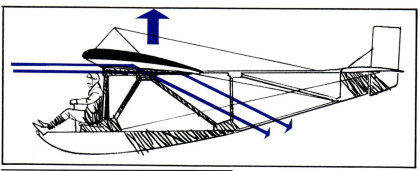

LET'S GET A WORKING THEORY

To develop a working theory it's necessary to find a starting point. Remember the paper planes you used to make? They flew, and they had no curved upper section. When you gave the plane the forward thrust with your arm, it sailed, and when the forward thrust was dissipated, it took a new course and flew downward. It planed through the air that rushed past its wings.

To get that paper plane all the way up to the front of the classroom so it would hit the teacher as she wrote on the board, you'd put a great deal of force into your throw. But to your dismay, the plane may have fluttered to the ground in erratic flight. Here's what happened. You pointed it wrong. The nose went up too sharply, so the wings were placed at a sharp angle to the air, or broadside to it. There was no flow of air over the top of the wing. Yes, there was force against the underside, but there was turbulence or drag behind the upper surface. Drag overpowered the lift produced by the planing action, and the plane fluttered out of control. In flying this is referred to as stalling of the wing. Now let's get some more definitions so we can communicate. You have already gotten one: drag is produced by turbulence, so turbulence is a dragging force.

THE ALL-IMPORTANT ANGLE OF ATTACK

Before, we talked about the wing meeting the air at a sharp angle. From now on we'll call this Angle of Attack. The Angle of Attack is the angle at which the wing meets the air. You are going to have to mull this over to understand it. For the moment accept it.

We also said that the wings made a sharp angle, or went broadside to the air. What air? The air a plane flies in is called Relative Wind. Relative Wind is caused by the motion of the plane itself. On a calm day, with still air, if you drive your car down the road at 60 and hold a handkerchief out the window it will flutter just as if it were a flag on a pole in a 60-mile-an-hour gale. Its direction will always be opposite to your direction of travel. When a plane climbs, its Relative Wind will be directed to the rear and down; when it dives, the relative wind will be rearward and up; during level flight it's straight back.

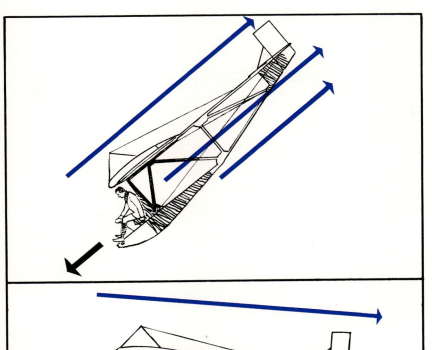

No matter which direction the wind is blowing a sailplane flies in its own envelope of air, called Relative Wind. Relative Wind flows opposite to the direction of travel. When a plane dives the Relative Wind will be rearward and up . . .

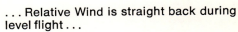

. . . Relative Wind is straight back during level flight . . .

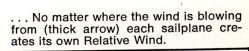

. . . No matter where the wind is blowing from (thick arrow) each sailplane creates its own Relative Wind.

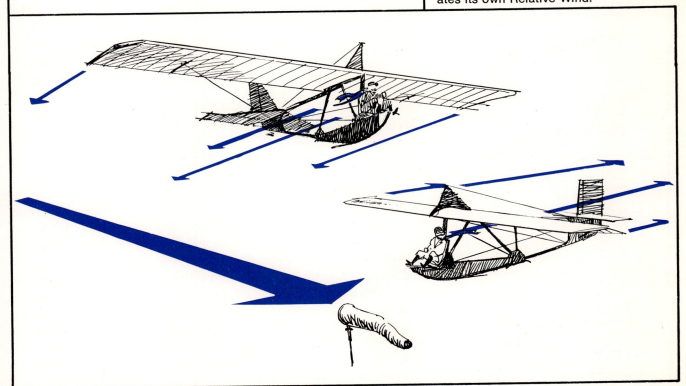

Why did the paper plane stall? The angle of flight (Angle of Attack) was so sharp that the Relative Wind could not curve enough to follow the upper surface of the wing. In that situation turbulence was created on the upper surface. Turbulence is drag. Drag plus weight overpowered lift, and the paper plane hit the girl sitting in front of you instead of the teacher.

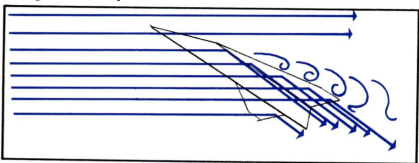

GRAVITY AND STRAIGHT GLIDING FLIGHT

The best way to understand and get a means to measure Angle of Attack is to observe what happens to a sailplane in straight gliding flight in calm air. To do this we'll have you try a simple experiment. This will also show how we are going to use gravity to our advantage.

We have already said that without an engine gravity provides our thrust. Here is what we mean. The force of gravity is always straight down, as any boy who ever sat under an apple tree knows. We will convert it to a forward thrust. Take a 3-by-5 file card and fold it in half. Open it up to form a V. Now you have a flying wing made up of two wings each 2½ inches long. Hold the card at arm's length over your head with the bottom of the V pointing down. Don't push it, just let it go. The wings barely support its descent as it slowly mushes straight down to the floor at your feet. In this "flight" the center of lift and center of gravity are at the same point. Try it again, but this time put a paperclip on the leading edge of the V. Hold the card at the other end. When you release the plane from your fingers, all the same forces will be at work. Although we have increased the over-all weight, we have moved the center of gravity forward, and the wing will now fly forward instead of mush to the floor.

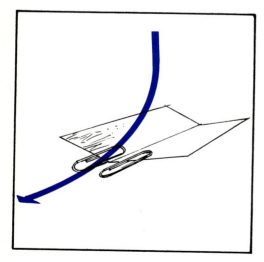

We have converted some of the downward force to a forward thrust. To attain flight the card acts as a wing because the air is flowing over its surfaces. With one paperclip it will glide to the floor about 6 feet in front of you. Now place a second paperclip on its leading edge, on either side of the V; it will fly further. A third clip will make the flying wing go across the room. A fourth clip will make it plummet in a dive.

What can we observe from the experiment?

1. When the center of gravity is moved forward of the center of lift, a forward thrust is produced.

2. When a wing moves through the air, it produces a lift that makes it support a weight.

3. Up to a point, an increase of weight produces an increase of speed. Remember four paperclips made it dive.

4. At slower speed the Angle of Attack is high. This is demonstrated in the flight of the card with one paperclip on its leading edge. If you watch its flight path carefully, you will see it's a series of short oscillations. At the top of each oscillation the wing stalls out. Each time it stalls the wing falls or pitches forward and picks up speed; this in turn increases its planing force, and as a result it lifts. As it angles up again, it is slowed by gravity until it enters its second stall.

5. As the speed increases, the Angle of Attack is reduced. This is shown in the comparative flights of the wing with one paperclip and with three clips. Two paperclips produced less frequent stalls, indicating the Angle of Attack was lowered. The faster flight of the wing with three clips appears to be one long swooping glide with no stalls indicated; obviously a low Angle of Attack.

IT'S GOING TO BE LIKE THIS

What's it going to be like the first time there is an empty harness in the seat behind you? You've given it a lot of thought and wondered about it. At certain phases of training we have all had our doubts; that's only natural. There is no uncertainty now about the mechanics; they've been drilled into you. Gradually your confidence has been built up until you're sure of yourself and the sailplane. The emotion you will have won't be fear, but rather apprehension. Sure, you'll be keyed up and alert. There is a certain amount of excitement about it. Your hands might feel damp, and you might stand off alone mentally checking procedures, even while you're still on the ground. You might think the worst time is going to be waiting before takeoff. Actually that time helps zero your thoughts in on the job that's to be done. You'll take off, you'll fly around the field, and you'll land all by yourself. Of course your instructor knew you could do it, and you knew it too. Still, there will be an uncontrolled grin from ear to ear when you open the canopy and wait for his extended hand. The guys around the airport may even cut your shirt tail off. Knowing is one thing, doing is another. Solo's not going to be a smug feeling, but it's going to be tremendously satisfying.

4
THE CONTROLS AND WHAT THEY DO

THE THREE AXES

Nothing that man does on earth is the same as what he does in the air. A whole new set of ground rules or, better, whole new set of instincts will have to be learned. It's like the farmer who had driven the horse and buggy all his life. When he was sold one of those newfangled horseless Model T contraptions and was headed smack-dab for the fence post, he yanked back on the steering wheel hollering "Whoa!"

The first thing is to understand the controls. There are three in a sailplane: ailerons, elevator, and rudder. They are the same as in the airplane, and the sailplane has ultimate controllability.

There are three axes of movement. The elevator controls the nose up or nose down attitude. This is called pitch. The ailerons control banking to the right or left. This is roll. The rudder moves the nose to the right or to the left. This is yaw.

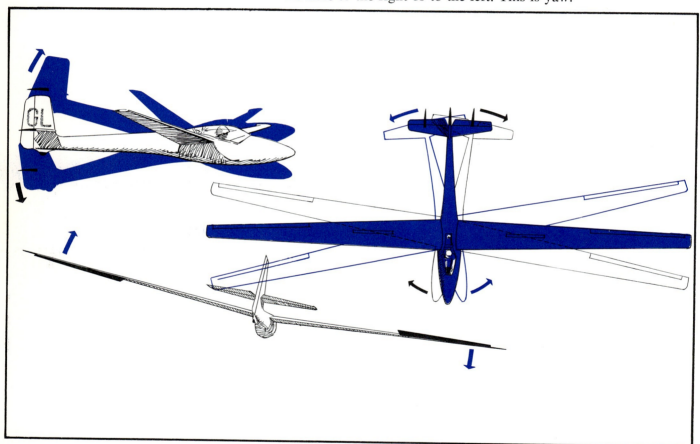

(Upper left) Pitch is controlled by the elevator.

(Center) Yaw is controlled by the rudder.

(Bottom) Roll is controlled by the ailerons.

There is one way of looking at the controls that will help you later to understand some of the problems we will encounter in flight. Consider all control sections as exercising their influence on the sailplane around the axis of the center of gravity. It's as if, while in flight, the plane were balanced on a pin placed at the CG and pitch, roll, and yaw revolved around this point. In flight the pin or point of center will move forward with the plane at the speed of flight. Later we'll want to stop the forward motion of that center-of-gravity axis and see what is happening to the control surfaces.

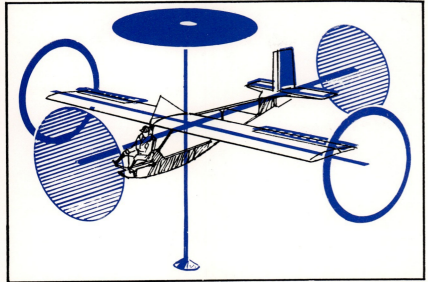

Around the center of gravity of the sail-plane: The circle shows the motion of pitch; the solid disk shows the motion of yaw and the striped disk shows roll. Which control produces each separate motion?

Now that you know how the plane moves around its three axes, let's look at the controls from earthbound experience, apply what appears to be logical thinking, and see just how *wrong* we're going to be.

By way of definition we said the rudder moves the nose to the right or left. Like the rudder on a boat, we might think, it points the nose or bow in the direction we wish to head. So far this seems natural. We might conclude that the rudder steers the sailplane.

When a motorcycle makes a turn, the cyclist banks toward the inside of the curve. The banking allows him to take the curve faster. Does a sailplane operate like the motorcycle? If so, it would follow then that the ailerons bank the plane to make it possible to turn at the necessary speeds, and for pilot comfort; otherwise the pilot would be thrown by centrifugal force toward the outside of his seat in a turn. This, too, seems logical.

The third control is the elevator, a most contradictory name since it will make the plane go up or down. Push forward on the stick which controls the elevator and a plane will go down. Pull back on the stick and the plane will go up. Except that if you pull back too fast and the Angle of Attack becomes too large, the plane will go down—a stall. Pulling back on the stick and hollering "Whoa" in that situation won't help. This can be compared to turning a car to the right by turning the steering wheel to the right and having the car go left. As we have said, nothing a man does when he touches the earth's surface can give him a reference to what he does in the air. Earthbound ways have to be forgotten. Earthbound theories won't work in the air, no matter how logical they seem. Now let's see what the controls *really* do.

To completely understand the controls, let's observe a sailplane in a turn. The rudder does *not* turn it! The wings turn the plane. The ailerons, which we will look at more closely later, put the plane into a bank. Push the stick to the right and the right wing will drop;

HOW WRONG CAN WE BE?

UNDERSTANDING THE CONTROLS

In level flight the lift is in one direction, up. In turning flight the lift splits into two directions; part keeps the plane up and part turns it by moving the plane sidewise.

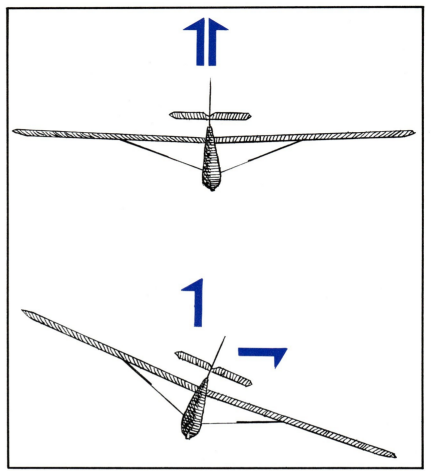

the left wing will go up. The ailerons do this. Let's start by putting the wings at a 20-degree angle. At this angle the wing lift is also tilted. Part of the plane's lift will be directed to the right. The wing no longer is only holding the plane up, it's shoving the plane to the right.

Increase the angle of bank to 45 degrees; more of the wing's action is shoving the plane toward the horizon. The tail weathercocks faster, and the turning rate is increased. Shallow banks give you a wide turn; steep banks give narrow turns. We can do this without even moving the rudder.

Now let's look at the wing lift. According to the amount of bank, some of the lift is going to be directed sideways, toward the horizon, and some in an upward direction. We still must support all the plane's weight. Since part of the support is being directed to the side, it's obvious that we'll need more of an upward force. The way to obtain it is to increase the Angle of Attack, which means more lift. When we do this the wing will create more lift. Our plan is to add enough lift in an upward direction to compensate for the amount of lift used to shove the sailplane sideways. We do this by a slight back pressure on the stick. The elevator changes the pitch of the sailplane, and the Angle of Attack is increased.

It would be so much more accurate to call the elevator the Angle of Attack control. What would happen if we made this turn without back pressure on the stick? Since we wouldn't have enough support for the plane's weight, the nose would drop and our turn would become a diving turn, air speed would increase, and much height would be lost. Note that as yet we still haven't introduced the rudder.

The tighter the turn, the steeper the bank, and the tail will always act like a feather on an arrow. It will weathercock the plane around into its Relative Wind. The elevator will be used to increase the Angle of Attack by pointing the nose up. The speed will not increase, but the amount of lift the wing exerts will increase, and we *almost* have a successful turn.

At last, now, about the rudder. To understand the function of this control we have to really go back and examine the action of the wings, their Angle of Attack, and the ailerons. You may go through your whole training and never hear the term "Angle of Attack" from your instructor, but what you will hear umpteen times is "Coordinate your turns."

What he means is for you to apply rudder with your feet as you initiate a bank with your hands. Making the hands and feet work together is a skill that presents a problem for all students. It's mastered very shortly. It's like throwing in the clutch of a car, shifting, and feeding the gas. It becomes second nature.

In an airplane the rudder is considered to be a secondary control. It's much more important than that to the sailplane pilot. Later we'll see how it's used to steer the sailplane when it is on tow and to steer on landing after touchdown. But remember, in free flight it does not steer the plane. The rudder gives us the coordinated turn your instructor will speak so much about. This is extremely important since it will reduce fuselage drag in the turn. Drag means loss of height to a sailplane, and that's not good. Of the three controls, the rudder is the least understood by the average pilot; let's see how it works.

First, whenever you increase the Angle of Attack, you increase lift and thereby increase drag. Drag decreases air speed.

Now back to the wing to understand the rudder. From straight and level-wing flight we put the stick over to the right. Two things happen. The aileron on the left wing goes down, increasing the Angle of Attack, and that wing will rise. The aileron on the right wing goes up, and the wing will go down as the aileron decreases the Angle of Attack of that wing. Since this lowered right wing tip will be flying at a decreased Angle of Attack, it will not produce as much lift or drag as the left wing, and will be flying faster. With more lift on one side than on the other, the sailplane banks. The lowered aileron on the upper wing causes more drag than the raised aileron on the lowered wing. The upper wing also has a greater Angle of Attack, and that too causes more drag. Obviously, that upper wing has more drag than the lowered wing, so the wing tips

THE TURNING DEFECT

on a banked plane will be flying at different rates around its own center of gravity.

Because the lower wing tip has less drag, the lower wing will tend to stay slightly ahead of the upper wing tip; therefore the nose of the sailplane also tends to be pushed toward the left in a right-hand turn. The plane is banked to the right and turning to the right, but the nose is now cocked left. This is called adverse yaw.

In a turn each wing tip is flying at a different rate of speed causing the sailplane to yaw.

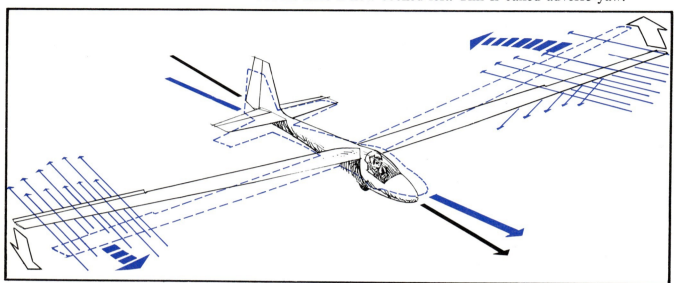

It's the rudder that overcomes this shortcoming in the sailplane's turning efficiency. It keeps the nose pointed in the direction of the turn. If you coordinate ailerons and rudder the plane will always fly and point in the right direction. Without this correction the nose of the plane will point off to the side and the broadside of the fuselage will be presented to the Relative Wind. This causes excess fuselage drag. Drag cuts efficiency and is the enemy; valuable height is lost. The rudder overcomes adverse yaw by turning the sailplane so it presents its most streamlined shape to the air. In some ways it's like the driver on the back end of a hook and ladder.

Adverse yaw causes excess drag. The Relative Wind is striking the fuselage broadside.

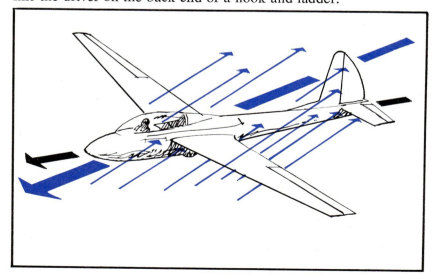

This all has to be thoroughly understood, and it's not easy. It might be well worthwhile to reread it. Too often the instructor will try to put this important idea across by merely telling the student to coordinate the controls and make good clean turns, and will let it go at that. Not as many pilots as you might think have a working knowledge of what actually is happening, and the misuse of the rudder can wrinkle sailplanes.

Now we know what the controls do. A lateral motion of the stick turns the plane, the rudder makes the turn more efficient, and a forward or back motion of the stick controls the Angle of Attack or attitude of flight.

Launching a boat is a matter of getting in and shoving off. Making the wagon work is a matter of applying a force to the wheel and getting the motion started. To achieve flight man has tried everything. He's pushed planes off cliffs, run them down hills, pulled them behind wagons, dropped them off balloons, shot them off with slingshots, and attached rockets. The latest device employs a small motor-driven propeller. Although the motor gets turned off once altitude is reached, purists feel this takes the sport out of the soaring. Today there are three accepted methods to get the sailplane airborne: auto tow, winching, and aero tow. The safest and the most practical is aero tow. In auto and winch towing the cable is attached to a hook well back toward the center of gravity of the sailplane. The plane is drawn through the air much as a kite is pulled on a string. The Angle of Attack is very high, and if there were a cable break at this point the plane would be close to a stall attitude and the height at this point gives little time for keeping the wings flying. The Angle of Attack must be decreased . . . shove the nose down . . . increase the speed . . . flying control is resumed and a landing is made. If this happened on aero tow, the possibility of a stall would not exist. The tow rope is connected to the nose of the sail-

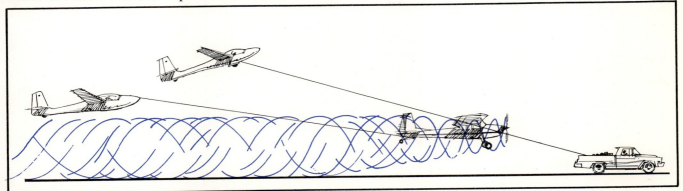

plane, and the towing flight is always at a relatively low Angle of Attack. If the rope breaks at 3 feet or 3,000 the sailplane is in a flying attitude with extra flying speed. Aero towing gives the pilot flexibility. He can be towed to any height and hold on tow until he gets into a thermal. Auto and winch will produce about 1,000 to 1,500 feet, and the release is always in about the same area. Air tow is almost exclusively used in the United States.

THE TAKEOFF

THE PROCEDURE

You are strapped in the front seat of the two-place training sailplane. This is about your fourth flight. The instruments are not staring at you quite as blankly as they did on that first flight. Your instructor says, "Well, I guess we'll let you take it off this time." Your hands dampen.

The tow plane lumbers into place, and the line boy hooks the 200-foot nylon or polyethylene rope to its tail hook. You go over the check list that you have tried to remember:

A. Altimeter set at zero. (You plan to land back at the same field.)
B. Brake, air brakes are closed and locked.
C. Canopy closed and locked.
C. Check wind sock for direction.
C. Controls all working.

The ground crew boy calls, "Open!" You pull on the tow release knob. He inserts the tow rope ring into the hook under the sailplane nose and calls, "Close." He'll give it a yank, and when he calls release you pull the knob again to ensure proper operation of the release. Then he hooks you up again and runs to his position at the wing tip. The tug plane slowly creeps forward taking up the slack in the rope. The line boy calls, "Ready?" You respond with a circular motion of the index finger. The tow plane waggles his rudder. You respond with yours, hard right, hard left.

Your instructor is sitting right behind you so there is no real problem, except you want to show him that you can do it.

Wing boy in action

On a heavy sailplane like the two-seat trainer the stick is moved well forward before you start to roll. As soon as the plane moves forward the control stick should be brought back to a neutral position. The wing boy, whose job it is to keep the plane on an even keel until the forward speed is sufficient to get the controls working, will be running the wing tip until you have aileron control. Some students have a tendency to watch their wings to see that they stay level. Keep your eye glued on the tow plane. The level of your wings can be judged by an imaginary line drawn across the top of the instrument panel and the horizon. Within 30 yards you should

There is no need to look out to the side to see if the wings are level, especially on take-off, eyes forward! The angle the instrument panel makes with the horizon gives you the answer as to what the wings are doing

(Top pair) Instrument panel level with the horizon indicates the wings are level

(Bottom pair) The panel off level indicates the left wing is low

be airborne. A slight backward pressure on the stick will get you up.

Here are the things to watch for.

Once the forward motion starts, the stick should be pressured back slowly so the weight will be taken off the front skid and put on the wheel as quickly as possible. This will keep ground friction to a minimum.

The glider will be airborne much sooner than the tow plane. You pressured the stick back to increase your Angle of Attack, making you airborne. Now that you're aloft you must reduce the angle again, or the increased speed of the tug will pull you up like a kite on a string. You must now help the tow plane get up by not lifting his tail before he is up to flying speed. A slight forward pressure on the stick will keep you about 5 to 10 feet off the ground, just above the prop wash from the tow plane's propeller.

The imaginary line between the top of the instrument panel and the horizon will indicate if you are in level flight. If a wing goes up, pressure it down with the stick. Rudder control should not be applied to make this correction.

Tow speed will be above the normal cruising speed. The more air that passes over the controls, the more effective they become. You can do one of two things to fly in level flight behind the fast-moving tug: trim the ship forward or keep forward pressure on the stick. As speed increases, the pressure forward should be increased. A delicate hand is required. If you shove in too much correction, you'll be all over the place.

Here is where the student gets into trouble. What's a little or a lot of control movement? How can words tell you? You'll hear your instructor say, "That was pretty good, but you overcontrolled." What he is really saying is that you thought you were driving a bulldozer. Don't shove, don't push—slight pressures do it. The only way you will learn what "slight" means is by experience.

THINK SAFETY

There are two safety precautions that you should be ready to perform.

If you are not prepared when the line boy asks you, even if he has the wing up and all is ready to go, give the stop signal with your hand. The motion you make is this: slice your neck as if to cut your head off with your hand. The boy will put the wing down. If any delay is necessary, pull the release knob to disengage the tow hook. That might be a little embarrassing, but embarrassment is preferable to trouble.

The other thing you should be ready for is to release from tow if it appears that the tow plane is going to have a hard time getting off before he runs out of runway. If he appears in trouble he might not have a hand free to release you. You do it. Without your extra weight he'll get off. You will settle back to the runway and apply your brake.

It is also a good practice to watch for knots in the line as it is being hooked. After a sailplane releases, the tug carries the rope back to the landing strip and drops it for the next hookup. Knots can develop in the free end whipping around. The normal pull on a rope during launch is about 20 to 35 percent of the sailplane's gross weight. Gusts or jerks could load this pull to almost 100 percent of the sailplane's weight. A knot in the tow rope will reduce its tensile strength by almost half.

Your instructor will have you handle this first takeoff only if you have rather calm conditions. The sailplane will almost take itself off. There is never a need to force it off with a sharp back stick movement. In turbulent or gusty conditions, or while taking off in a crosswind, the sailplane should get above the prop wash as soon as possible to avoid gusts that might push it back to the ground. As the tow plane is about to take off the sailplane should dip its nose by slight forward pressure on the stick to help the tug take off.

With a crosswind the wingman should run the tip from the upwind side and hold the upwind wing a little lower to keep the wind from getting under the wing and throwing it up. On such a day he should run a little faster to be sure he doesn't release you until you have enough speed to make your controls operative. Then you must be alert to feed in aileron and keep that upwind wing slightly lower until you are airborne. Once in the air the sailplane should track over the path that the tow plane makes. The rudder will be used to start the "crab" into the wind. (See drawing.) This will

In a cross wind, even before the tow plane is off the ground, get the sailplane headed into the wind in order to track the same path as the tow plane

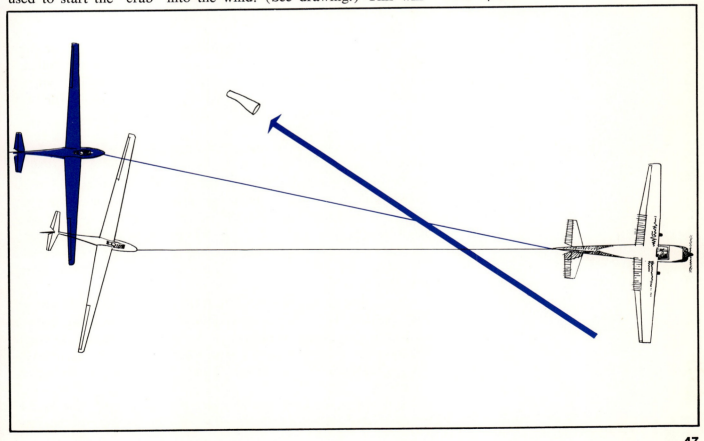

prevent the sailplane from blowing off to the side and creating directional problems for the tow plane. Once the tow plane is off the ground he'll correct for drift and the sailplane will follow.

The cross wind is from the left. When the tug leaves the ground, he'll also crab into the wind

After about the tenth flight nearly every student says, "I can't understand why the tow gave me such trouble." The tow always seems to produce problems, but once you get the hang of it, you've got it.

The embarrassing thing about the tow is that most students put the trainer through a spectacular series of gyrations that any Navy dive bomber would be proud to emulate. When the instructor comes to the rescue, before the bombs are dropped, his voice from the rear seat will say, "Look, you're making it too hard. Take your hands and feet off the controls; let me show you something. Now my feet are off the rudder pedals and I'm holding the position with one finger on top of the stick." The sailplane follows the tug as if it were glued to it.

A CERTAIN AMOUNT OF PANIC

The problem starts as soon as the tow plane is airborne on takeoff. The tug pilot will climb out, operating at full throttle, so the speed will rapidly increase. The sailplane will have a high Angle of Attack and a fast forward speed. Gravity is not working as its source of thrust; the tow plane is supplying that. If allowed to fly on its own the sailplane would fly up and over the tug. A forward pressure on the stick with one finger could hold it in place. But that's not what happens for the student. The sailplane climbs and gets out of position. The student overreacts with a certain amount of panic. He shoves the stick forward, the sailplane dives back into position, then past it, and before he knows it he's looking up at the belly of the tow plane. One such "correction" leads to an overcorrection. A good instructor will let the student fight his way out of this "paper bag" just as long as he's within the general area of the tow position. Unfortunately there is something comical about it —to everyone except the man in the pilot's seat, who's usually awash in cool perspiration.

A NEW TRAINING TOOL

A good training machine for a student learning to fly a sailplane is a small tape recorder. The student should strap it to his chest; the microphone can be attached at any convenient place in the cockpit so that it'll pick up both the student and the instructor In the silent flight of soaring every word and every exasperated breath will be recorded. When a person learns to drive a car, the instructor can, if necessary, pull to the curb, stop the car, and take all the time needed to explain in detail any problem. Not so in a sailplane. As the instructor is explaining what went wrong with the last maneuver, the student is already facing a new problem. While you're on tow and diving on the tow plane, how do you expect to really comprehend what your instructor was saying about your takeoff? By playing the tape back in the quiet of your study at home, you'll relive the whole lesson, second by second. Without the emotional stress you'll hear what the instructor was saying.

It's possible, by listening to the tape over and over, to develop new conditioned reflexes. From the tape you'll be able to reconstruct and visualize what the plane was doing when the instructor called for a correction; even the hiss of the speed of flight will be recorded.

The tow is formation flying. There are two accepted positions. High tow is above the tug's propeller wash, and low tow is below it. You're in the correct high-tow position when you can sight a line across the top of the tow plane's vertical stabilizer and have it line up on the spot in the tug where the tow pilot's head would be. Another good method is to maintain position by keeping the tow plane landing gear on the horizon. High tow is used most of the time, and it's the safest. On low tow, if the rope broke and slapped back it could

HIGH AND LOW TOW

High tow, the normal position. The top of the tow plane's vertical stabilizer is centered on the pilot's head

damage the sailplane or get snarled in its controls. On high tow a snapped rope would invariably fall below the sailplane. There are two circumstances when low tow is preferred. On long cross-country flights, the low position is easier for the sailplane pilot. The rope and the tug can be kept in view, making it an easier position to sustain. Low position is also used when the tow plane is having difficulty climbing out on takeoff or in a strong downdraft.

A CONTRADICTION

How is the sailplane flown on tow? Unfortunately, to explain the practical technique on tow, we're going to partially contradict what we have been saying about the theory of free flight. Flight on tow is not the same as free flight; the controls are used differently.

In free flight we used the turn as a means of explaining the controls. Let's do the same thing for the tow. The function of the elevator stays the same in both towing and free flight, but its use will be limited on tow. If you find yourself too low on tow, back pressure is used and you will climb; that's as we would expect it to be. If you are too high, stick forward will only make the correction up to a point. The stick is your up-and-down regulator in relation to the tug. But—and this is very important—remember that when we reduce the Angle of Attack, stick forward, we increase speed. This becomes a serious problem on tow. If we get high, way out of position, we can't allow the speed to increase by diving down on the tug to get back into the correct position, because the increased speed will place too much slack in the tow line. Therefore, we can only use this forward-stick elevator control for minor descending movement on tow. The sailplane should never be allowed to speed up to a point where it could be flying over the tow plane. That's way out of position, but it could happen. This means that the elevator alone can't be used for sharp descents, which is one of its functions in free flight.

ON TOW, STEER BY RUDDER

The rudder also takes on a different and important function on tow. It's more like the tail on a kid's kite. After all we have said about it not steering the sailplane in free flight, now we're going to say that on tow it does exactly that. The rudder now is used to control the lateral movements, from side to side.

LET'S TRY IT

Now we'll put you back at the controls and continue the flight and explain what the controls do on tow. You have taken off and ridden the blanket of air just high enough over the runway to avoid the prop wash. As the tow plane lifts off, you dip down to help the tug off the ground. The climbout presents the first problem. To correct for overclimbing the desired position, the stick is pushed forward. All stick motions must be small on tow, since the high speed of the tow makes control response extremely sensitive. The tow line must be kept as a straight line. If you can see one side of the fuselage of the tow plane and not the other, the line will not be straight. To correct for this, rudder is used. The plane is skidded back to its proper position; addition of bank by ailerons would only complicate the situation. For minor corrections use only the rudder. The introduction of the aileron into this maneuver is only necessary if very large horizontal movements are necessary.

Unlike free flight, where once the new direction has been made all controls are neutralized, on tow the rudder must be held in its deflecting position until the correction is completed. It's just like driving a car through a turn. The wheels are turned until the turn is completed.

Anticipate what the tug is doing but don't jump the gun. What happens when you respond too fast to the turning tug? When the tow plane starts the turn, if you don't wait until you've reached its position in space to start yours, the sailplane is going to turn inside

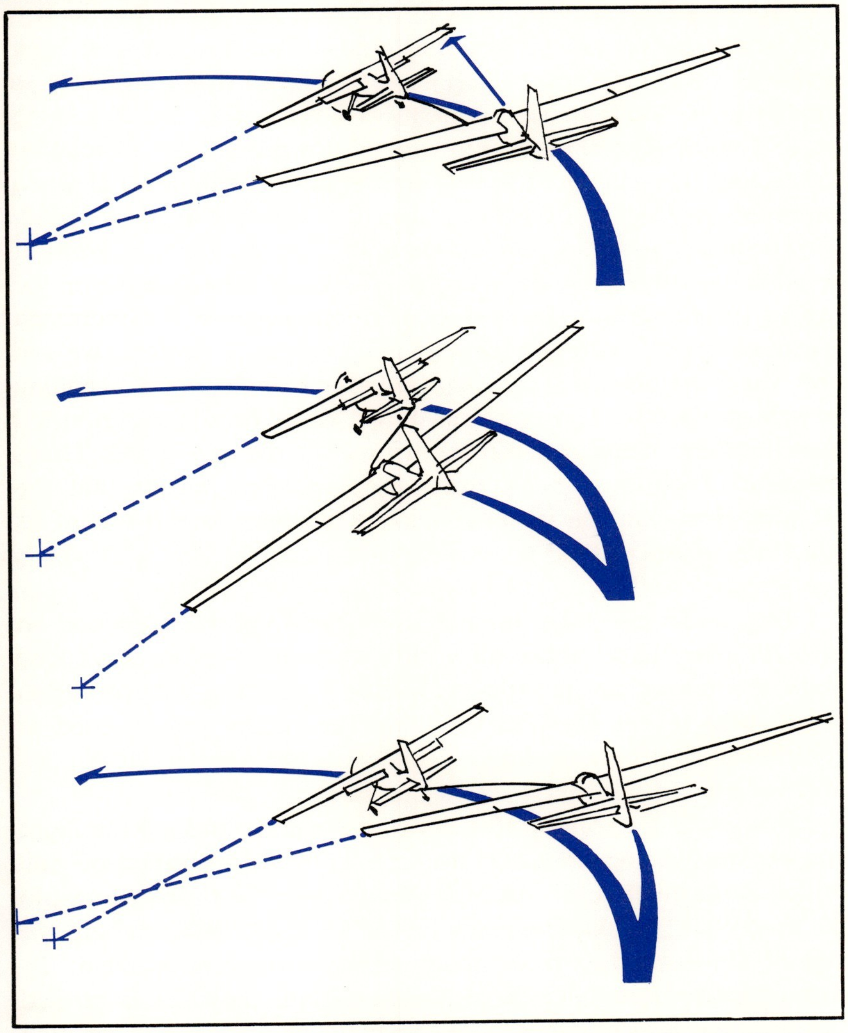

TURN WHEN IT'S YOUR TURN

Correct turn . . .

. . . Too early

. . . Too late

the tug's turn and you'll start to overtake it. The tow rope will slacken, and your air speed will start to decrease. The airplane will surge forward, since its dragging weight has been momentarily removed, and to take the slack up with a jerk is a good way to break a tow rope. If it doesn't break, the sailplane will be catapulted forward with a surge of speed that will initiate a climb. At the same time the nylon rope, which acts like a rubber band, has gone slack again. The tow plane shoots ahead and the whole slingshot procedure starts all over. This time when you find yourself high on the tug in a turn and with a slack rope, apply the up rudder pedal, cross the controls, and skid the sailplane toward the outside of your turn. When this slip is over, you're going to be where you want to be, behind the tow plane, and the drag of the fuselage is going to cause you to lose height, which is also what you are after. Then, just as the rope is about to straighten out and the slack removed, drop the nose of the sailplane by a forward pressure on the stick. This will increase your speed and reduce the rubber-band effect of the nylon tow rope.

What will happen if you wait too long and pass the point in space where the tug started its turn? Have you ever played crack-the-whip? Speed is sharply increased. Now where will you be? High, and to the outside of the turn. The excess speed causes a climb. You can get back down by crossing the controls. Increase the bank with the stick and up-rudder pedal to cause a slip. The drag will bring you down, and the bank will get you back behind the tow plane.

It's possible to get so high that the cross-controlled slip won't be enough. In that case, you can apply a small amount of dive brakes. However, this is reserved for extreme situations.

There are other conditions to watch for on tow. Turbulence can throw the best of pilots out of position. If the tow plane is buffeted, about three seconds later the sailplane will experience the same problem. There are two ways to anticipate the effects of turbulence. One is to wait for the up- or downdraft and then make the correction. The other method is to make a correction and stay in formation as soon as the tug has been hit; then make the correction again as the sailplane receives the buffeting. But it's possible, through no fault of the pilot, for the sailplane to be buffeted out of tow position. To learn to get back into formation, the student is taught transitions around the tow plane.

First you'll be introduced to the propeller wash from the tug. Prop wash is the air that washes past the airplane's fuselage, describing an area about 30 feet in diameter. From high tow position the instructor will suggest that you drop straight down until you feel the buffeting. You'll recognize it from the rattling of your teeth. You'll be told to climb straight up to the high tow position again. These maneuvers are done with the stick. Now you'll have a feel of where the turbulence is. That will be the first step in learning to make a clockwise transition around the prop wash.

There are a number of reasons for teaching this maneuver. One, as we have stated, to get you back into tow formation if you were buffeted out of position. Two, to teach you how to change tow position, from high tow to low or the reverse. Three, if you do not have radio contact with the tow plane, there are signals the sailplane can communicate to the tow pilot by his change of position on tow.

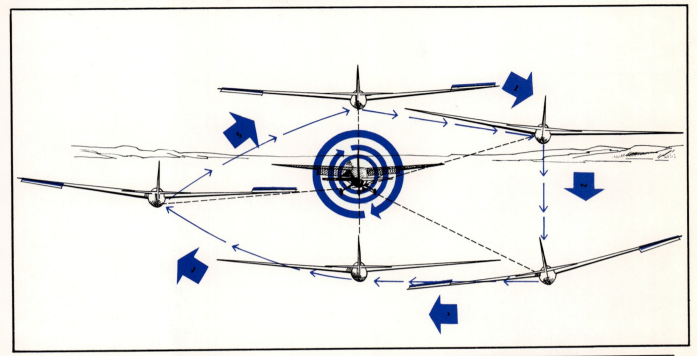

THE TRANSITIONS

To move out to the right from high tow, the stick is depressed very slightly to the right to drop the wing slightly; simultaneously right rudder is applied and the controls are held until the lateral movement is completed. The plane is held out in that position (position 1) with the rudder, and the wing is leveled. To get into position 2, the stick is pressured slowly forward and the rudder held. The sailplane starts to descend. When the pilot looks up to the left and can sight the tow plane at 10 o'clock with the horizontal stabilizer in line with the wing tip, he has droppped far enough; he relaxes the forward pressure. The right rudder is still holding him out to the side. Now he will start left rudder and move the plane to the left under the wash. When he has reached position 3, the tug is above, at 12 o'clock, and he should pressure the stick back and raise the sailplane until he feels the buffeting of the wash. Forward stick will drop him back down out of the turbulence. Now he knows just how far below the prop wash he is. He should continue his clockwise movement to position 4. But on the second half of his trip he can go to the 9 o'clock position directly. This diagonal movement will be accomplished by the simultaneous pressuring of two controls: gradual stick back and left rudder in, with a "dash" of right aileron to keep him from getting out too far. To get back to the original high tow from position 4, right rudder is fed in as the stick is pressured back to raise the sailplane. The dash of aileron can stay in until the position has been reached. When the wings are brought level, rudder neutralized, the student pilot will sight the tug's vertical stabilizer back on the tow pilot's "head."

Here's what it all looks like. Start here. Go clockwise around the wash from the tow plane

5

1

4

3

2

Next to the difficulties of climbing out of position is the problem of swaying on tow. It's caused by overcontrolling. The classic axiom of flying being "a continual series of small corrections" applies here also. Don't kick the rudders, easy pressure will do the trick. Concentrate on your feet and what they are doing; as you swing back into position, ease off the rubber. Don't freeze on the control, or you'll only swing out in the opposite direction. As you approach the correct spot in space, be ready to give a touch to the opposite pedal. Getting too high or out to one side is always the start of a more serious problem. Relax and concentrate on slight corrections and you won't need to make the big ones.

Remember, embarrassment is common on the first few tows. Most students experience it, but it's really not as difficult as we might have made it sound. We've tried to tell you what can go wrong and why. That doesn't mean that all these things will happen, or at least not all of them at once.

When you have reached altitude, the release should be made from the high tow position. Then the flying metal tow ring will have no chance of hitting the sailplane. As you approach the prearranged dropoff height, the sailplane pilot should look around to see that his air is clear. Student pilots should only release upwind of the airport to ensure comfortable gliding distance to the landing strip. The release should be made from a normal straight-flying attitude when the rope is not under heavy tension.

CUTTING THE UMBILICAL CORD

Wait until you see the line spring free before you start to make your separation turn to the right

There are two levers to pull in a sailplane. One is the tow release, and the other is for the dive brakes. It may sound stupid to say, but be sure you pull the right one. If you do pull the dive brakes by mistake, you won't be the first to do so. In these early lessons, as you reach for the release knob, glance at it and say to yourself, "Release knob." Memorize its position. If you do inadvertently pull the wrong one, shove the dive brakes off immediately and then quickly pull the release knob.

When you pull the knob, you will be traveling well above normal cruising speed. The sailplane should make a climbing turn to the right. Not only will the climbing turn convert the excess speed into extra height, but you'll be getting away from the rope and the tug as soon as possible. The tow plane will make a diving turn to the left to clear the area. Caution. When you pull the release, don't start your climbing turn until you actually see the tow rope spring ahead like a released rubber band. One pilot, who didn't look, assuming when he pulled the knob that the rope released, went into his climbing turn to discover that in the tight confines of a cockpit one has a tough time retrieving false teeth from under the rudder pedal.

If you find yourself in a position where you are banked sharply away from the direction the tow plane is turning and you are in a climbing attitude, release from tow. A correction from such a situation could overstress the craft.

Handling the controls as if you were driving a bulldozer causes this problem. The best way out is to release

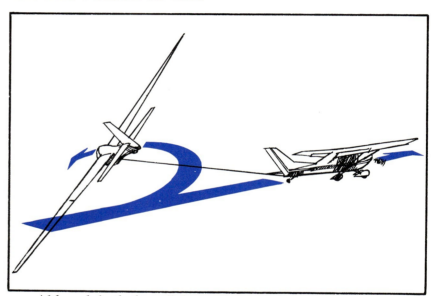

EMERGENCIES AND SIGNALS ON TOW

Although both the sailplane pilot and the tow pilot are in command of their respective planes, neither has a responsibility to the other if his ship is in danger.

If the tug develops power problems on takeoff, the tow plane pilot has a right to release the sailplane without a signal. If he must land, he will try to do so to the left of the runway in order to permit the sailplane to land to the right. If the tug can make it off, he should fly out in order to leave a clear runway for the sailplane to make a straight forward landing.

If, at any time during tow, the tug pilot wants the sailplane to release because of an unforeseen problem, his signal to the sailplane is a vigorous rocking of the tow plane wings. That means, "Either you release or I'll release you."

The tug pilot won't use this emergency procedure unless it's necessary. Loss of power would be a good example. Or, if the ceiling suddenly closes in, conditions are no longer visual flight rules, and the sailplane pilot doesn't realize what is happening, the tug will signal for a release. The tow plane won't attempt to tow a sail plane downward; this is a very tricky maneuver. Remember, the sailplane has a tendency to climb at tow speeds. If the tug loses altitude on tow, it accentuates the sailplane's climbing. It is better for the sailplane to descend on its own.

If visual contact is lost between the sailplane and the tug, the sailplane must release. The tug should never head into a cloud because there is no way for the sailplane to fly blind on tow.

Towing is a team operation. Radio communications are desirable, but this is an expensive luxury. If there are no radios and the sailplane pilot sees a good cumulus cloud forming while on tow, the sailplane can swing out to the side and by using full rudder turn the tow plane's tail into the desired direction. At first the tow pilot may think the sailplane has gotten out of position and may try to hold course with full opposite rudder. His leg will soon get tired; he'll get the point and head in the new direction.

WHAT HAPPENS IF YOU HAVE A RELEASE FAILURE?

Don't panic! There are two ends to every rope. The tow plane has a release too. Pull the release again, and again. If it doesn't let go, descend to low tow and try again. If that doesn't work, ascend to high tow and yaw with hard rudders; then pull the release. If you're still attached, it's time to signal the tow pilot. He should know something is wrong because he has reached release height and you're still attached. To signal him, use hard rudder and steer off to the right as far as the tow line will allow you to go. This should get the tow pilot's attention. Waggle your wings. Rock them by stick right, stick left, right, left until he gets your signal. He'll take you back over the airport and pull his release, and you'll be off and free except for a 200-foot rope dangling from your nose. Prepare to land. You'll have plenty of time to work out your landing pattern. If you usually come over the airport fence at 50 feet, now you'll have to come over it at 250 feet; otherwise the rope might catch around the limb of a tree or a fence post. The rope would break or the hitch release before you got nosed into the ground, but there's no need to test the tensile strength under these conditions.

An episode like this might never occur in a lifetime of soaring, but every pilot should know the procedure.

WHAT IF THE TUG CAN'T RELEASE?

Although the records do not show a case where both the sailplane and the tug can't release, the procedure should be anticipated and understood. Both planes will have to descend together and land together. The "I can't release either" signal from the tug to the sailplane will be a slow fishtailing of the rudder. The tug will start to descend as slowly as possible to help prevent the sailplane from climbing over him. The sailplane pilot must keep the rope taut by using a side slip and/or by the use of the dive brakes.

A long shallow descent will prevent the sailplane overrunning the tug, and will set them both up for a wide gradual landing pattern. If there is a danger of overrunning and a serious sag can't be controlled, low tow should be entered to prevent the risk of the rope falling over the tug's control surfaces. Under any condition the sailplane should enter low tow by the time they're both on the final landing approach. The tug should make a high approach over the airport fence. On final, the sailplane prepares to land first, on the right side of the runway. Dive brakes and/or a side slip must be used to maintain the line tension. As the tug makes a power-on, wheel landing, the sailplane should stay out to the right with rudder as the tug lands on the left side. At the tug's touchdown both should gradually stop.

A TOW ROPE BREAK

Looking at the airport's wind sock for wind direction should be part of your flight preparation. Wind direction not only is important for takeoff but will tell you what to be ready for if there is an emergency and a fast landing is required. Get familiar with the takeoff strip. If it's a field you fly out of regularly, you will know its plan. If the field is new to you, study its layout; plan ahead for any eventuality such as a rope break on tow. It's so much better to have a procedure in mind than be caught by surprise. On your first flight out of a field, ask about landing conditions just over the airport fence, then look it over from the air during takeoff. We'll talk a good deal about landing patterns later, but we just want to quell any fears that you might have about a rope break. Fast decisions will preclude its becoming a dangerous situation.

If a break occurs just after takeoff, before or immediately after the towplane leaves the ground, hold the forward pressure on the stick and the sailplane will land straight ahead. If you are 50 feet up and running out of landing space, use the spoilers or dive brakes to get down; they also keep you from becoming airborne once you've touched down.

THE CRITICAL POINT

From 50 feet to slightly less than 200 feet above the runway is the altitude that requires the preplanning. If the farmer's field over the airport fence is good, a straight landing should be used. This means the ship will have to be disassembled to be brought back to the field. It's better to be safe than consider the extra problems you are making for a crew.

If your altitude is close to 200 feet and there is no landing field ahead, a fast decision to turn downwind must be made. A 180-degree turn will get you back over the airport, and a downwind landing will be accomplished by employing the spoilers or dive brakes. The cardinal rule: keep the air speed extra fast when turning at low altitude.

If a rope break occurs at about 1,000 feet, there's no problem. Release the part of the rope that's dangling from the tow hook when you're over a safe area and proceed with the flight, or make a 180-degree turn, go downwind, and enter a normal landing pattern.

In contrast to the car or winch tow, the attitude of the sailplane on aero tow has many factors in its favor. The speed is high and the Angle of Attack of the wings is within the normal flying range, and a stall will not be imminent.

The tow is just formation flying. We have pointed out all the problems and solutions. This makes it sound very difficult. After the first half-dozen flights you'll get the feel of it and it will all become automatic. The tow will teach you the feel of the controls, and when you learn that it's duck soup.

ONE LAST WORD

IT'S GOING TO BE LIKE THIS

There are two kinds of flight, gliding and soaring. The training period is mostly gliding flight. You'll be towed aloft, and your instruction will take place on the glide down. You'll know about thermal updrafts; you can't see them, and many a pilot has taken his whole training without ever encountering them. You'll hear about them; you'll read about them; you'll see pilots make long flights using them, but you won't really believe they exist. The first one is truly exciting. You'll stumble into it, but you'll know what it is . . . instantly. Then you'll become a believer! It'll push up right from the seat of your pants. Its strength will astonish you, and you will truly climb on wings. The landscape falls away, while the ceiling seems limitless. This is the power; to use it is the skill. This is what the whole thing is about.

6
HOW TO FLY

AIR SPEED

You now know the basic theory and how the controls work on tow and in free flight, but before we put them together in practice, we need some more information. First, let's look at air speed. It does not tell you how fast you are going over the ground. It tells you how fast the Relative Wind is passing around and over the sailplane.

Only in absolutely still air will your air speed indicate your approximate ground speed.

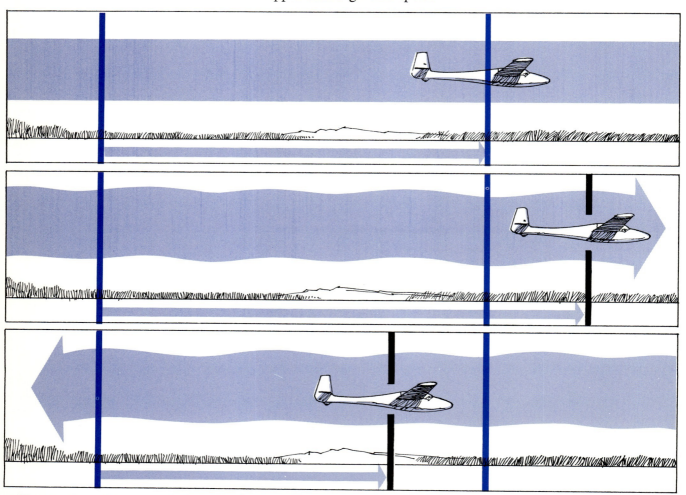

The top plane flying in still air at 40 mph will cover 40 miles over the ground. The middle plane will go farther if he flies at the same speed with a tail wind. The bottom plane flying at the same speed but bucking a head wind will cover less distance

If you are going 40 mph and have a tail wind blowing at 10 mph, your ground speed will be about 50 mph.

If you are bucking a head wind of 10 mph and the air speed indicator reads 40, you'll have a ground speed somewhere about 30 mph.

The reason these speeds were expressed as approximations is that as a miles-per-hour-recording device, the air speed indicator is inaccurate. It's really a pressure-measuring instrument, like the tire gauge you use on your car. It measures the dynamic pressure built up by the impact of the plane as it travels through the air. The higher the speed, the higher the reading, and at slow speed the impact will be less and will read low. Density has a great effect on the reading. At high altitudes it will read low because the air is thinner. It will read higher on cold dry days and lower on hot muggy days. As a navigational instrument, the air speed indicator is just an approximator.

Early gliding pilots sneered at air speed indicators. They could approximate their air speed by the sound the wind made as it rushed by the struts. You'll still use your ears in soaring, but in certain maneuvers the air speed indicator will be more accurate. It's important to note that there is a time lag of a few seconds in this instrument. The pictures of the stall (see page 70) will demonstrate that, so we too will come to depend on our ears and the feel of things.

(see page 70)

THE SAFETY INDICATOR

There is no question that the air speed indicator is the sailplane pilot's best friend. It's the only instrument that indicates anything about Angle of Attack.

The air speed indicator tells the Relative Wind speed. The force of gravity produces the Relative Wind. Attitude—nose up, nose down—which is the same as Angle of Attack under these circumstances, will determine the amount or speed of the Relative Wind. There is a point where the amount of lift gets out of balance with the amount of drag produced by too large an Angle of Attack, resulting in a wing stall. Every sailplane, according to its design, has a specific slow stall speed. It is here that the air speed indicator becomes an accurate device. Air density has no effect on the instrument when it is indicating the stall; if the stall occurs at 30 mph, the instrument will read 30 at any altitude or in any kind of weather, hot or cold. What we are saying is that the plane is not concerned with the actual speed, it only cares about the dynamic pressure produced by impact. If it has to fly at 40 mph to get a 30 reading, that's OK with the plane. Impact is relative to speed, and speed is relative to attitude; therefore as an Angle of Attack indicator in straight flight the air speed indicator is an accurate stall-warning device. For the specific plane you are flying, the slow stall speed is important to know.

The air speed indicator in this respect is a safety indicator. There are some other important safe air speeds you should know, such as maximum air speed on tow and manufacturer's recommended speeds for flying in smooth and rough air. Exceeding the speed limits may create a dangerous situation that could result in structural damage. These should be observed; sailplanes don't fly well without all their parts.

THE STALL SPEED . . . UP CLOSE

What happens when we try to defy gravity by gliding in still air? Let's point the nose of the sailplane up very slightly so the canopy is lined up on the horizon. We have increased the Angle of Attack. As we increase the angle by bringing the nose up more, our forward speed slows down. The plane comes to a point where it sinks faster. But in doing so, the flat underside of the wing strikes more and more air, thus finding a cushion of new lift. While this happens the Relative Wind is taking a new direction; part comes up from below and part from in front. We'll come to a point, as we keep raising the nose higher and higher, when the Relative Wind can no longer get over the front of the wing and travel along its top surface. The forward motion is slowed down by drag and gravity; we have lost thrust and at the same time air flow over the upper surface of the wing. We still have the buoyant cushion under the wing, but instead of an efficient airfoil there is a turbulent glob on the top surface of the wing. The Angle of Attack is too high, the speed too slow. Drag plus weight become too much for the wing to support, and it stalls. Every plane has a specific speed at which the wings stop flying, the nose drops down, and it acts like a dead duck. The recovery will be simple.

MINIMUM SINK

Minimum sink is that speed where the ship will sink at its slowest rate during straight flight in still air.

There is, of course, a flying speed for your ship somewhere between the 30-mph near-stall, mushing descent, and the high-speed glide that will be a compromise between the pull of gravity and the effective use of the wings to support the weight of the ship. What we are seeking in this compromise is the exact Angle of Attack that will give the amount of lift that produces the minimum downward component of gravity. This flight attitude expressed in miles per hour is our minimum sink speed. Let's assume that the plane we are flying in the book has a manufacturer's minimum sink speed of 36 mph.

BEST ANGLE OF GLIDE

Wherever soaring pilots meet, the phrase "L over D," written L/D, is bandied about. This inside jargon for lift over drag is more easily understood if you consider it as a simple ratio and think of it as the sailplane's best angle of glide in straight flight. This angle of descent produces the maximum distance covered over the ground for every foot of altitude lost in still air. That's the way the L/D ratio is expressed. For example, 30/1 means that that particular plane will travel 30 feet forward in still air for every foot of descent.

L/D is discussed extensively because it tells much about a sailplane. There is a direct correlation between L/D and price. A sailplane with a 44/1 ratio costs more than twice as much as one that has a 23/1 ratio. Asking a fellow the L/D of his sailplane is like asking him how much his mistress costs.

There is only one attitude of flight where the Angle of Attack produces the optimum conditions of minimum sink and maximum forward thrust. It too can be translated into air speed. In the average plane it is about 15 mph over the stalling speed. That could be 45 mph for the plane we're going to be flying here.

Remember the experiment with the folded-file-card plane and the paperclips? Minimum sink results when the clip is placed on the paper wing and balanced so it takes the longest time to reach the floor when released without thrust. You have best angle of glide when the file card lands furthest from your feet. To achieve this, three paperclips were used; the center of gravity has now been changed, altering the angle of flight. In the sailplane, the elevator controls this attitude; it's the stick that changes this Angle of Attack.

Now we have three important flying speeds: stall speed, 30 mph; minimum sink, 36 mph; best glide angle, 45 mph. We're going to refer to them as we progress into soaring flight.

Let's return to the flight. We have released from tow. The clearing turn was made, now we go into straight and level-wing flight. If there is a trim tab to balance out the controls, it should be set. Once it's set, you'll be able to take your hands and feet off the controls and the sailplane will fly itself. Training planes and most medium-performance sailplanes (under 30 to 1 L/D) are very forgiving. Do something wrong and the plane will automatically right itself if you let it.

If turbulence lifts a wing, use your controls to bring the wings level. Pressure the aileron toward the wing that lifts and push it down. Simultaneously, push on the rudder pedal. Aileron alone will cause a yaw; rudder will correct the yaw before it starts. Right hand, right foot coordinate the two even on minor corrections. Neutralize the controls as soon as the correction is made and the plane will keep that attitude until either you change the controls or the conditions change.

Level-wing, straight flight is easy for the student to master—seemingly duck soup. The student can do it without the help of the instructor; the plane can do it without either of them.

MORE ABOUT STRAIGHT FLIGHT

The stick controls attitude. We have said this many times. Now let's show it to you. The sequence of pictures taken as the plane's speed increases in 10-mph increments demonstrates the attitude of flight at each speed. It's interesting to note that if you wish to maintain a specific speed, the stick must be held in that position to keep the attitude or speed constant. This is unlike controlling the aileron and rudder where you neutralize the stick once the desired attitude is achieved. The sailplane holds the turning direction until you pressure the stick out of the neutral position. That's not so with air speed. A sailplane has to be held constantly at its correct Angle of Attack. The only exception is trim speed, which is the neutral air speed.

In these pictures you will see what attitudes you will fly once you learn the rudiments of gliding and start to soar. The instructor isn't going to waste valuable altitude to show you this.

It is obvious from these pictures that the sailplane is going to be on the ground a lot faster traveling at 80 mph than at 40.

When the power pilot wants more speed he can either open the throttle or reduce the Angle of Attack by putting the nose down.

SPEED OF THE GLIDE

1 Upper right dial is the air speed. Normal flight, the needle reads 40 mph. Picture below shows the attitude of the plane relative to the horizon

2 Air speed now reads 50 mph. The nose is dropped. Below, the plane makes a slight angle with the horizon

These photographs and the following sequences were taken by simultaneous exposure of electric-drive Nikon cameras. One was in the cockpit, and one was attached under the wing of a 2-33 Schweizer trainer. One camera shows what the student sees: the instruments and the horizon. The wing camera shows the attitude of the plane in relationship to the horizon. The important instrument in these pictures is above the square placard on the right

THE WHIP OR ACCELERATED STALL

The soaring pilot only has one choice to make: to put the nose down.

There is an interesting thing about the relationship of speed and height in a sailplane. To get one you have to pay for it with the other. If you want speed, you have to give up height. If you have speed, you have to sacrifice it to get height. One is always being traded off for the other.

There is one situation in which the soaring pilot should never find himself, and that is low and slow, because he will have nothing left to trade. He should always bear in mind that to get out of a stall he's going to have to pay out altitude to purchase speed.

To accomplish the sequence of speed pictures, the stick was pressured, not yanked. The reason is important. We have been saying all along that air speed, attitude, and Angle of Attack are much the same thing. The stick is the controller of air speed. The stick is also the controller of Angle of Attack! When the Angle of Attack is increased we gain altitude, but at the same time have to pay for it with speed. If the plane is gradually slowed down and held in that attitude, it will eventually be slow enough to stall out.

3 At 60 mph the nose is pointed down farther. Below, the angle with the horizon becomes obvious

4 The elevator, controlled by the stick, is pressured forward to get this change of flight attitude and increased speed. At 70 mph the plane's tail is well above the horizon

There is another way to stall it. If we *abruptly* increase the Angle of Attack at *high* speeds, we can also produce a stall.

Here is what happens. The stick is pressured forward and the air speed is reading 80 mph. The plane is diving for the ground. For this particular plane that is the attitude at 80.

You have no problem at this moment with any of the controls; they are functioning very well. You know your plane stalls at 30 mph so we have no fear. Yank the stick back at 80 and, surprisingly, the plane stalls. The controls feel like spaghetti. Before you even know what's happened, "back" stick, which always meant upward flight, suddenly meant downward flight . . . straight down. How is it possible to not have flying speed at 80 mph? It's the stall, a high-speed stall. If you are taught your flying by air speed, disregarding Angle of Attack, it will be like painting by numbers. The instructor tells you to put green in one block and red in another; you may end up with a pretty picture, but it won't teach you to be an artist.

Flying by the air speed numbers means nothing if you don't relate it to Angle of Attack. A large, abrupt interruption of the Relative Wind will cause a stall at any speed. Inertia and G loading

The sequence starting on the next page is discussed on page 74. It's the slow level-wing stall. The instruments on the panel will tell the student what is happening. The left dial is the altimeter. The air speed is on the right above the square placard, and the variometer, which indicates whether the plane is going up or down, is to the right. These pictures were taken at the rate of about two per second

1 The straight-ahead stall starts from a normal flight position. Speed 45 mph; altimeter reads 2820 feet

2 The stick is pressured back. The nose comes up, as seen in lower picture. Wings are held level

5 The wings have stopped flying and plane falls nose down. Air speed still reads under 40 mph

6 This proves and shows the lag in the air speed indicator

3   Nose goes above horizon. Note air speed reads 40 mph. Hold stick back almost in your lap

4   Plane starts to fall nose first. Air speed now reads about 38 mph

7   The altimeter shows the plane has dropped 30 feet, and the air speed starts to climb. Back pressure on the stick is released

8   From the attitude of the plane as compared to the pictures of the speed dive on page 69, our plane is flying at about 70 mph

...71

9   With a slight forward stick, speed builds, wings are flying again

10   Altitude is lost rapidly, and the plane is now ready for the recovery

13   The air speed indicator now starts to catch up with what has just happened

14   The altimeter shows a loss of almost 120 feet in this gentle stall

11   If a wing starts to drop, it's leveled out with aileron control

12   The nose is gradually raised with the stick from about the time of picture 10

15   The plane is brought back to a normal flying attitude with the stick

16   In most sailplanes, the recovery from a stall can be accomplished by the plane itself, no hands

enter into the picture here also and will be discussed later. You might ask, "Why are you discussing pulling out of a dive, which is really turning flight, under a section headed straight flight?" The answer is that the accelerated stall is an excellent demonstration of the importance of understanding Angle of Attack. Out of a high-speed glide can come a high-speed stall. Student pilots are given the false impression that fast speeds alone will keep them free of the stalling problem. Air speed is a variable in relation to stalls.

THE SLOW LEVEL-WING STALL

Every student will go through a series of stalls as part of his training. The student is shown how to accomplish it and then will do it himself. It's learned in a few flights. The stick is slowly pressured back. If a wing starts to drop, it's leveled with the stick and rudder as the back pressure is applied. The nose of the sailplane is brought above the horizon. The attitude is pointing up. The Angle of Attack is gradually being increased. The air speed falls off. Just hold the stick in your lap. There won't be sufficient Relative Wind passing over the controls, and they'll feel ineffectual and limp. The hissing sound of flight will gradually disappear. Just before absolute silence, the controls will start to shudder. You'll feel it on your hands and feet. The whole plane will creak and groan. From a nose-up attitude to one of nose down will be a matter of a second.

The altimeter in the sequence shows the altitude loss in feet from the start of the stall to recovery. The stall pictures also demonstrate the lag in the air speed indicator.

These pictures should demonstrate to you that in flying near the the ground the stall becomes the critical and dangerous part of soaring. The loss of altitude is so rapid that recovery time may not become possible.

What is the recovery procedure? Reduce the Angle of Attack and increase the speed by taking the back pressure off the stick. This alone will stop the stall. The excess Angle of Attack produced the excess drag; the wings of the plane could no longer support its weight. The plane is designed so its center of gravity makes it fall nose down. With its nose down, speed will automatically increase, and the wings will begin to function again. So, strange as it may seem, to get the nose up, you've got to point the nose down. If you can remember to do this, the plane will do the rest itself. Your instructor will demonstrate it if you ask. He'll go into a stall, relax the back pressure, help the nose down with a slight amount of forward pressure on the stick, and then take his hands and feet off the controls. The Relative Wind will once again flow over the control surfaces, and the wing will start to fly again. With all controls neutralized the sailplane will right itself. It's a very forgiving machine.

You can quicken the recovery process by a slight forward pressure on the stick to get the speed back faster. A shove will produce a dive. That would mean more altitude loss. Once again, it's a pressuring. As soon as the controls resume functioning, gradual back pressure will return the plane to normal flight. This has to be accomplished by watching the attitude change in relationship to the horizon, since the air speed lag will not produce a true reading or true attitude. If you gradually pressure the stick back on recovery and hold it back until the air speed indicator slows down, the nose will go above the horizon, again causing another stall.

A true secondary stall, or the whip stall, presents a serious problem for the beginner. The student can easily get into this situation because of his old earthbound instincts. As the sailplane becomes stalled and falls earthward, the student's reflexes tell him that up is survival and down is trouble. He responds. Back comes the stick, just as when the old farmer yanked back on the steering wheel hollering "Whoa!"

The abrupt change in the Angle of Attack, just as the Relative Wind was about to get everything going nicely again, causes the secondary stall. More back pressure at this point, which is the instinctive thing for the student to apply, is only going to increase the Angle of Attack. The procedure here is the same as that already discussed for stall recovery.

The straight stall is a very important part of your training, as you will see as we go along. (The turn stall is even more important, but it will be discussed in the section on turns.) This simple stall teaches you to recognize the characteristics of an approaching stall and the stall itself. This is not a dangerous maneuver when practiced at good height. It should demonstrate to the student why an extra margin of speed is necessary when he flies close to the ground, but also that speed alone is not the answer; an abrupt change in the Angle of Attack can get him into just as much trouble as slow speeds.

It's interesting to note that 30 mph is the stalling speed, 36 mph the best minimum sink, and 45 mph the best gliding angle. We're working with comparatively small margins of speed: 36 will hold you up longest and 30 will drop you like a shot duck. The low air speed, sudden silence, unresponsive controls, and the shuddering of the whole sailplane are the signals. They tell you to do one thing: relax back pressure on the stick so as to reduce the Angle of Attack. Get the wings flying.

One of the first questions asked by people who have no contact with soaring is, "How do you get down?" It's a legitimate question, even for the student pilot. Instructors have a habit of concentrating on turns, stalls, and precise landing patterns and neglecting descending level flight until the student is about to land. Although we'll discuss the landing pattern later, there are things to say about descending flight that should not be jammed in with teaching the landing approach. Too many other things are happening all at once on landing. There are really two separate problems in descending level flight: you have one of them when you are high and want to get down; you have the other when you are low and want to stay up.

MORE ABOUT THE STRAIGHT GLIDE

DIVE BRAKES AND SPOILERS TO GET YOU DOWN

Most sailplanes are equipped with dive brakes or spoilers or both to get you down. They do it by killing part of the wing lift and increasing drag. There are a few high-performance planes that use flaps and/or drag chutes to do this. We'll confine ourselves to the brakes and spoilers because they're what the student will be using.

Spoilers only operate on the upper wing surfaces; dive brakes operate on the lower surfaces. Both are activated by a lever in the cockpit and can be applied in degrees. Panels come out of the wing surfaces and interfere with the flow of the air as it passes over those portions of the wings that house the brakes.

When you want to descend you select the desired flying speed and assume that flight altitude. Then you apply the dive brakes. Lift is reduced at those sections on the wing by the amount the brakes are extended. No matter what your attitude is, your sink rate will increase. The increased drag will reduce your air speed somewhat. A quick descent can be made with full brakes extended. If you're about to be sucked into a cloud by an updraft, you'll think dive brakes are the greatest invention since the wheel. They'll get you down out of trouble, and many brakes are designed so that even with the plane's nose pointed to the ground, the brakes will keep terminal velocity within structural limits.

The speed of the glide is maintained by the attitude of the plane and is held constant. The angle of descent is regulated by the amount of dive brakes extended. It can constantly be changed. The glide can be extended by retracting the brakes back into the wing. The descent can be steepened by extending them.

You can constantly regulate and control the amount of induced drag and lift that is being killed.

STAYING UP

Now comes the other problem. We've just solved how to get down when you are too high. How do you stay up when you are too low? If we had a motor our problems would be solved, and you'll wish many times that you had one.

The problem is simply stated. You are low and you must cover X distance over the ground to reach a ridge where you can get lift or a place to land. What do you do? You're going to have to learn new responses because your normal instincts will lead you astray.

The instinct in flying is to stay up. Instinct says the longer you are up, the better chance you have to cover the required distance. Stretch the glide! Lift the nose! Keep it up! Following this instinct is a sure way to increase the sink rate or to spin in and wrinkle yourself. The cardinal rule in soaring is to maintain flying speed; don't stall and you won't spin in.

Any time you are flying between the minimum sink speed and

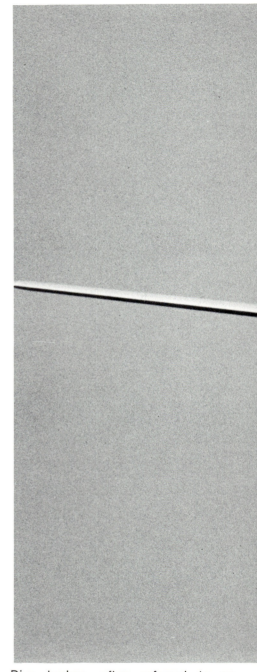

Dive brakes, often referred to as boards, kill the lift over their area of the wings and cause the plane to descend gradually

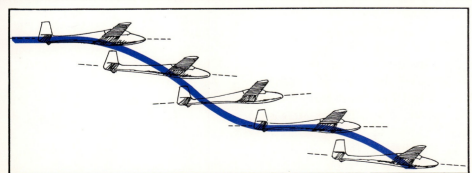

Lifting the nose and pointing the ship up in order to stretch a glide is an action based on a false premise. A mushing descent results, and that's dangerous

the stalling speed you may have the illusion that you are traveling forward at a good rate because your nose is high, but actually the high nose is deceptive. It points the way up, but you are mushing down at a fast rate with little over-the-ground coverage. At slow speed, the high Angle of Attack brakes the plane by mush-induced drag. We have already discussed mushing, descending flight where the wings continually find new levels of planing action and lift only to be slowed up, thus causing more descent. The descent increases the speed and another cushion of support is found. The rule is, if you want to go down steeply, point the nose up slightly. If you want to go down less steeply, point the nose down. That is, of course, within certain limitations. If you are in still air, you should know that your best speed to fly will be best angle of glide, 45 mph.

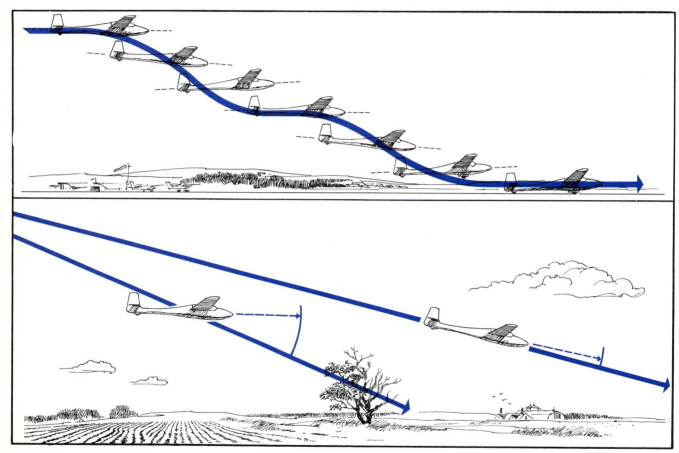

(Top) Mushing descent is dangerous at low altitude

(Bottom) You can't point a sailplane like an arrow. It's hard for the beginner to realize that nose down will carry you farther

It means just what it says, best angle of glide. At this speed you will go further forward for every foot of descent. Slower speed will produce a descending mush, and faster speed, up to a point, will get you ahead faster, with good over-the-ground coverage. The best L/D, or angle of glide, is the exact compromise to do the job for you. But still-air figures are all relative and as such are meaningless. They do tell you something about your plane, but it all has to be translated from still-air conditions to the kind of air you are flying. Still air or stable air itself is the kind of condition that should keep you on the ground, if you're smart. It's not what you would consider soaring weather.

It's difficult for most beginners to understand that a sailplane doesn't have to be held in a turn. Once the attitude of the bank is initiated, the controls are put back to a neutral position and the plane will assume that amount of turn until something changes it. Neutral in a sailplane is different from neutral in a car. It's not in one exact position. But once the neutral position is achieved, if all the forces on the sailplane are in balance, it'll turn as easily as it will fly straight.

There is one similarity between turning a sailplane and a car: you have to watch where you are going. But in a plane you're going in three dimensions. Visibility is not as good in a glider as in a car, and you don't have a rear-view mirror. Before you turn, clear the air: see that there is no traffic in your intended flight path.

Once the air is clear, your eyes should be focused ahead. Note the position of the nose of the ship in relationship to the horizon. In a correctly executed turn, that position won't change as you enter and go through the maneuver. Beginners often have the habit of looking down toward the ground on the inside of the turn. Don't. It's all right to glance, but the eyes should be ahead. Watch the nose; it's going to tell you much about the quality of the turn, and the top of the panel is going to tell you what the wings are doing by the angle it makes with the horizon.

THE TURN

Note in the turn sequence taken every 90 degrees of the 360-degree turn that the panel cuts the horizon at the same place throughout the turn. The secret to this is keeping the air speed constant. The turn is coordinated, as yaw string shows: it's constantly pointing straight back.

Sit squarely in your seat. If you make a correct turn, you'll stay that way. If not, you'll feel the tug of your body to the outside or inside of the turn. At times the seat of your pants is going to tell you more than your head.

Think it through. The turn is to be to the left. Apply the bank to the wings with the stick, a gentle pressure in that direction. At the same time apply a little left rudder. Don't kick it, apply pressure. These two movements are simultaneous. It's like the arm motion and footwork in tennis. If the timing of one or the other is off, it's the fence the ball goes over, not only the net.

When the desired amount of bank has been achieved, the controls should be neutralized. Remember as a kid when you were showing off to the girls by walking the fence? Your body had to do some fancy gyrating to stay above it and not under it. The same theory applies here. The air disturbances will continually upset the balance of the turn so you constantly have to make slight corrections. Opposite aileron will be a most common correction. But it must be accompanied with a slight pressure on the up rudder pedal. Never make corrections without using *both* aileron control and rudder.

Remember what we said in the section on controls about the way a plane turns? A very slight back stick pressure should be applied in the turn; a steeper bank will necessitate more back pressure. This is where our old friend Angle of Attack comes back into the picture. The turn is not only a banking of the wings and the application of rudder to correct for the inefficiency built into the plane's turning mechanism; also, the Angle of Attack must be increased to compensate for the loss of lift. Part of the lift that had

The lift is split into two directions

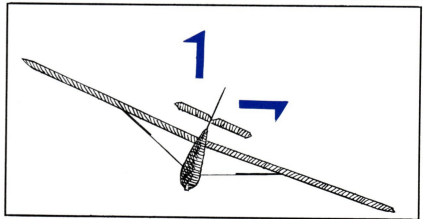

been supporting the plane in level flight has now been transferred toward the side. Less wing support is available to carry the weight of the plane. Where do we get the extra support? An increase of the Angle of Attack increases lift. Bring the stick back or the nose of the ship will start to fall.

Since turning flight is such an important phase of soaring, you should know more about it than just which way you push the controls.

Remember when as a kid you tied a rock to the end of a rope and then swung it around? It didn't make any difference whether you swung it out to the side or around your head, it took two hands to hold the same rock that was easily picked up with one hand. A half-pound rock requires a support of many times its weight to keep it from breaking free and flying off. The rock doesn't actually get heavier, but the centrifugal force causes the additional pull. This pull is exactly as if it were real weight. The same thing happens to a plane in a turn, and it makes no difference in which direction it's turning. We landlubbers consider turns as being either right or left. In flight they can also be up or down.

The curving flight, or centrifugal force, loads the plane with weight just as if it were real weight. Now the wings have to perform more of a job to support the "heavier" plane. This can be accomplished two ways. Either the wings must fly faster to produce the extra lift or the Angle of Attack must be increased. In order to accomplish a level turn in a sailplane, the Angle of Attack will have to be increased to keep the nose at a constant place relative to the horizon.

You as a pilot will be subject to the same increase in weight, and this sometimes is very confusing to the student pilot. But the thing to remember is that if the pilot feels heavier, the plane is getting heavier at the same time.

Turns up to 30 degrees add very little discomfort to the pilot and a very small increase to the weight of the plane. But when you get to a 45-degree bank, things start to happen. You will weigh about half again your normal sopping-wet weight. When you bank over to 60 degrees, you'll weigh twice as much as your bathroom scales indicate. In the pilot's language, you and the plane are under 2 G load.

Stall speed increases as the angle of bank increases

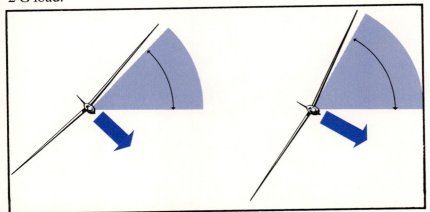

In straight flight, speed and Angle of Attack are much the same, but in curving flight, because of the extra wing loading, or extra weight, the stall speed is going to be increased. We established the stalling speed for the plane we are flying at 30 mph. In a 45-degree bank the stall speed will increase by about 17 percent, to 35 mph. In a 60-degree bank the stall speed will increase by 40 percent to 42 mph.

TIGHT TURN

What does all this G-loading theory mean to the pilot while in flight? It's this simple. If the stick is not given back pressure to increase the Angle of Attack, the sailplane will go into a dive while curving under the weight of the G load. A balance between two forces is necessary: the plane will have a tendency to increase speed; the increase of Angle of Attack counteracts this. But the pilot should balance out these two actions and fly at an increased speed that will prevent a stall for his particular angle of bank.

At this point you may question the wisdom of flying at such a steep angle of bank. Flying an airplane at a 45- or 60-degree bank might be considered hot-rod stuff. In soaring those angles are going to be commonplace; as you will read later, this is the way you exploit a thermal.

It's interesting to note that in straight flight we stall at 30 mph and in a 45-degree bank we stall at 35. We're playing with very small speed differentials.

Your first experience at flying under 2 Gs may make your head spin, but if it does you can bet you are not holding your speed constant. Watch the horizon; a steady nose will mean constant speed.

COORDINATED TURNS

Every student tangles with his instructor when learning the turns. Coordination becomes the bone of contention between them. If the stick is moved to the side before the rudder is applied, the plane side slips toward the lower wing. A skid develops if the rudder is applied before the bank is initiated. Both of these are easily seen and felt. Exact coordination of the rudder and the stick will come in time, but what is even more important and often neglected is that the coordination should include the correct amount of back pressure with the bank.

We have to recognize that a correct turn is a function of three factors: ailerons for the amount of bank, rudder to make the turn work smoothly, and an increase of the Angle of Attack to compensate for the loss of vertical lift, overcome centrifugal force, and literally lift the ship around in the turn. It also prevents an increase of speed and loss of altitude.

Since the whole purpose of soaring is to get altitude and cherish every foot of it, turns should be made as smoothly as possible. To increase the supporting power of the wings to overcome the G load, to give them the extra lift to perform their dual task in a turn, the Angle of Attack must be increased. The amount of back pressure on the stick depends on the angle of bank. The steeper the turn, the more back pressure must be added. In the core of a thermal, in a tight 50-degree bank, the stick will be back in your lap; it's the increased Angle of Attack that keeps the nose up.

A MISCONCEPTION: THE INTERCHANGEABLE FUNCTION OF RUDDER AND ELEVATOR

There are many pilots today who are convinced that there is a degree of bank after which the functions of elevator and rudder interchange. One pilot once stated that in a very steep bank the rudder is so far over in a horizontal position that it now replaces the elevator, and conversely, the elevator becomes the rudder as it approaches the vertical.

He then compared the tail section of a sailplane to that of a dirigible and said that the dirigible didn't really care which of its four tail fins was up.

It is true that in a steep bank there are times when the pilot will momentarily kick rudder alone to get the flight back to a coordinated condition. A buffet can upset the balance, and instead of using coordinated motions that would reduce his angle of bank and possibly fly the sailplane out of the core of the thermal, kicking rudder will skid the ship back into a nose-up attitude. In that case, the slight drag produced by the short skids is the better of two evils —a lost thermal is the devil of a thing to find again. No matter what the plane's attitude, kick rudder and it'll yaw, even if it's upside down. The rudder and elevator retain their control function by virtue of their relationship to the wings.

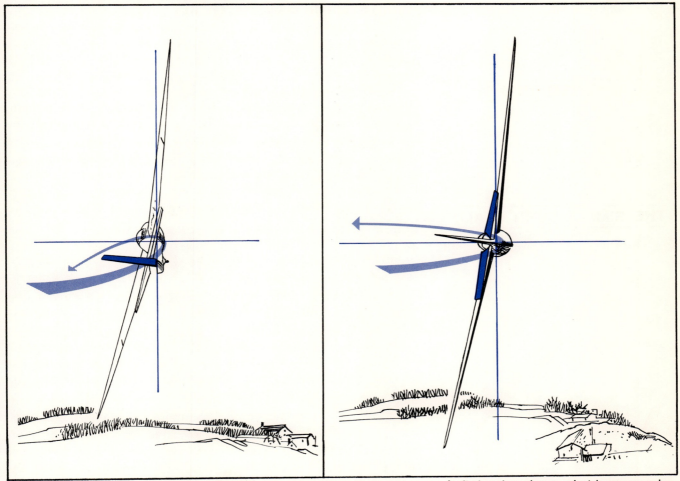

Our friend's misuse of the rudder is tempting the fates. The question he never seemed to ask himself was, "Why was the nose falling?" The answer is not found in the strange notion that the controls switch function. The nose is down for a reason. In his case, it was down because there was insufficient wing lift.

Left drawing shows what happens when rudder is used to keep nose up in a turn. Fuselage is presented to the slipstream and excess drag is introduced. If elevator is used, as in right drawing, the Angle of Attack is increased, and the turn is coordinated. Controls are not crossed

NEUTRAL STICK

We have said that when you initiate a turn and the correct attitude is reached, the controls are brought back to neutral. The neutral position should be examined more closely.

In shallow turns, because of the built-in stability of the sailplane, it will tend to come out of the turn in order to right itself and fly level. Therefore, in shallow turns neutral means a small amount of inside aileron pressure is held.

In medium turns the forces are quite neutral requiring very little, if any, aileron trim or pressure. Controls are centered.

In steep turns there is a relatively large increase in speed of the outside wing. Because of the excess speed, lift on that wing will be increased. This will tend to steepen the bank; therefore neutral in this case will require outside aileron pressure, or a small amount of opposite stick. Neutral for a steep left bank means stick to the up side or right. The slightly depressed aileron on the down wing produces lift to keep it from dropping. Here is how you do it. Let's make a steep turn to the left. The stick is put over to the left, the left rudder pedal is depressed. The turn is started. The stick is held over and rudder held in until the desired amount of bank is achieved. Then the controls are neutralized. The right pedal is depressed to bring the rudder back straight. But the stick is brought back past the center position and is moved a little to the right. This slight opposite stick moves the aileron down on the down wing (the left wing). The down aileron gives that wing a very small touch of lift to keep it from sinking. Now the bank is neutralized and the sailplane will continue to fly in that attitude until something changes one of the forces under which it's flying.

THE SIMPLE TURN STALL

As a student you will learn how to put a sailplane through a turn stall maneuver so that you will know how to recover from such a situation.

We'll go through an explanation of how the turn stall is done and how the recovery is made.

You will be asked to fly the plane very slowly. That's already a high Angle of Attack. Then you'll be told to initiate a very shallow bank, say to the left. You will be instructed to slowly bring the stick back and simultaneously keep that right wing up in its shallow bank. Unlike the level-wing stall where you brought the stick straight back, you'll have to bring the stick back in a diagonal direction: back to make it stall, and to the up-wing side to keep the lower wing from falling. The slower you go, the more ineffectual the controls become, because less air is flowing over the control surfaces; more back stick is needed to compensate. The symptoms of a stall will appear and then suddenly the nose will drop and the sailplane will be heading for the ground and pivoting on that lower wing. A full-fledged spin will develop if it's allowed to continue.

Recovery must be instinctive. Opposite rudder is applied, back pressure on the stick is released, and as the turning is stopped, the wings are brought level. Normal flight is resumed.

You will find the cross-control stall a little harder to learn than the straight or turn stalls; rudder has to be added to the maneuver. Here's the way you do it. Clear the air below you with an S turn, then enter slow level flight. Initiate a slight bank. Once you have this going well, slowly bring the stick back to assume a nose high attitude. This will increase the Angle of Attack of the wings and get you close to the stall. As in the turn stall, you will keep the bank constant, slight up stick, which requires opposite down aileron in the neutral position. As you gradually bring the stick back to complete the stall, it will be necessary to move the stick further and further toward the up-wing side to keep the lower wing from falling. Simultaneously with this final stick maneuver you'll introduce hard pressure on the lower rudder. There'll be silence, a shuddering, then the nose will drop fast and the top wing will fly around the lower wing with increasing speed. You are in a cross-control stall.

The recovery must be quick and instinctive. Kick opposite rudder to stop the turn and relax the back pressure on the stick to reduce the Angle of Attack and increase speed to get the wings unstalled. Level the wings and return the sailplane to normal cruise speed with slight back pressure on the stick.

This stall is very similar to the turn stall except that in the cross-control stall the wing didn't stall itself. In the turn stall the ensuing yaw, caused the drag of the aileron on the nearly stalled lower wing, was the final culprit. In the cross-control stall the guilt falls on the kicked rudder. The speed and the direction of movement of the wing tips have been affected.

Yaw, by our original definition, swings a sailplane around its center of gravity and moves the nose to the side. To understand this, put your arms out to the side like wings. Your head is the nose of the plane. Hold head and arms rigid. The "flight path" is toward the ceiling. Swing from the hips sideways to the left. What happens to your hands? The right hand moves forward, toward the ceiling. The left hand moves back. If your right hand were a wing tip it would be flying fast into the Relative Wind. If the left hand were a wing tip it would be moving backward, or in the same direction as the Relative Wind. It stalls out.

Now do you see why I fear for our friend who flies by kicked rudder? Skidding into a thermal ain't the game.

Let's look at this in a situation that can really mean trouble, close to the ground. We'll discuss landing patterns later, but here is the place to make this observation. Suppose you are in the landing pattern and about to make the final turn onto the glide that will lead to your touchdown. This is referred to as being on final. You approach that turn onto final and see that you are about to pass the point of turn to the runway. You decide to do something about this miscalculation. You have been making the turn and adjusting the degree of turn by holding the angle of bank with opposite stick, the neutral position. If you hit bottom rudder to prevent overshooting the turn and skid the plane around, you will have crossed the con-

TURN STALL

1 Turn stall and cross control stall are started the same way. Initiate a slight turn

2 Stick is brought back to raise the nose above the horizon. Speed is reduced

5 Stall starts. It's accompanied by a buffeting noise. The nose starts to fall fast

6 Plane slips sideways and lower wing drops more

9 Kick top rudder to stop the turn. Relax back pressure on stick to increase speed

10 Wings now have enough speed to fly again. Note what the yaw string has been doing in this sequence

3 Stick is held back and toward the up wing to hold lower wing from dropping

4 In turn stall, hold nose up until wings stall. In cross control, kick the lower rudder

7 Plane starts to turn around its lowered wing tip

8 Recovery is started and completed before the sailplane can go through a 90-degree turn

11 Back pressure will slow plane up and normal flight will be resumed when stomach catches up with pilot

Turn stall and cross control stall produced pictures that were much the same, therefore only one sequence was used to demonstrate both. Wing camera pictures were not used because attitude of the plane is rather obvious from what the pilot sees. Note in these stalls that air speed lags as it did in the straight stall. Altitude loss is only slightly over 100 feet. Bernie Carris, who flew from back seat as pictures were taken, has flown these maneuvers thousands of times as test pilot for Schweizer aircraft

trols. The yaw starts. If you are not carrying an excess of speed, the lower wing stalls. The extra drag of the down aileron and the "backward" motion of the wing tip in relationship to the flow of air are the offenders. The top wing, still flying, will take you over on your back and down, with no room for recovery. This kind of stall causes a spin-in that wrinkles sailplanes and people. Your instructor will keep hammering home to you the necessity of excess speed in the landing pattern to prevent just such a situation. Excess speed will prevent the stall.

SLOW SPEED . . . TURN STALL

Stumbling over your own ailerons

There will be times when you will be flying at very slow speed. Such an occasion could be while working very light ridge lift. Let's say you're flying at minimum sink, 36 mph. You wish to turn and by some error you slow up a mile or two per hour. You will be flying very close to the stall speed. If you initiate a steep turn by putting stick over hard, you are going to place an excess amount of drag on

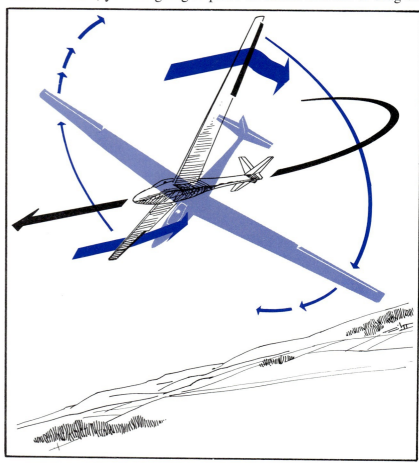

the wing tip that is supposed to rise to accomplish the bank. The aileron on the supposedly up wing goes down. The increased drag stalls out the wing. The other wing is still flying. You "stumble" over your ailerons. The wing doesn't come up; on the contrary, it drops. The other wing, still flying, flips over the top, providing you with an excellent view of the ground. The recovery is always the

The Spin. The most spectacular maneuver of your training. Since wing camera pictures were consistently the same throughout the sequence, only one was used. You're diving for the ground, as angle with the horizon shows. This is the attitude of the spin

THE SPIN AS YOU SEE IT

1 Spin is started, setting up a cross control stall. At stall point, kick rudder

2 As plane starts to fall to right, recovery procedures are not initiated

5 Rapid-fire camera shows how sailplane swings to nose-down position

6 Air speed starts to catch up and altitude is lost fast

9 Cameras are now working at about two pictures a second

10 Ground comes up fast. You are held firmly in your seat by centrifugal force...

3 Altimeter reads 2700 feet. Altitude is needed for this maneuver

4 Horizon falls off fast. The sensation starts to reach you

7 Turning of plane can be seen by following path of plane...

8 ...around shadow of cloud on ground

11 ...the feeling is sensational but not frightening. Every pilot should have this training

12 A complete revolution has been made since picture 6, as cloud shadow shows

13 As spin continues well into second turn, recovery will soon be necessary

14 Five hundred feet has been lost in a matter of seconds. Actual speed is about 80 mph

17 Normal flight is resumed and stick is gradually brought back

18 The spin is over. It has cost 800 feet of altitude

15 Stop rotation. Kick up-wing rudder. Release back stick pressure

16 Get both wings flying again. Road on ground to left of panel is the mark

19 Even experienced pilots take dual training in spins at least once a year

20 It's fun!

same: stick forward, to get flying speed; kick opposite rudder to "un-yaw."

The rule here is simple. Never, but *never* handle the controls in a rough manner at slow speeds. Turn out of slow straight flight with minimal stick and rudder. You won't be loading the sailplane with excess Gs, and the stalling speed in turn will not be increased to a point where the extra aileron drag will be the culprit. In some ways this is similar to the whip stall that we discussed earlier. Rough handling of the controls brought on an abrupt change in the Angle of Attack, and the stall developed in spite of the fast air speed.

THE BUFFET STALL

The stall speed of our plane we have established as 30 mph. That's in still air! If you were flying slow on a very gusty day, what do you think would happen if a gust hit you from the rear? What happens to the Relative Wind that is flowing over the wings and control surfaces in normal flight when a gust from behind in effect

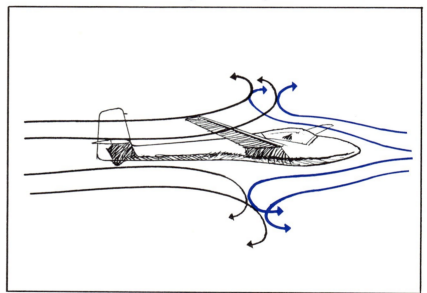

pushes at the air with a speed equal to your forward motion? The gust cancels out the Relative Wind and wings stop flying. On a gusty day keep the air speed well above the best glide speed. For our plane that's 45 to 50 mph.

Now that we have covered the stalls, let's go back and look at our friend the rudder.

THE VILLAIN RUDDER CAN BE THE HERO

You might think that because coordinated turns are so important, they should design the plane with the stick tied in with the rudder. It would be easy to do mechanically; push the stick to the side and the rudder would move with it. There are times when cross controls are extremely important, so the controls are kept separate. At this juncture you might start to think that learning to fly is in some ways like courting a woman—thinks keep changing. After all we have said about the need for coordinated controls, now we'll start to take the opposite tack.

After you learn all the stalls your instructor will teach you two types of slips; both are performed by crossing the controls. Slipping is not often used in flying sailplanes, but it is important under certain conditions. It's a useful way to lose altitude quickly without increasing the speed excessively. It's not often called for in modern sailplanes, since the dive brakes and spoilers do the same job and more efficiently. But there will be occasions, as in wave flying or landing, when you will want to add the descent produced by the side slip to that of the dive brakes to get down in a hurry.

Slips are classified by their intended track over the ground, thereby giving straight slips and side slips.

Slips are entered by lowering a wing and then applying opposite rudder to the degree necessary to control the track.

SIDE SLIPS

Both planes are making same track over ground: top one is flying coordinated controls; lower plane is in a slip and losing altitude as it moves ahead

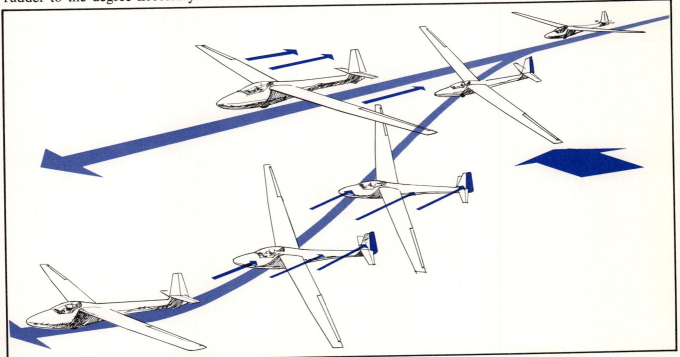

STRAIGHT SLIP

The sailplane is put into a straight side slip by applying stick to the side, slight bank, and then enough opposite rudder to prevent the nose from turning. To also prevent the nose from falling, the stick should be pressured back slightly, but since this is a cross-control situation it is very important to keep the air speed up. Excess speed will prevent stalling. The rate of descent can be adjusted by the angle of bank. The greater the angle, the more rudder is needed. If there is a crosswind, the upwind wing should be down.

Different planes have different slipping characteristics. In some trainer planes slight forward pressure will be necessary in slips because top rudder tends to raise the nose.

The loss of altitude in slip is caused by presenting the side of the fuselage to the Relative Wind, but this causes an instrument problem in some planes. The pitot tube, or air intake tube, which operates the air speed indicator, is also flying sideways and the air speed reading in some planes becomes meaningless. You must depend on attitude and control response to ascertain your speed. Sound will indicate it also, but you must realize that because of the excess drag the noise level will be high.

The tendency in learning the slips is to develop too much air speed, thereby canceling some of the benefits of slipping.

A situation that sometimes calls for a side slip is the off-field landing, when a last-moment decision is made to drop in sooner than you had anticipated. In this case the side slip or slipping turn is used. The added descent of the slipping turn, over and above the descending angle set up with the dive brakes, will enable you to turn on final lower and shorten the glide to touchdown.

With full rudder, the slip produces a turning flight path. That's an important maneuver to know: advanced students will practice landings using slips to descend instead of dive brakes

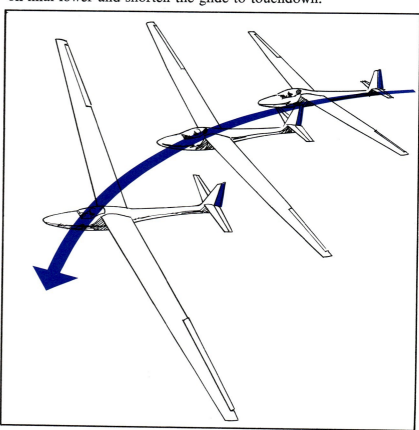

SLIPPING TURN

The sailplane is put into a turn and the opposite or top rudder is applied. Since it's not necessary to keep the plane flying straight, full rudder can be used. But the rate of turn and descent can be controlled by the angle of bank and the amount of top rudder. Learn how to adjust the amount of top rudder and convert a turning slip into a straight slip. This should be practiced at altitude; it's not a good idea to learn this maneuver on landings.

Recovery from slips should be accomplished by leveling the wings and then slowly releasing rudder pressure so the nose will wind up in the desired direction of flight.

Every cross-country pilot should know how to do side slips and constantly practice them.

We've talked a lot about the turn and have said nothing about how you come out of one. Just consider coming out the same as entrance, which is a turn in the opposite direction. Level the wings with the stick and take the back pressure off; use the rudder at the same time. If you want to come out of a turn on a specific heading, start to unbank about 30 degrees before the desired direction. Then neutralize all controls and settle back into cruising flight.

A good air speed indicator will cost about $70 and it's the most important instrument in the panel. But there is an instrument that only costs a fraction of a penny that is of great value. It's called the yaw string. Any 4-inch piece of yarn will do. When attached to the canopy of the sailplane, it indicates with delicate sensitivity the exact direction of the Relative Wind. It's like the masthead pennant on a sailboat; this tells the skipper the precise direction of the wind, and thus corrections can be made to increase the efficiency of the sail. For the sailplane pilot the yaw string does even more; it's his quality control. It constantly tells whether the plane is flying efficiently.

Care should be taken on the positioning of the string, so that there will be no interference of the slip-stream.

If the sailplane's controls are handled correctly, the plane will always present its most streamlined shape to the Relative Wind. If such is the case, no matter what your maneuver, the yaw string will always point directly back at the pilot. The only intentional exceptions are the slips. The free end of the string will point between the pilot's eyes if the controls are coordinated, whether in straight glides, tight turns, up flight, or down flight.

If the string points off to either side, something is wrong.

What happens to the string when we yaw? The Relative Wind is being presented to the side of the fuselage. The string will point to the opposite side.

What happens when we start a turn applying the rudder before the ailerons, or engaging excess rudder for the amount of bank? The string will point toward the inside of the turn. That's a skidding turn. If we apply too much aileron for the amount of rudder or apply the rudder late, that will be a slipping turn and the Relative Wind will be coming from the direction of the turn. The string will point to the outside of the turn. Where would the string point in a stall? Straight up.

It's not important to memorize what happens to the string with each kind of error; just memorize the correction, and you have a choice of controls to use.

Whichever side the yaw string points toward, pressure the opposite rudder pedal to pull it back straight, or use the stick. If for example it points off to the right, put in left rudder, or increase the bank to the right with the stick. If it's off to the left, move the stick to the left, or hit right rudder. The string will then point straight back. The rule to center the string: *follow the string with the stick, or pull the string back to center with opposite rudder*.

1 Coordinated flight. The yaw string points straight back: the air is passing smoothly over all surfaces

2 A slip. Pull string back with left rudder, or follow string with the stick

3 A skid. Plane is turning left but skidding to right, creating drag. Correction made as in picture 2

4 In a stall, string points straight up. Plane is falling: relative wind is from below

Although you have a choice in making the correction, usually rudder makes more sense. While soaring in a thermal the angle of bank is an important factor in staying within the confines of the core of the updraft. By making the yaw string correction with the stick and changing your rate of turn, you could affect your position in the thermal. On the other hand, if the yaw string is askew during the landing pattern, the stick, or angle of bank, should be used as a corrective measure *if* the change in the amount of turn will improve your landing pattern.

If a turn turns sour, do one thing: get the stick forward. Then start the corrective measures. With forward pressure on the stick a sailplane is well behaved and stable. The rule: any trouble, stick forward! Keep up your air speed.

In actual practice you're going to discover that turns are not as complicated or as troublesome as they might seem. We've been analyzing all the problems so that you will understand them. As one old hangar pilot put it, "Flying is like a marriage. It's a lot of fun, and it's even better if you know the theory so you can avoid trouble before it starts."

A LAST WORD ABOUT THE TURN

IT'S GOING TO BE LIKE THIS

The heat of the day scorches the earth and everything on it. The bottom of the sea of air boils and with tremendous energy breaks and surges upward. The release, a waterfall in reverse, and what excitement to ride its rapids! The boat? Outspread wings and a cocoon that silently seek out the boiling bubble. Finding and exploiting the energy of the invisible force is the challenge. Defeat means ignominious return to earth, while triumph is an exhilarating ride on the updraft of air until it mushrooms into a celestial fabric, white and fleecy, or until it has spent itself and can rise no more. Triumphantly from on top, the pilot can now take time to loll in the silence and see what only few men can see, a reward for his skill and concentration. Soaring is a sport of deep concentration. The rewards are the beauties, but they are fleeting. The pilot does not ride as a passenger through this marvel of beauty. He has no time. He is working. He's plotting, calculating, he's challenging a force and defending his place. The reward is short-lived unless it's committed to memory. Short-lived because every triumph over gravity invites potential threat, and the sweet taste of triumph will shortly sour. Like the millions of faces below, no two thermals are the same; experience teaches, some are false, some tricky, some strong. Some hide and some show themselves. Some are being born while some are dying. You cannot marvel at the environment, the silence, or the vista when your opponent is so nebulous.

7
LANDING

Any old-timer will tell you the same thing: set up a good landing pattern, give yourself room and time to make a final glide, and you'll have no trouble

1 Pilot turns onto final

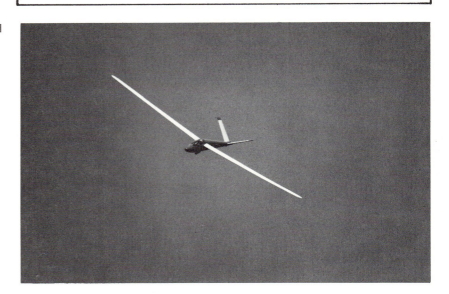

2 Dive brakes are extended

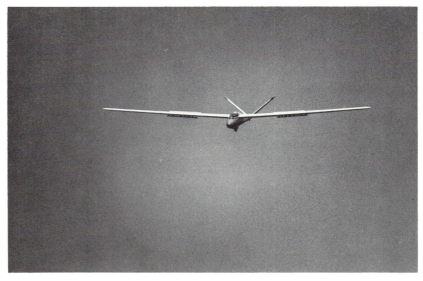

3 Descent is gauged

4 More brake is used

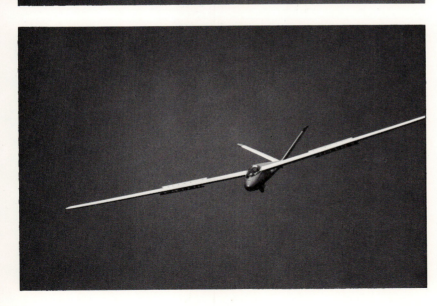

5 Pilot jockeys position

6 Lineup is made for touchdown

7 Pilot's eyes are now on far end of field

8 Air speed has been constant

9 Brakes are retracted in glide for touchdown point

10 Steady and level

11 On the ground: brakes extended and wheel brake applied to stop as quickly as possible

THE PROCEDURE:
IT CLICKS OFF FAST

Many things happen fast. That's why landing is the most frustrating part of the student's training. Once you're halfway into the landing pattern, you're irreversibly committed. But it's not really difficult, it's just a matter of organizing a procedure, ticking things off as they come, and getting used to seeing common objects from a new and rapidly changing perspective.

The landing can be broken down into two parts: things that should always be happening and the variables. You'll hear a lot from your instructor about the landing pattern. He'll want you to make it as routinely consistent as possible each time you come in. It's not only the safe way, but the sooner certain aspects of it become second nature to you, the sooner you'll be able to relax and your time can be more efficiently spent handling the variables. It's only going to take a minute or so from the time you enter the landing pattern to touch down; things click off fast.

THE PATTERN

The final touchdown should always be made into the wind; at that point ground speed will be at a minimum, and the roll-out short. Working backward from that fact, the safest and best way

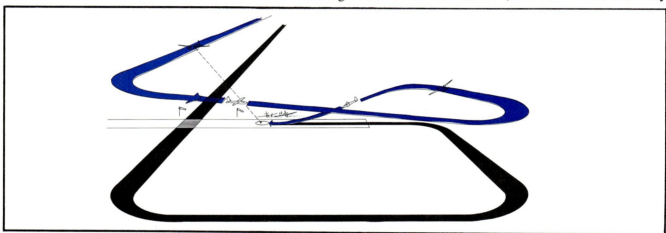

Throughout the pattern the pilot should constantly eyeball his landing spot. This prepares him for off-field landings. Seeing objects from a new perspective is often confusing at first. The wind sock shows the direction of the wind, and pattern is built backward from that fact. Final glide is into the wind, the base leg should put you into position for final, downwind leg must set you up for base leg, and it all starts on the crosswind leg

to enter that final phase is to fly an oblong pattern. There are four legs: first crosswind, downwind, base, and the final. The normal way to fly it is counterclockwise, all pattern turns to the left unless otherwise designated.

Flying a good pattern will be one of the constants in the landing procedure. At least knowing this much, flight path, you're not going to have to stop and think which way to go. Your instructor will run you through this a few times, pointing out the flight path. He'll want you to know where to go and how high you should be at each turn point. He'll also point out landmarks at each turn point. This makes three pieces of information that are constant: which way to go, exactly where each turn point is, and how high to be at each turn point.

Here is where the tape recorder becomes useful. Later, in calmer surroundings, you can visualize the whole procedure without the tensions of performance. Like an actor you study your script. Once you know your lines, the stage action becomes meaningful and easier.

The FAA rules recommend entrance into the pattern at a 45-degree angle to the downwind leg, thus eliminating the first crosswind leg. This recommendation should be followed at active airports where there is a good deal of power traffic. At gliderports it's good practice to include the crosswind leg in the pattern in order to

FIRST CROSSWIND LEG

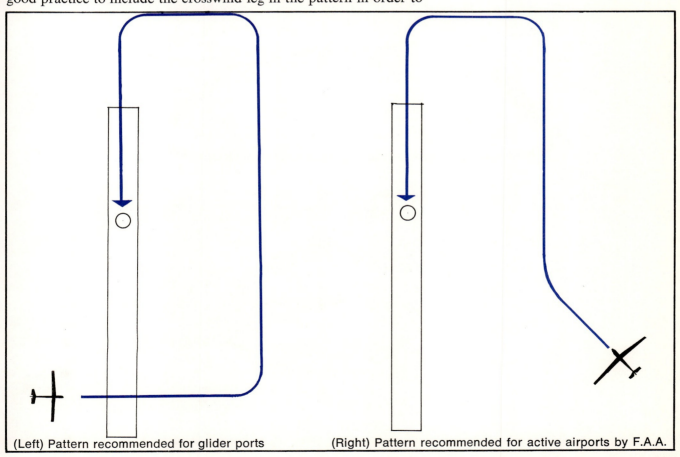

(Left) Pattern recommended for glider ports   (Right) Pattern recommended for active airports by F.A.A.

prepare for off-field landings in farmers' fields. It is good for the student to learn this as part of a normal pattern. It'll give him that much more time to make some important observations. At the start of the leg he should be at about 1,000 feet. He will pass over the airport to see any traffic problems that he should be aware of in the air and on the ground. The wind sock will show wind direction. From this position he will see other air traffic that might be on a longer downwind run, or any planes about to land.

The first crosswind leg is a good habit for the pilot who expects to soar cross-country. This gives him one more look at the landing area to select a touchdown point and roll-out free of obstructions.

There are other observations the pilot should make on the first crosswind leg: wind direction and strength. From his drift or over-the-ground speed he'll be able to tell much about how he will fly the rest of the pattern. For example: If there is a strong tail wind, the over-the-ground speed will be fast. This means that on the downwind leg he might be blown off course, away from the field; he should correct for this, since the downwind run should be flown parallel to the landing strip. It also means that when he gets to the base leg he'll be bucking a head wind and lose altitude faster than he might have expected. Then he'll have to make the necessary adjustments; either the downwind leg should be shortened or the downwind leg should be moved closer to the landing strip.

If on the first cross leg the wind is strong from the right causing drift to the left, it will signal certain conditions about the rest of the circuit. The downwind leg will be very fast because when he turns onto it he'll have a tail wind. On the base leg he'll drift to his right, or away from the landing spot. He'll face a head wind on the final leg. In this case the downwind leg should be cut short, and the turn onto base should be made closer to the fence line of the landing strip.

A head wind on the first cross leg will indicate corrections on the downwind leg. This leg should be moved slightly away from the field or he'll find the base leg will be too short and fast.

The reason we must consider all these factors is that as we traverse from point to point, a gradual descent is necessary.

Altitude will be lost by the use of the dive brakes between points, not by pointing the nose of the sailplane down. The brakes enable you to lose altitude without increasing speed. The further out you put the "boards," the greater your sink rate. Critical judgment is required here. If you make your turn onto the downwind leg at 900 feet and you know you want to be between 600 and 700, as you turn onto the base the brakes can be extended or retracted as needed to achieve the correct altitude at the right spot.

The descent should never be accomplished by a variation of speed. Pattern speed should be constant until flairout on the final leg. This speed can be determined, again, by the observations in that first crosswind leg. If it's a calm day and the wind sock shows it, and the air you are flying displays the same stillness, the pattern speed for our plane would be about 55. If there are strong winds aloft and/or on the ground (not necessarily in the same direction), the speed should be increased by 5 mph.

We'll talk later about the final approach in a crosswind, but as you fly through the pattern you're really setting yourself up for the last leg. The first three legs will give you all the information needed for the final touchdown. Think and plan ahead to avoid being confused by things that should become strictly routine.

DOWNWIND LEG

Learning to fly the pattern has one major difference from learning to drive a car around the block: there's a third dimension added. When you enter the pattern you'll be at about 1,000 feet above the field; when the pattern is completed you'll be on the ground at a spot one-third down the runway.

You determined your flying speed by the observations of the wind speed at your altitude and the observations on the ground. The last thing you do on the crosswind leg is to set up your attitude for the selected air speed and hold it constant. We'll assume the conditions are relatively calm, so the speed will be 55 to 60 mph. A glance at the altimeter will indicate if you are going along as planned. The landmarks will show if you are in the correct position. The turn to the left is made. Coordinate it! Glance at the runway, note its position. Fly parallel to it. Check the air speed. Keep it constant. Crack open the dive brakes. Now apply them if necessary to be at the correct height for the turn onto the base leg. If you get too low, bleed off the dive brakes. Mark your spot ahead for the turn onto base leg.

On this leg the first corrections will be made. You should always be considering the landing point, and glancing at it. If you are too high, you can apply more dive brake. If that isn't enough of a correction you can fly slightly to the right, which will necessitate a longer base leg. If you are too low, you should bleed off the dive brakes. If that isn't enough, move in closer to the landing strip, which will necessitate a shorter base leg. Whatever your decision, don't tamper with the speed.

BASE LEG

As you turn left onto the base leg you have a further opportunity to make minor corrections. Speed is still sustained at 55 to 60 mph for the conditions we have set up. Your object will be to reach the end of the base leg between 300 and 400 feet above the ground. Your first means of achieving this descent are the dive brakes. If you feel you are too low, close the dive brakes. If you're still too low the pattern can be cut short, but a turn toward the field will give you a shorter final glide. A long final gives more time for setting the plane up for the touchdown. But a shorter final is better than sitting on top of a tree short of the field.

If you are too high and full dive brakes aren't making your descent rapid enough, the pattern can be lengthened. Fly to the right, a few degrees away from the field. During the base leg run,

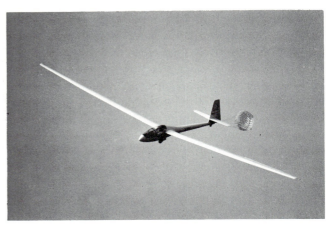

Chute landings are spectacular: because of their much greater landing speeds, high-performance open-class sailplanes use these drogue chutes to facilitate landing in short fields

constantly glance toward the field. Seek out the spot where you expect to touch down.

Check your flying speed; remember turns close to the ground are the ones that lead to problems. Make your last turn onto the final leg at pattern speed.

It's good practice to learn to change the angle of glide on final, as a preparation for off-field landings. With dive brakes retracted you'll glide the farthest. To shorten the final glide, full dive brakes should be used. If that's not enough, a straight slip can be added, and it's considered good procedure.

There is another technique, but it is rarely used. With dive brakes extended the ship can be yawed by rudder, from side to side. The excess drag increases the descent.

Toward the end of your training, your instructor will have you try both straight and turning slips in the pattern. Sometimes in off-field landings judgments of height are difficult. The slip with extended dive brakes can get you down in a hurry, for a last-minute change of touchdown point.

Dive brakes should be cracked open and tested before the pattern is started. There have been cases where the dive brakes have been frozen and inoperative. The student should always be ready for such a situation and have an alternate plan in mind. The slip and a slightly larger pattern would be the main descending technique. Yawing by rudder could be used on final. All slips and yawing must be stopped at about 30 feet in low-performance planes.

A word of warning. Making a 360-degree turn any place in the pattern in order to lose altitude is extremely poor judgment. And never—but never—decide to thermal once you have started the landing pattern, no matter how much lift you encounter. At that height the thermal is very narrow, and your chances of getting much out of it are slim. In the meantime, you have messed up your pattern, and there might be a plane behind you coming in for a landing and you could mess him up too. Sailplanes don't have rear-view mirrors. The rule is, once you have started the circuit you're committed to it.

ON FINAL AND THE TOUCHDOWN

The air speed throughout the pattern has been between 55 and 60 mph for our plane. Once the turn onto final has been completed the air speed can be reduced to the low side of the bracketed speed, or 55 mph. The absolute minimum speed for the approach should be 10 mph above the best glide angle speed. Some pilots prefer to think of pattern speed in relation to stall speed. Their rule is that pattern speed should be 25 mph above stall speed. This will still be safe for relatively calm conditions, and things won't be happening quite so fast. Speed will be held constant to within a few feet of the ground.

If there is any wing tipping due to turbulence, corrections should be made immediately or the sailplane will turn off course. The dive brakes are used to regulate the last rate of descent. The flight path can be extended by bleeding them off, or it can be shortened by extending them.

Unlike a power plane, a sailplane is never full-stalled in for final touchdown. This is the big thing that power pilots must unlearn to get their glider rating. A sailplane is flown all the way onto the ground.

The turn onto final should be made no lower than 300 feet. This will then give a long final glide, and enough time to get oriented and touch down. As the sailplane approaches the ground, a very slight back pressure on the stick will begin to slow the glide up. This rounding out should be done so the plane will fly parallel to the ground within 1 foot of the ground to prevent the ship from dropping in. It'll fly on a cushion of air, lose speed, and sink onto the main wheel.

After touchdown the sailplane must still be flown, wings level and straight. Once on the ground you can steer the direction of runout with the rudder. The stick is still used to keep the wing tips level. Apply the rudder, point the nose to the side of the runway to clear it for other planes behind you. Once your roll-out heading is obtained, neutralize the rudder. If necessary slowly apply the wheel brake until the wings are no longer producing lift. When the speed is reduced the sailplane will nose up on its skid and stop. Put the stick over, lay a wing down.

All this may sound relatively simple. Reading and thinking will help some, but until you experience the meaning of "slight back pressure on the stick" at the moment of flairout, the meaning of the word "slight" will be relative. Flairout will seem difficult at first.

Too much back pressure at that moment will balloon the sailplane. If this happens, the amount of ballooning becomes the next consideration. If it's only a few feet or so, no action is necessary. Neutralize the stick and pause. The wings will find a new cushion, and the plane will settle in, making a slightly longer flight to touchdown; just proceed, holding off as for a normal landing. If, on the other hand, the ballooning is 10 feet or so, corrective action must be taken so that the plane won't stall 5 to 10 feet in the air. Forward pressure on the stick will bring the nose down and will point you toward the far end of the field. Then the ship will settle in and you will make a second attempt at the landing. If you do balloon, don't rush things. The longer it's held off the ground the better.

THE EYES: WHERE AND WHAT THEY SHOULD SEE

Ballooning is an error of judgment and then overcontrolling. Every student experiences it. Its cause is related to what the pilot sees and where he is looking. It's hard to judge where the ground is on flairout, especially if the student is looking at the spot where he hopes to land. In the last stages of the final approach, the eyes should be focused about 500 feet ahead or the distance he normally looks ahead while driving his car. The closer to touchdown, the closer in he may look. What's happening to the sailplane can best be observed by the relationship of the top of the instrument panel to this boundary horizon. The plane will fly itself onto the ground. The panel top will tell you if the wings are level and its relative horizontal flight path.

When flying in lively air the speed should be increased for the whole pattern. There are two reasons: wind gradient and turbulence. The effects of both are critical near the ground. This is why we have set the height of the turn points in the pattern as high as we have. Some instructors will feel that we have established too high a pattern with the turn onto final at absolutely no lower than 300 feet, but actually 400 is better. This will prevent flying through the effects of a wind gradient while turning, and as you will see, it will be a good habit to develop.

When the wind is brisk, ground obstacles cause a change in its velocity; surface winds are slowed up by friction, winds aloft are only slightly affected. Trees, buildings, hills, general landscape slow the air at the surface causing turbulence; this in turn slows the air above. The effect diminishes gradually with altitude. Only under severe conditions will the gradient effect reach 1,000 feet. This means that on landing you will fly through layers of changing wind speed.

LANDING IN STRONG WINDS

WIND GRADIENT

One thing to remember—put the retractable gear down. At 200 feet the wind can be blowing 30 mph, but only 10 mph on the ground. This can cause trouble. The rule: fly fast

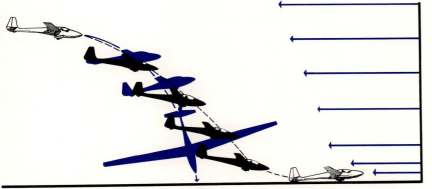

Wind gradient will be much greater over rough terrain than smooth. That's one reason why hurricanes peter out over land. The higher the wind, the steeper the gradient will be; it will be more effective on the lee side of hills and obstacles than on the windward side. The critical area can be up to 300 feet above the ground. For example, a 30 mph wind at 200 feet could be as slow as 10 mph on the ground. This means that a sailplane on final flying through the reducing layers of wind speed will experience sudden drops of air speed as it flies into the lighter winds. Its own inertia will carry it on over the ground, but the reduction of wind speed will cause a drop of air speed. In an extreme case, this could stall the plane out. The sudden reduction of air speed causes the sailplane to sink. As the plane descends at a sudden increasing rate, the pilot's instinct might be to slow it up, flare out with back stick, and prepare to land. This is erroneous thinking. Checking the rate of descent with back stick will increase the Angle of Attack. Less Relative Wind will be passing over the control surfaces because of the diminishing wind velocity. As descent is made through the gradient, an increase of the Angle of Attack could set up a stall condition.

Air speed through wind gradient should be maintained at the higher end of the bracket, or 60. This will ensure enough speed for leveling out to land. Here, once again, you can't fly by instinct. The stick must be pressured forward to increase your speed; the reduction of wind speed will cause a slowup, so actually with stick forward you will be touching down at normal speed.

In a high wind gradient condition the air brakes should be used sparingly. There is no use increasing the rate of descent and causing a heavy landing.

When the wind gradient is high the turn onto final should be high and shallow. The wings of the sailplane are very long. A steep bank with a 50-foot wing could have one tip reaching into air traveling at 30 mph and the other dipping into 20-mph wind. The upper tip will be flying faster, at a higher Angle of Attack producing more lift, and could spin you in, over the top. Excess speed will prevent trouble.

A turning plane's wing tips can be flying in air of different wind velocity: upper wing tip could be flying in 30-mph wind while lower tip flies in 20-mph wind. The rule: fly fast

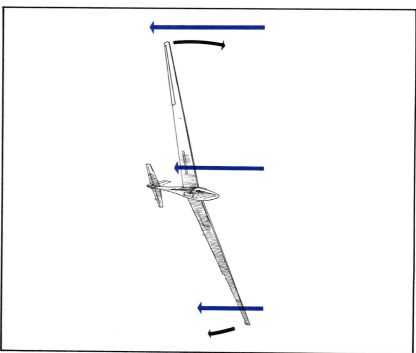

TURBULENCE

Turbulence should be handled like wind gradient when it occurs near the ground; excess speed will prevent problems. Gustiness is caused by high winds spilling over buildings, trees, etc. In normal flight aloft gustiness is caused by unstable air; it will be rough but controllable. Air speeds should be kept high. Under these conditions the landing pattern should be high and fast. Turns should be shallow in preparation for a wind gradient effect on final. Faster air speed gives better control response if the ship is hit with a gust from the side or rear.

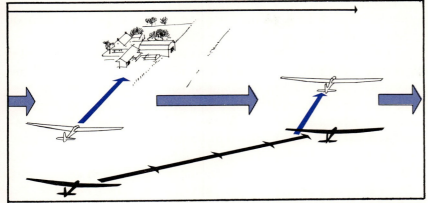

CROSSWIND LANDINGS

Before a student finishes his training he will have to demonstrate crosswind landings. If he uses the pattern legs to gather information before he gets on final, he will know whether or not a crosswind procedure will be involved in the landing. The wind sock will show it. Smoke, flags, wash out drying, movements of trees are a few of the things sailplane pilots should always observe for wind direction. Even more significant will be the flight path on the downwind leg. If a crab into the wind is necessary in order to keep a ground track parallel to the runway, the same thing will be experienced, but in the opposite direction, when the pilot turns 180 degrees to final. A fast or slow over-the-ground coverage on the base leg is another signal revealing that the wind will be coming from your right or left when you turn onto the final leg.

THE CRAB METHOD

When the sailplane is turned onto final the over-the-ground path should be a line extended out from the runway. The plane will not follow this line if the nose is pointed straight down the runway, because the wind from the side will cause a drift. After all, the glider is flying in a mass of air, and as the mass moves the glider will move

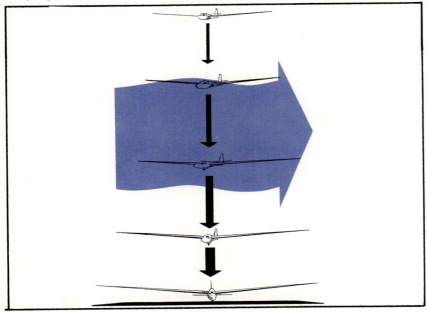

with it even though the sailplane is flying straight and has no lateral motion relative to the air mass. It's the air mass that's moving and carries the plane with it.

By pointing the nose slightly into the wind, the over-the-ground track will be corrected. The sailplane will not weathercock as the landlubber might imagine. The yaw string will be centered and the flight will be coordinated. The sailplane's lateral motion is drift. Correcting a little, heading the plane slightly into the wind, counteracts the drift. There is another way to explain this. If the drift is to the east, pointing the ship to slightly west of north will result in a path to the north.

So as the plane is turned onto final in a crosswind, it should be headed into the wind enough to make the correct over-the-ground path. The wings should be flown level and rudder neutralized. This attitude should be maintained until the flairout and touchdown. The moment before touchdown the sailplane should be swung parallel to the landing strip with the rudder. If the rudder is applied too early, the sideways drift will take effect. If the nose is swung too late and the sailplane lands in a crabbed attitude, it will place excess side load on the landing wheel and possibly cause damage.

Once the plane touches the ground it will have a tendency to weathercock into the wind. Care must be taken that the upwind wing is lowered to prevent a gust from getting under it. When the plane is brought to a stop the upwind wing should be put down to the ground with the stick.

UPWIND WING DOWN IN A CROSSWIND

The nose is headed right down the runway. The windward wing is lowered and opposite rudder is applied. This is a side slip. The slip counteracts the drift of the wind. At the last moment before touchdown the wing has to be leveled so as not to touch the wing tip on landing.

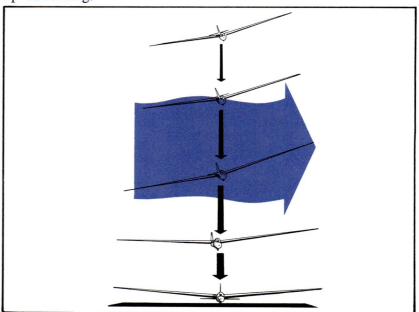

However, the crab method is the easiest to learn and best suited for the student pilot. In a crosswind give yourself plenty of room between parked gliders and plan to turn the plane into the wind on final runout.

Practice glance reading of the instruments. This is not only important for the landing pattern, it applies to all your flying. You're not going to see much with your eyes glued to the board.

After the first few landings with your instructor, start to gauge your height above the turn points and use the altimeter as a check. Then learn to go through the pattern without the altimeter. It's not very accurate below 300 feet anyway.

Except in training planes, it's not good practice to use full dive brakes on touchdown. The descent will be rapid and could lead to a heavy landing. If it is necessary because the landing is being overshot, remember that full brakes kill a good part of the wings' lift, so the flairout should be made only a foot or so off the ground and the air speed kept high.

SOME LANDING TIPS

This is what you'll see if a perfect landing has been set up. At 120 feet the airspeed is 60 mph; heading is right down the grass strip; yaw string is centered. But keep your eyes off the instruments at this point. Focus eyes at the far end of the field

A bad landing, in most cases, can be traced to a faulty pattern.

In your first landings, the instructor pointed out the circuit, its landmarks, heights, etc. This method was satisfactory for those early flights because he wanted you to have as few variables as possible. Once you have the hang of landing, it will be necessary to learn to set the pattern up yourself.

Some old-timers do what they call "feeling" the landing pattern. They don't land by being at defined heights at specific points in a pattern. What they do when they land at a strange airport or a farmer's field is watch their landing spot and add another piece of information to their calculations—the angle to the landing spot below them. This angle is measured by the amount their eyes must drop below a line parallel to their level wings to the touchdown point. While on the downwind leg they glance over and keep the runway parallel to their flight.

PLOTTING YOUR LANDING PATTERN

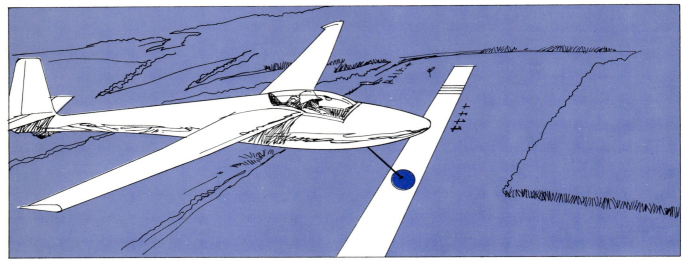

1 Make decision as to landing spot on crosswind leg. This gives time needed to set up pattern

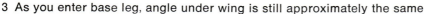

3 As you enter base leg, angle under wing is still approximately the same

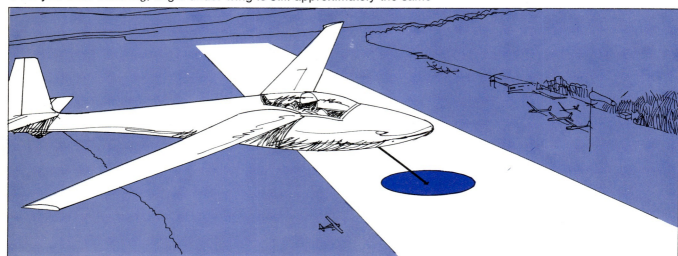

When they fly opposite their touchdown point, the angle down to it should be about 40 degrees. If they are at the correct altitude and angle, then their distance from the field will enable them to make a normal landing pattern. If the angle is not correct, it's changed by either moving away from the field to reduce the angle or moving toward it to increase it to the 40 degrees.

Now they are set up for the rest of the pattern. This is just another way of keeping the variables in landing to a minimum.

One of the major problems all beginners have is that of moving in too close to "Mother," the landing strip. When they approach a new landing situation they cut into the downwind leg too early. When they do this the base leg is cut short and they're on final before they know it. Too many things are now happening all at once. A well-planned pattern will give you all the time in the world, especially on base leg, to make slight minor corrections.

Learn the correct angle between the level wing and the touch-

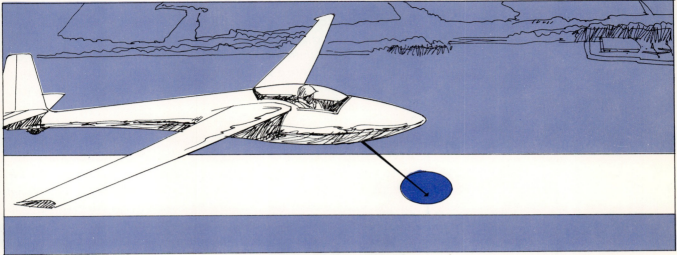

2 Keep "eyeballing" prospective spot as you descend on downwind leg

4 Make a broad pattern. Keep the legs long enough so that things won't happen too fast. It's good to start learning landing procedure by making your spot about one-third down the runway; later you can practice dropping just over the fence

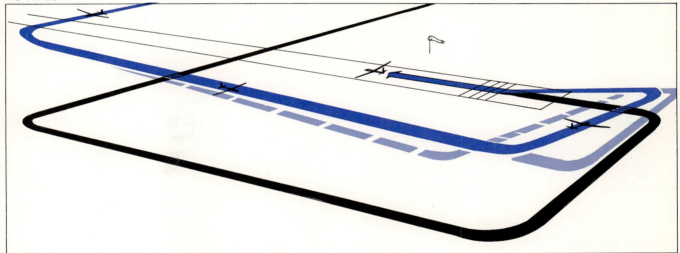

down point, and you'll be able to set the sailplane down where you want to in any field that's large enough. This 40-degree angle gives you time, an all-important commodity: time to handle the wind; time to consider ground obstacles; time to set your correct air speed; time to bleed off dive brakes or extend them on the final descent; time to consider the flairout; time to perform each part of the landing, step by step.

The perspective of objects on the ground is much the same as perspective in the air. Things that appear below you are lower than you; objects above you are higher than you. When an object cuts through your horizon, while you're on the ground or at 1,000 feet, it's at your altitude. This is important to know when flying a landing pattern with other air traffic. Planes above your horizon are above you, those below it are lower. Traffic cutting through your horizon is at your same altitude.

THE CHANGING PERSPECTIVE

The important thing to learn to observe while on final glide to the touchdown spot is the changing relationship between objects on the ground in the flight path and the horizon. On the final descent, objects that move up toward the horizon will *not* be cleared by the plane. Those that move down, away from the horizon, will be flown over. The touchdown point never changes in its relationship with the horizon.

At first, the student pilot looks at the whole landscape scene without seeing the perspective relationship of individual objects. The direction and position of objects on your canopy in relation to the horizon will tell you much about the landing point. During descent on final, buildings at the far end of the field will move up on the canopy. The fence at the near end of the runway will move down. But closer observations than that have to be made.

Once you understand this you can put it to practical use. Here's an example: If you are landing in a farmer's field and observe that the area beyond the far side of the ditch is clear for landing, that establishes your desired touchdown spot. Then on the final glide, as the ditch appears before you, note its exact position on the canopy. If it starts to rise toward the horizon, the dive brakes must be bled off to extend the glide. If the ditch appears to be dropping away from the horizon, the brakes should be extended or the landing may be long. If the far side of the ditch stays steady in its position on the canopy and does not change in relationship to the horizon, fly as you are—your landing point is good.

Observe the details, for example, how trees seem to move with the changing perspective. Watch the relationship of motion. From your altitude, line up the top of a tree you expect to fly over and a tuft of grass on the field behind it. If the tree starts to rise in relationship to the grass, you may not clear the tree, but if the tree starts to fall away from the grass, you're clear.

Problem is set up in left-hand drawing: will the telephone wires be cleared on final glide? If the pole and wires move down on the canopy as you approach (middle drawing), and the space opens up between pole and landing spot, your flight path is safe. If, as in the right-hand drawing, the pole moves up on the canopy, or the space between pole and landing spot diminishes, you're in trouble

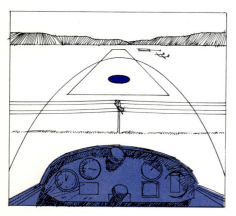 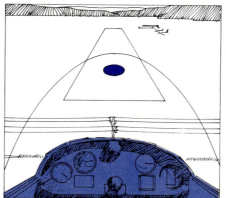 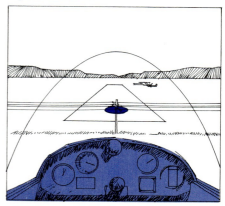

As you descend, all objects rapidly increase in apparent size. This is what tends to confuse the student. Judging these rapidly growing objects by absolute heights and distances and committing your judgment to memory won't do you much good in landings off field or at a strange airport. Being three times the height of the tree at the airport fence won't do you much good when you land in a farmer's field where the tallest thing around is the bull.

Train your memory, imprint on your mind the shape of the landing strip. If you are too high as you come over the airport fence, the field will appear more as a square. The amount of foreshortening of a good landing is the perspective to commit to memory. How do you learn this? By experience and remembering the various fast-changing relationships of objects and the over-all changing shape of the field.

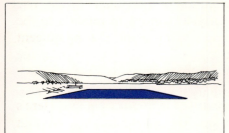 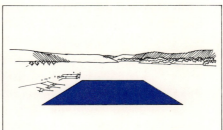 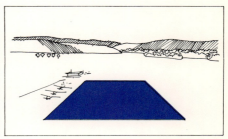

Train your memory to recognize the proper shape of the landing strip. In left drawing, you're too low; center one has correct perspective; you're too high if it looks like right-hand drawing

IT'S GOING TO BE LIKE THIS

The first bite in the air is a signal for the hawks to convene for their migration southward.

The ventilators are closed, but the autumn chill still seeps into the cocoon. The body nags for release from its harness to undo its crampedness, but there is still work to be done. Twenty miles to go. One more good thermal will get you home. Just one more. Then a few knee bends and a cup of coffee will satisfy the body needs, but they are secondary. Slowly the altimeter unwinds, foot by foot. The whole instrument panel seems to be saying, "Negative, negative . . . negative." A glance at the lowering sun reinforces the accuracy of the instruments. The splash of fiery color subsides in the trees below. Above, the cottony clouds dissipate to clear the way for the evening star. It seems that only moments ago success was so close its flavor could almost be tasted. Such a perfect flight, now to end this way. The fellows at the field will have a good laugh. "He's down! In a farmer's pasture, this side of the river. Hook up his trailer and let's go get him." Reevaluate . . . stick with it . . . find the answer to success. The sink rate is very slow. At other times this is a blessing, but in these ebbing conditions it spells the end of the vertical flow, when even hawks must flap their wings. Safety is no problem, there is a freshly mowed field by the river that has been hayed for the last time this year. The wagon marks still show the rhythm of the farmer's work. . . . No time for idle thoughts. . . . Stay in the area and search it out . . . turn to the right . . . to the left . . . move over toward the ridge . . . the plowed field has cooled. . . . Could the trees have held the ground heat and now allow it to release? . . . Try it . . . 2,000 feet . . . time runs out . . . a hawk at a distance flaps his wings. . . . Oh, if the sailplane could do the same . . . turn, follow him, keep him in sight . . . he too is seeking. The hawk makes a correction, heads southward, flies faster, and shortly joins his kind. Now there is hope. Lazily, three . . . no, five hawks circle. A glance heavenward surely spells salvation . . . home. Fifty, not five, hawks circle in the last thermal of the day. The instrument panel comes alive, the weary body relaxes. The flight ends in a crescendo. The hawks allow the giant within their midst as if he were one of them. With graceful ease they bob and weave out of the path of the stiff, awkward giant as he tightly turns, passing up through them. Up . . . up . . . up to 5,000 feet. The big bird rocks his wings in salute and thanks and heads north . . . home. The final glide is already calculated; the slight evening breeze helps. Now it's only mechanics; the work of the day is over. The aching back will soon be relieved, and the coffee will circulate its warmth throughout the numb body. Will the redtail hawks remember this extraordinary day when a white titan joined them? The titan will never forget.

8
SOARING FLIGHT

GLIDING AND SOARING FLIGHT . . . TOGETHER

A sailplane flies by gliding down under the influence of gravity. Gravity is converted into the forward thrust that enables the wings to produce their lift. In reality, a sailplane is always descending, even as it climbs. Sail a paper plane across the room and its flight will be a continuous descent. Fly the same paper plane over a campfire and it will glide down until it gets into the rising warm air; then it will climb. As it climbs it's still under the influence of gravity, but the rate of sink is not as fast as the rate of climb produced by the column of rising air.

Think of it this way. Try walking down an up escalator. If the escalator is going up faster than you are walking down, you'll end up on top. Your walking is similar to the sailplane's gliding flight, the escalator similar to the updrafts.

THE VARIOMETER

Flying an updraft is similar to walking on the escalator with your eyes closed, since we cannot see updrafts. The variometer becomes our eyes. It tells us if the air mass we are flying in is going up or down, and how fast, or if we are flying in zero sink, where our sink rate balances the rising air.

There are three main types of instruments, none of which should be confused with the rate-of-climb indicators in airplanes. The vario is a very sensitive instrument and has a much quicker response than the rate-of-climb indicator. The function of the vario is to measure a change in the rate of pressure while ascending or descending. The vario responds to minuscule variations of pressure.

The principle behind the variometer is simple. The panel instrument is connected to an insulated reservoir of air, like a thermos bottle, inside the plane, and then to the outside by a static pressure line. When the sailplane ascends, the reservoir of air is at a higher pressure than the air outside, so the air, to equalize itself, will flow toward the outside. When the reservoir of air descends, it is at lower pressure than the outside; the flow of air is inward. The instrument measures the direction and the amount of air flow, which is calibrated in feet, meters, or knots per second or minute.

Pellet-type variometer, inexpensive, sensitive and reliable, is usually found only in training ships. Change of pressure in and out of the vacuum reservoir indicates direction of air flow

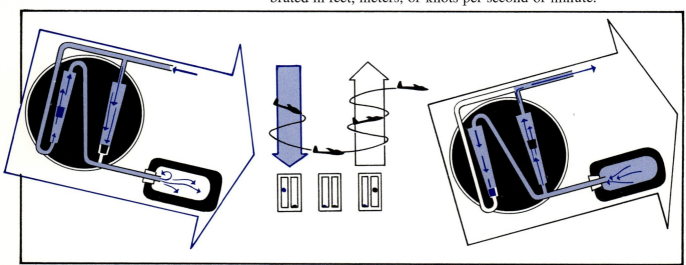

The least expensive but a very sensitive vario is the pellet type. The instrument consists of two tapered tubes with a colored plastic pellet in each which is pushed up the tube by the changing air flow. The red pellet indicates sink and the green pellet means ascent, or "green air," a phrase coined by the old-time glider pilots.

One of the best types of mechanical instruments is the vane type. The principle is the same as the pellet vario. A very close-fitting vane pivoted on a jewelled bearing is mounted in a cylinder. A hair spring keeps it centered. The vane is deflected up or down by a jet of air. It's connected to a needle that gives a direct reading on the dial, according to the direction of air flow.

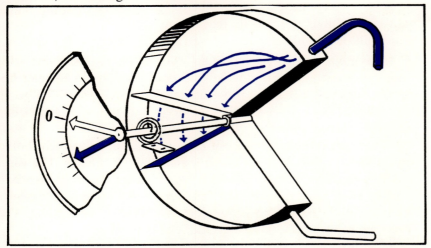

Vane-type vario works on same principle, but is more accurate

The latest development is the electrically operated variometer. Its quicker response and extreme sensitivity make this a must in competition flying. The flow of air from or to the reservoir is detected by the cooling effect on a hot wire or thermistor. By means of a switch, ultrafine variations can be amplified so that weak or strong conditions can be read most accurately on full scale.

A transistorized audio attachment can be fitted to the vane or electric variometer so that the pilot does not have to watch the instrument panel. Since the audible output is in direct ratio to the intensity of the lift, the pilot can center in a thermal by sound and at the same time watch out for other aircraft flying the same updraft.

When a sailplane is flying in still air and the stick is brought back, the plane will climb. The ordinary variometer will indicate the change in altitude and the pilot might assume he's encountered an updraft. This is what the old-timers call a "stick thermal." In like manner the variometer will indicate descent or sink air when the stick is pressured forward. Since the function of the vario is to measure rising or falling air currents exclusive of pilot controls, these readings could be misleading. In unstable air this can mean success or failure while flying thermals. While flying through a mass of rising or sinking air, the vario must distinguish between it and the pilot's maneuvering the plane up or down, since changes in air speed could easily be mistaken for rising or sinking air.

TOTAL ENERGY

A deflecting diaphragm and/or a venturi tube placed in the pitot line will compensate for this error. Any variometer can be compensated, so that irrespective of varying flying speeds it will only deal with and record the effect of air mass on the ship. This is called total energy. The concept is not difficult to understand, nor is its importance unappreciated, but you might have to be an engineer to understand how it is mechanically accomplished. As a pilot it's only important to know whether or not your variometers are compensated for total energy. No serious pilot will fly without total energy. But even more important, without a good working variometer, soaring flight would almost be an impossibility.

RIDGE SOARING

In 1901 Wilbur Wright said that it would be easy to *soar* in front of any hill of suitable slope whenever the wind blew with sufficient force to furnish support, providing the wind was steady; 10 years later Wilbur made a 10-minute flight that remained a record for over 10 years. Germany's aviation magazine *Flugsport* announced on August 30, 1921, that Herr Klemperer had made a soaring flight of historic significance. He flew for 13 minutes, covered a distance of 6 miles along a ridge, and landed at a point only 1,200 feet lower than his starting point. This was the beginning of ridge soaring.

By 1922, one year after Klemperer's "glide parallel to a range of hills," flights of two hours were being accomplished. It took almost 20 years to learn how to use ridge lift, and for the next 8 years the glider would be confined to only ridge soaring.

There is no limit to the duration of ridge flying except humans' endurance and prevailing wind conditions. Flights of over 60 hours are on record, and the record would have been extended even longer if the pilot hadn't overextended himself foolishly and fatally fallen asleep at the controls.

Did you ever watch a newspaper blow down the street on a windy day and instead of being flattened against a wall skim right over? When a steady wind blows against an obstruction the air is deflected upward for a considerable height above it. Ridge soaring uses this principle. The strength and direction of the wind and height and shape of the hill are the determining factors. The vertical flow of the air as it moves over the obstruction forms the cushion that supports flight.

THE RIDGE

For the beginner, nothing could be more ideal than to have a gliderport with a nearby ridge running perpendicular to the prevailing wind. Ridge soaring is the easiest to fly of all the sources of updraft.

How do you go about flying a ridge? The first thing you have to understand is that wind is a fluid, and like water it'll always take the path of least resistance. With that in mind, there are then three things that will constantly require your consideration: the shape of the obstructing slope, the wind's direction, and its velocity.

A direct flow of air against the slope or ridge provides the best conditions, but good soaring is possible even if the wind is 30 to 40 degrees off the perpendicular. A steady wind source is a necessity, and there are none more constant than ocean winds. Torry Pines is a prime example of an ideally located ridge-oriented gliderport. The constant westerly Pacific winds striking the high California coastal cliffs provide excellent ridge soaring conditions. The takeoff point, on top of the cliffs, puts the plane directly in the vertical air flow. The beach below makes an emergency landing area for those that get caught below the crest and can't "scratch" their way back up to the top.

Even modest mountain ranges provide innumerable ridge-soaring possibilities. In the East, a range of foothills only 900 to 1,000 feet, running NNE. by SSW., provide over a hundred miles of cross-country ridge soaring. Starting only 75 miles northwest of New York City, at Wurtsboro Airport, situated next to the Shawangunk Ridge, it's possible to fly this eastern foothill ridge of the Appalachian Mountains southwesterly to the Kittatinny Ridge and the Blue Mountain Ridge. With luck, one of these days a flight into Virginia will be made. The interesting part of this kind of cross-country flying is that it's possible to fly out and back on the same ridge if the northwesterly wind condition prevails.

A slope need not be long to provide good flying, especially the Sunday afternoon variety. It's not uncommon to have as many as 20 planes flying a 5- to 8-mile section of a ridge.

Long ridges are made up of a series of small ones with many different components, and each component presents a different problem. There are ridges with hills and crests of varying height, some with cliffs, gentle or steep slopes, wooded and smooth ones. Some ridges have large gaps, and some small gullies. Some have indentations or protrusions, and the ridge may veer, presenting a whole new set of wind problems for the pilot.

A few simple rules can provide even the beginner enough information so that shortly after his first solo he can successfully fly a ridge.

The best lift is in front of and above the crest.

If a ridge has sloping ends, the wind will seek the path of least resistance and skirt around it if possible. These sloping end areas, therefore, provide little or no lift and are relatively likely to produce turbulence and downdraft. Increase speed to fly out of these areas as fast as possible.

If the ridge has a cliff facing the wind, its center section produces the best updraft. In close to the face there is usually a layer of turbulence. It acts like a covering to the cliff. The steady wind blowing against this will pile up against the turbulence and directs the flow of the air, which itself will form a pathway for the oncoming winds up and over the cliff. The thickness of the layer of turbulence will be a function of the wind velocity. The higher the rate of flow, the more will pile against the face of the cliff.

In weak conditions you will be able to work within a wing span

Ridge lift. Fly fast . . . you're close to the trees

of the rock face without feeling turbulence. In brisk air it might be necessary to work hundreds of feet away. All ridge soaring is cross-wind flying. This must be remembered when flying below the crest of the cliff face. The plane should be flown on a crabbed heading slightly into the wind to prevent drifting toward the ridge. At first, flying along close enough to see the birds sitting in the trees can be a rather nerve-shattering experience, but after a few flights you'll gain confidence in the ship and it'll become fun.

Air speed in ridge soaring is very important. It is obvious that the minimum sink speed produces the best results. With the rate of sink at a minimum, we are taking full advantage of the vertical updraft. Any faster speed will increase our sink rate and sacrifice lift for speed. But safety and control are more important than lift. Wind velocity is the determining factor in determining the air speed to fly.

We've established 36 mph as the minimum sink speed for the sailplane we're flying in the book.

When the conditions are steady but brisk, add an extra 5 mph to the minimum sink speed for safety; this will make our air speed 41 or 42 mph. Lift will be stronger under these conditions, so it won't really affect your ability to keep the balance between descending flight and the vertical component of air on the "green air" side of the variometer.

When the wind is brisk and gusty, an additional 5 mph should be added. Now we'll be flying at 46 to 48 mph. Air speed in ridge soaring is extremely important since you will be flying close to the ground with little or no altitude for stall recovery.

At the top of the ridge the maximum lift will be found at about a 45-degree angle out and above the slope. The distance will depend on the wind velocity. You'll be making your decisions by trial and error.

Your altimeter and variometer are your guides. The altimeter is your over-all reference. It accumulates and averages out the vario readings. But the variometer instantaneously senses sink and lift; it's the instrument to fly by.

As you fly along the ridge, by moving in toward or away from the crest, the vario will record the amount of lift. When the variometer reads maximum lift, note the position of the plane in relationship to the ridge. Follow the contour of the highest point and maintain a constant angle and distance. Note landmarks below, so that when you fly back along the ridge in the opposite direction you'll know the best heading to take.

If the ridge has a gully between crests, increase your speed as you fly over it; this area produces little or no lift, and usually turbulence. When you reach the peak on the far side of the gully, resume your former attitude if this second section of the ridge is parallel to the ridge you just flew; good lift will be found in the same relative position.

While ridge flying, it's important to always keep in mind the

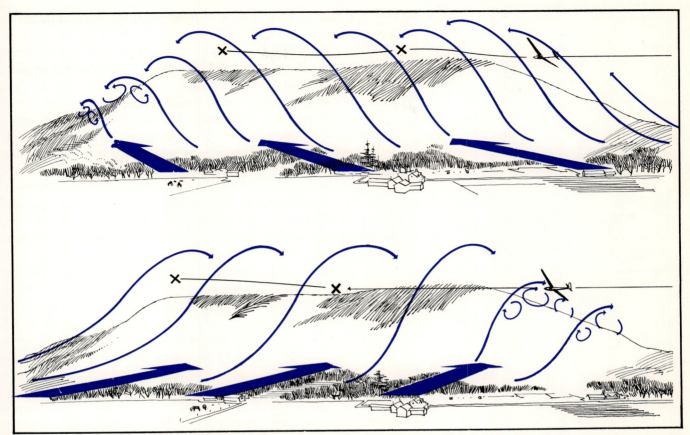

direction of the wind in relation to the flight path. Let's assume you have just flown a part of a ridge and are now flying toward the next section, which has a sloping gully or gap at each end. As you approach it, you'll want to know where to find maximum lift. Let's assume that the upcoming ridge takes a new direction, so the angle of the wind striking it will change; so will the places where you'll find maximum lift. If you have turned to line up with the new direction of the ridge and the prevailing wind in effect has swung so that it is now angling from behind you, good lift will be found over the first crest. On the other hand, if the new direction is more of a head wind for you, the crest will produce turbulence and downdraft; accelerate past the first crest. Head for the center section of the upcoming ridge, and lift will be good. With this wind angle, the far end of the ridge will also be good. Now lift will be found even out over the gap or gully.

Ridge soaring is like playing billiards. You always have to figure the angles. Keep the prevailing wind direction in mind. A constant or rising altimeter and the rising variometer show that you are flying right.

In good conditions you should be able to fly hundreds of feet above the ridge. In moderate conditions you may only be able to hold your own above it, and weak winds may have you scratching along under the crest. It's always important to remember while flying above the ridge not to drift behind the spine of the crest,

Wind direction plays a vital part in how you work a ridge. In top drawing, plane would fly at normal speed to get to X points where lift is good. In bottom drawing, sailplane should be flown fast to get out of turbulence, then slow to normal speed on reaching X-point areas. Sink air will be found at opposite ends of the ridge, depending on wind direction

especially if you're low. The lee side of the ridge always produces turbulence, eddies, and strong downdrafts.

Much can be learned by observing the topography of the ridge. Strangely enough, a small isolated hill produces the best lift behind it, where the diverted winds meet again.

If the foot of a ridge is wooded or has broken ground, the wind will be impeded and cause turbulence at low levels.

Spurs and indentations that make up the shape of the ridge have their effects on the flow of the wind. A more complicated problem is presented by a ridge that ascends in a series of steps. The air above each "terrace" is like that of the lee side of a small ridge. At low altitude, you must fly the contour of the land formation below you. Once you sink below the level of the ridge's crest, you should always have a landing area picked out and a procedure for landing in mind.

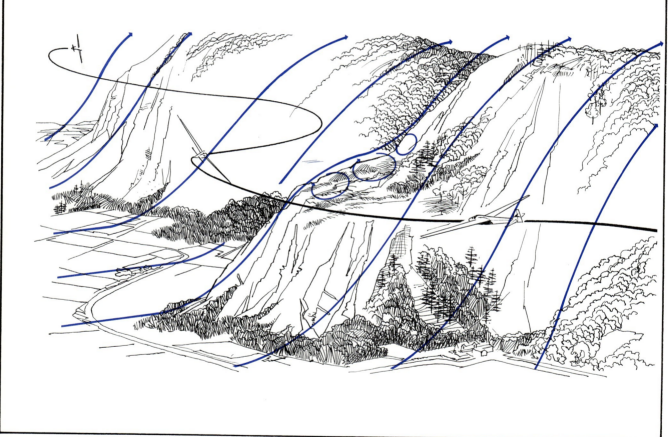

RULES OF THE ROAD

Traffic procedure is a very important part of ridge soaring. Whether you are flying alone or at a local ridge site with other gliders, all turns must be made away from the ridge. There are two reasons for this. If you turn upwind the drift will keep you very close to your relative position along the ridge during a 180-degree turn. If you turn downwind you could drift over the ridge by time you completed a 180-degree turn. The wind will also allow you to use a much shallower bank turning upwind than downwind. The second consideration is other traffic. If a plane behind you were closer to the ridge than you and at your same altitude, a turn on your part toward the ridge would force him into the ridge or set up a possible collision course. The rule of the road: all turns while ridge soaring are to be made away from the ridge.

If you wish to pass another plane at his altitude, you must pass between him and the ridge. This works along with the first rule. If you are following, you'll have no way of knowing when he's going to turn out. If you pass on his windward side, he could turn and cut right in front of you. Also, never fly directly above or below another sailplane. If the upper plane hits sink, it could cause a midair collision.

Remember, in all turns increase your speed to prevent a stall, and if you are flying close to the minimum sink speed, it's advisable to make shallow banked turns.

If your ridge has sloping ends, don't wait until you get into the downdraft at the end of the ridge to make your turn. In still air, a 180-degree turn will cost over a hundred feet in altitude. So if the turn itself costs you altitude, you should make it in lift.

A FEW THINGS TO REMEMBER

Don't wait till you reach sink air to make your turn—it can cost you altitude

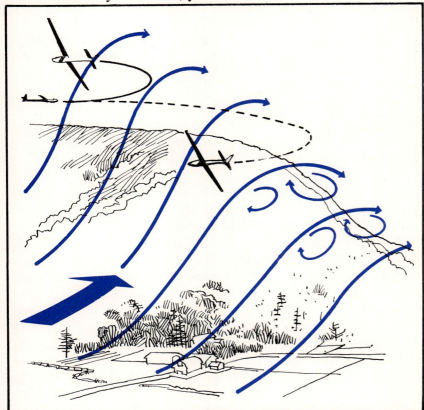

One of the problems that the beginner may encounter when flying below the crest of a slope is the desire to keep the sailplane up by "steering" it up to regain the crest. Guard against this earthbound instinct. A high nose means a decrease of speed, and you're

already flying close to the stall. At such a slow speed you have no leeway to trade off speed for altitude. Height can only be maintained in ridge soaring by encountering a vertical lifting air mass.

Don't keep your eyes glued to the instrument panel while ridge soaring. Your decisions are made by conditions outside—topography, wind direction and velocity, traffic—and also by keeping a wary eye out for suitable landing spots.

Ridge soaring is a good way to learn to fly because it makes available many hours aloft, and it's also an important part of cross-country flying. Many a contest has been won by smart pilots who, on finding themselves trapped by weak thermaling conditions, take to a ridge, soaring up and down waiting for the conditions to change. Ridges are also an excellent source of thermals, especially late in the day.

THERMAL FLIGHT

On September 13, 1921, two weeks to the day after Herr Klemperer broke Wilbur Wright's 10-year record by soaring a ridge for 13 minutes, Fredrick Harth made a significant flight of 21½ minutes. J. Bernard Weiss, a member of the Royal Flying Corps and leading British aeronautical historian of the day, described the event thus: "The flight was confined to the neighborhood of the starting point, the landing being made within a distance of 150 yards, on a spot that was not more than 40 feet lower. During the flight the machine had risen upwards of 400 feet. The slope of the land below was one of only six degrees, and it was claimed that the flight was made by taking advantage of the energy supplied by gusts, and not due solely to rising currents."

It is obvious when reading this account today that Herr Harth got caught up in a thermal, which was an unknown phenomenon of that day, and almost as mysterious today. The average person, in this day of jets, has more understanding of flights to the moon than he has of thermal flights.

Sailplane pilots who have made a cross-country flight are usually greeted by the farmer whose field they have just landed in with, "What happened, mister, did you run out of wind?"

Thermals exert tons of energy, but since we can't see thermals or observe any work being done by them, we ignore them. Only painters, photographers, and lovers seem to have paid any attention to them, and then they only admired the signature the thermal leaves in the sky, the fluffy cumulus cloud.

To define it simply, a thermal is a rising body of warm air. Thermals have existed ever since the day there was atmosphere and are caused by the different rates of heating of the earth. They erupt over every area, whether it be in the Arctic regions or on the equator.

The requirements for thermals are twofold: First, there can be no general overcast. There must be enough clear sky for the sun to warm the land. Second, the conditions of the atmosphere have to be such that the movement of the air can be vertical. This is known as *unstable* air.

Stable air is horizontal motion of the atmosphere; the common name for it is wind. Wind, it could be argued, is the result of changes of temperature and pressure of the air. Actually, winds affect their very originators. There is a never-ending struggle between masses of air to obtain a constant equilibrium. In doing so, the motion that is set up is horizontal. Wind has an effect on temperature distribution, and wind is the means by which the masses of air are shifted around; thus it causes pressure changes. But winds occur because there are pressure differences. Defining wind is like trying to find the beginning of a rolling hoop.

There is another struggle that goes on at the same time, but on a much smaller scale. It's the upward and downward movement of air. This vertical motion is caused by warm air rising since it is lighter than its surrounding cool air.

Since the normal flow of the large masses of air tends to be horizontal, it's considered the stable condition, and that's why wind is called stable air. Stable air will resist any vertical flow and tends to get things moving horizontally. But when the up and down movements become too much for the wind and the vertical motion is allowed to take place, get out your sailplane. That's unstable air.

What are the conditions that allow the upward and downward movement?

SIGNS OF STABILITY

Gliderports rarely have meteorological equipment or trained weather personnel, thus leaving the glider pilot to rely on his own thumb-sucking guesstimates.

Much can be established about stability from some general observations, and a change in these conditions for better or worse is itself an indicator.

Good visibility can mean good soaring, since the first requirement for developing a thermal is ground heat. Poor visibility in the low levels of the atmosphere means stable condition; a lid is placed over the smoke and haze cutting the effect of the sun. A change to crisp, clear air will bring about the possibility of good convection.

In your region the winds that initiate a cold front will also give the signs of unstable air, since cold fronts are followed by good soaring conditions. A cold front is usually ushered in with turbulence, winds, and squalls. The signal that the cold front has passed is a rapid improvement in the weather conditions.

High, thin, fleecy clouds usually signal stable weather is on the way but still quite a few hours away. Heavy overcast needs little or no comment here, but flat, horizontal, layer-like cloud formations indicate stable air. Fluffy, irregular, or vertical cloud developments are a sign of instability.

Swirling dust devils are a sign of instability. Incidentally, if one is observed while landing, avoid it. Land to the upwind side of it if possible.

Swirls or puffs of white milky clouds appearing at low level are just what we want. They indicate not only that unstable moist air is present, but that thermals have begun to develop. These milky swirls usually start about noon. If they start in the early morning, don't wait for even further improvement; if there is a lot of water vapor in the air, an overdevelopment of cumuliform clouds could take place and obscure the sun. Conditions would continue to be unstable, but without ground heating by the sun, thermals will stop.

LAPSE RATE

A local sounding made by the tow plane equipped with an outside thermometer and the standard rate-of-climb indicator is the best weather tool the glider pilot has at his disposal.

The variations between temperature readings every 500 feet of altitude will give a do-it-yourself lapse rate chart.

Since the temperature of the air is an index of its stability, comparison of the temperatures at ascending levels will indicate the degree of the atmospheric stability.

The lapse rate temperatures will give an indication of what will happen to warm, ground-heated air. The lapse rate will show how warm the lower air will have to get in order to rise through the first few thousand feet in order to make useful thermals. The warm air will cool as it rises, and will rise until it strikes warmer air or is neutralized.

The rate of temperature decrease with altitude indicates the amount of instability, and the higher into the atmosphere the decreasing rate goes, the better the convection will be. When the reverse occurs and the air increases in temperature with an increase of altitude, you have what is called an inversion. It's important to know where this takes place, since an inversion puts a lid on the rising air and indicates a stable condition. If it occurs at 5,000 feet, you could get good flying. If it occurs from the ground on up, or even starts at 1,000 feet, *and there is no strong sun,* you might as well wait for another day.

On the other hand, if there is a low-level inversion, but strong sun radiation is getting through to the ground, all is not lost. The hotter the ground gets, the hotter the air above it becomes, and this can make the low-level air warmer than the inversion layer, causing it to rise and start convection. How does one go about getting this information?

Since most glider sites have practically no weather equipment, conditions for the day are usually assessed by one of the old hands who looks up and makes his prediction. With four simple items, a good bit of the guesswork can be taken out of it: the tow plane, an outside thermometer for the plane, a standard broadcast radio, and an adiabatic chart.

The accompanying chart is a simplified version for our soaring purpose. The basic form of the chart shows that when dry air rises to higher altitudes without exchanging heat with the surrounding areas, it cools by expanding. The rate of cooling is 5.5 degrees Fahrenheit per thousand feet, and that's what this chart is all about.

First, by tracing onto paper the coordinates, legends, and solid diagonal lines (all the graph lines and language of the drawing), you will have your own basic form to chart a lapse rate. It's a very simple affair to use and understand. Temperatures in degrees Fahrenheit are marked along the base line. The vertical coordinate is the altitude above sea level, in thousands of feet. The diagonal lines represent the rate at which dry air cools as it rises. For example, trace with your finger the diagonal that starts on the base line at 66 degrees. Moving your finger up to the zero altitude line, the temperature would be read directly below—60 degrees. That means that air at zero, or sea level, would be 60. Following the diagonal up to where it crosses the 5,000-foot altitude coordinate shows that the rising parcel of dry air has been lowered to 33 degrees.

Here is the way we use the chart. A base line is drawn on the chart that will represent the altitude above sea level of the general area around the airport. The altimeter of the airplane is set at 29.92

A DO-IT-YOURSELF CONVECTION CHART

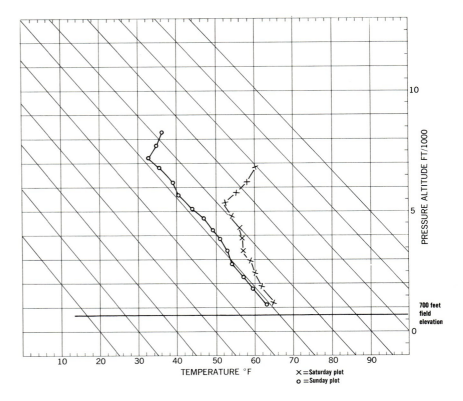

barometric reading, the average sea level reading. The airplane fitted with an outside thermometer will make a climb over the area. Temperature readings will be plotted at 500-foot intervals above the field elevation.

Two typical soundings are made on this chart. "X" plots are Saturday's readings, and "O" are Sunday's.

The plot marks are connected to form a line. In both cases the plane stopped climbing when a sudden increase in temperature was recorded. This is the point of a temperature inversion. That is the lid; thermals would have a hard time breaking through this layer.

Saturday's plot shows that thermals could go as high as 5,200 feet on the pressure altitude scale before the inversion started.

Here is how the plot is used. We know the 5,200-foot mark is as high as we can go with these conditions. We must find the temperature at ground level that will now make this possible. When the sounding was made in the morning, the ground temperature was 66 degrees; that is the first plot. It's made by taking the reading on the temperature scale and simply moving it directly up onto the field elevation line. The ground temperature needed to heat the air enough to enable it to reach 5,200 pressure altitude is read by projecting an imaginary line from the 5,200 mark parallel to the nearest diagonal, down to the field elevation. At the point of intersection drop a line to the bottom scale and read the temperature. We find that to reach 5,200 feet the temperature has to rise to 78 degrees. The local radio weather report will tell you the temperature every hour and what high temperature is expected for the day. One more step: convert pressure altitude to actual altitude by subtracting the field elevation from the reading. In this case 5,200 feet minus 700 feet field elevation will give you thermals to 4,500 feet above the ground.

The Sunday example is different. The starting temperature is the same, 66 degrees. The plotted lapse rate goes to 7,200 feet on the pressure altitude scale before it shows an inversion. By drawing the imaginary line down, parallel to the diagonal, you will see that the reading at 4,800 is critical. If the air is warm enough to get past this altitude it will go on to the 7,200 mark. Carrying the imaginary line down to the field elevation line, then to the temperature scale, you will see that the trigger temperature, or ground level temperature needed to kick off thermals to go up to the inversion level, will be 71 degrees, only a 5-degree increase.

Interesting observations can be made from these two plottings. If the plotting is parallel to the diagonal adiabatic lines, soaring conditions are good. If the plotting makes an angle to the nearest diagonal, that angle will be an indication of your soaring prospects. The larger the angle, the poorer the conditions. Sunday's flying was better than Saturday's; a larger volume of air had to be heated on Saturday to produce convection.

WATER: FRIEND OR FOE?

Water takes many forms. As liquid, or rain, it comes in packages of stable air, except when it's the advancing line of a cold front. Too much rainfall can cut off the development of thermals at their source. If all conditions are go—good visibility, a descending lapse rate showing unstable air, bright warm sunshine—but the ground is soggy from a heavy rain, the energy of the sun will first have to be used to evaporate the excess water before it can heat the ground sufficiently. This would have to be figured into the guesstimate. Knowledge of the drainage pattern of the local terrain can help. Thermals will pop off the areas that drain first.

The swirls of thin, milky clouds that seem to appear against the blue sky from out of nowhere are signs of water vapor condensing. Moisture is not a necessity in the production of thermals, but it helps. Dry thermals over hot arid areas can grow into giant boomers if they can break out of their lower warm surroundings. In the northern zones, dry thermals are usually weak and hard to find because there is no water vapor to condense and leave its sign. That's where the tow plane's rate-of-climb indicator comes into play. By making the climbout at a steady rate, if the plane hits a thermal and is carried up with it, it'll show on the instrument. If there are no clouds around, you can rest assured that it's a dry thermal day. This can be an important observation in the test sounding.

Water vapor helps the thermal. Moist air is less dense than dry air and will tend to rise easier. The lapse rate of moist air is slower than that of dry air; it gives up less heat as it ascends. If it were possible to make a comparison between a dry and wet thermal rising next to each other through the same atmosphere, it would show that the dry thermal would cool down faster. Its temperature would become equal to the surrounding air at a lower height, since it would be giving up heat at a faster rate.

CUMULUS CLOUD FORMATION

When the air at ground level becomes moist it's cooled by evaporation. Later, when this air is warmed by contact with the sun-drenched ground and rises as a thermal, the water vapor carried up in the air is cooled. When it reaches the point of condensation a cloud is formed. The latent heat absorbed during the original evaporation is now released upon condensation. This extra heat gives the lifting air another boost. It keeps the thermal that much warmer than the surrounding air.

The pilot has to learn to read these clouds as a driver reads road signs.

For the sailplane pilot, the first milky wisps of condensation are a visual signal that a thermal is starting. Under that wisp is the updraft. Within minutes, according to its strength and the amount of water vapor carried aloft, it will grow and can expand with astonishing rapidity.

If he's lucky enough to see the first wisps appear against a blue sky, there is no question about what he has found. If he notices a light, filmy cloud but didn't see it form, it could be the last stages of a cumulus cloud being reabsorbed by the surrounding air. This then is the evaporation process again, and a cooling of the air takes place. If a pilot flies for this wisp of cloud thinking it is a new thermal forming, it will come as a shocking revelation to him that he has flown into sinking air. So you can see that reading the "road signs" is not a cut and dried matter.

Thermals are like women—no two are alike, and no particular specimen can be described as typical of all others. It all depends on the environment in which you find it.

Once the blob of warm air starts its vertical movement, it quickly takes on the shape of a spherical bubble. Some will argue that it takes an elongated form like a chimney or tower, but most observers stick to the bubble concept. It's difficult to explain with the bubble theory how it is possible for one sailplane to fly up through the core and then many minutes later for another one to enter the same thermal at a low level and follow that first one up. Not only is this technique possible, but it's standard practice in competition flying. But from most observations and meteorological experiments the bubble theory explains best the air flow within the thermal. Supporting the bubble concept there is evidence that a volume of buoyant air that has gone up only 500 feet is much larger and more buoyant than the embryo, which may have been only a small bubble when it left the ground.

Thermals have three areas: the cap or cloud, the lower area or source, and the middle portion which is the most useful for soaring.

Pilots disagree about the form thermals take, but this will serve as a working explanation.

As the bubble breaks away and enters the middle-layer stage it takes on a doughnut shape. The core, or center of the doughnut, contains the strong updraft; the outer perimeter is an area of down-

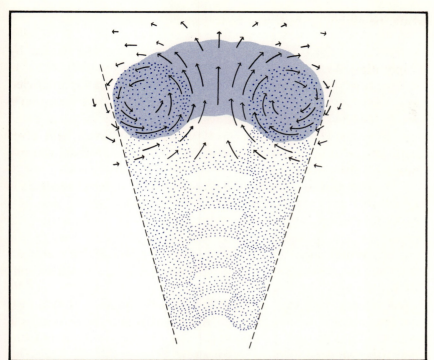

draft. The upward velocity of the center core is faster than that of the whole bubble; therefore the doughnut would be seen to take on a concave shape if it could be observed from below. There is an inflow of air from the surrounding atmosphere at the base of the doughnut. As long as the air in the center of the doughnut is rising at a faster rate than the whole thermal, a sailplane will rise up through it. As the warm air becomes diluted by the inflow of cooler air, the slower-rising air won't support soaring flight. As a sailplane flies through the core of a thermal, it will receive its strongest lift in the bottom two-thirds of the bubble.

The condensation level marks the base of the cloud but by no means the top of the thermal. As long as moisture and energy are fed up into the base of the cloud it will fight its way upward, the heat of condensation contributing additional boost. The signs of a growing cumulus are the huffing and puffing, and bulging at the sides and top. Although there is little visual difference between the first few minutes of a new cumulus and the last wisps of a dying one, the full-fledged cumulus has its own particular look. Its edges are firm and the bulges have a solid appearance. Do not be fooled by the winds aloft tearing at the bulges and giving them the ragged appearance of a dissipating cloud. Watch the ragged fingers that seem to tear away; if their edges don't dissolve it's a good indicator that the cloud is still alive and kicking.

The base of a working thermal cloud is flat when seen from a distance. When seen from up close the dark underside is not a solid wall, but a gradually increasing milky haze. In most cases, the bottom is concave, a sign of its strength.

There seems to be a debate among meteorologists as to whether there is a sucking effect at the base of a large cumulus just after the thermal has stopped. Some think continuing heat of condensation within the cloud produces this action, and others feel the sucking is a "catch feeding" of subsequent small thermals into the larger one. The novice or student pilot should not explore too close to the base except in very light cloud conditions. Getting sucked into a thunderhead could be a serious matter. A novice can become disoriented in a matter of seconds.

Cloud flying, so the rules say, should be attempted only by pilots with an instrument rating in a plane properly instrumented, and then only after a flight plan has been filed and permission granted. But a flight plan is impractical for a sailplane. Play it safe: get the knowledge but keep yourself out of the situation where you have to use it.

FINDING THE THERMAL

We have already described the cumulus cloud as the sign in the sky that a thermal is present. Don't wait until you're flying to learn to recognize the signs. You can learn just as much walking down the street, driving your car, or sitting in a meadow. Glance up if the cu's are forming and take a reading. Make a mental picture of the one you think has the best potential, then look away. Then, 15 seconds later, see what happened. Did it grow or dissipate? If you're not sure, try it again; give it another 15 seconds. Test out your findings the next time you're in the air; search underneath or close to the best potentials and see how much you have learned and how good your judgment is.

Without a little luck, chasing cu's can be a rather discouraging business. Some pilots express a desire for dry thermal days, claiming they don't waste their time flying into "has-beens."

If there are no cu's, the next place to look for thermals will be at their source—the ground. Where are the most likely places that thermals could develop?

Three main factors must be considered: the type of soil and cover, the terrain, and the wind strength.

Let's take a look at how the game has to be played.

Some areas absorb more heat than others; color is a basic factor. White reflects the sun's rays without heating the air, dark absorbs and heat is radiated to the air. It's obvious, then, that dark soil will absorb more heat and be a better thermal producer, but if the darkness is caused by dampness, then it's not going to be a producer. If the dark soil is on a slight elevation, it'll drain quickly, but if there is a brisk wind blowing across it, once again it won't be a producer. In the first case the moisture prevented it from getting warm enough; in the second case the air wasn't in contact with the warm ground long enough. Obviously, all factors have to be considered when trying to make a judgment as to where the thermals will be found.

A plowed field may reflect more heat than a grass field, but it's a better source because the furrows provide more area of radiation. Sand is a good producer for much the same reason. Although sand color will reflect the heat more than darker colors, there are so many tiny surfaces to receive the sun's rays that good heating takes place.

Thick dark crops or dense wooded areas would seem to be good thermal producers, but instead they intercept much of the incoming radiation before it reaches the ground. Many of the sun's rays are used up evaporating the moisture that comes up through the plant from the ground. A large tree transpires tons of water in a day. Conversely, during a drought, dark foliage areas would be excellent producers.

It takes a longer period of time to heat a wooded area, but once it is heated the foliage acts much like a blanket. In the evening when open fields have started to cool down, the wooded areas would be warmer and could still give off thermals.

Bare ground and short crops are good producers. Corn will have a tendency to trap the air and make it very warm, but once it does let go it can produce a boomer. It's been suggested that the foliage acts like a tunnel once the bubble breaks away. The surface air flows out as if the bubble were a leak in the dike, and the foliage prevents the cool air from rushing in and plugging it up.

On windy days, wind shadows or sheltered areas will have a better chance of warming. Although the wind shadow may not be over soil or a crop considered a good thermal producer, it could still be very active since it's not the absolute temperature that causes thermals, but the relative temperatures of adjacent areas. Groups of buildings, towns, and hilly country can produce wind shadow areas.

Thermals are often found in wind-shadow areas. The bluff here prevents wind from breaking up the thermal before it forms

Towns are dry, so they will produce. They also will have some internal heating. Fires, dumps, and smokestacks can keep the thermals popping off, but don't get caught downwind of a town where the smoke and haze forms an umbrella and cuts the sun off from the ground.

Ridge tops are good. The drainage is fast, and the air can be cooler than the air in the valley and still produce a thermal. The angle of the sun is a very important factor. A slope facing the sun will heat more than the valley floor. This is especially important to remember late in the day.

Often bubbles of warm air will sit around the ground just waiting to be triggered; trucks will launch them off a highway, airplanes will kick them off airports.

Asphalt parking lots and shopping centers have saved many a competition pilot. There are even stories of pilots flying long distances over bumper-to-bumper highway traffic, the heat of the engines being enough to produce zero sink. It's a strange phenomenon to have a sailplane fly on gasoline at the fine price of nothing per gallon.

FLYING THE THERMAL

Some time in the future heat-sensing devices will be developed that will discover and pinpoint the elusive and invisible thermal. Even now in this space age, microwave observations of earth from an aircraft are recording valuable data on thermal radiation indicating areas that are the thermal producers. It's not too farfetched to conceive of heat sensors set in the tip of each wing giving instantaneous temperature differentials of the air along the 50-foot wing span and transmitting their findings to the pilot's panel. At the moment, our trial and error method is the best technique available, and in many ways it's the great challenge of the sport.

Looking back to the time not too long ago, when pilots flew gliders with no instrumentation and comparing those conditions to what we fly with today, it would be understandable if they thought we were taking the fun out of the sport.

Thermal flying would be almost an impossibility without the variometer, but even with it many decisions, judgments, and quick responses still have to be made by the pilot.

At first, the inexperienced pilot is going to conclude either that thermals are a figment of someone's imagination or that finding them is mostly luck. First he must become a good pilot able to handle the plane smoothly, fly it at steady speed, and enter turns accurately and quickly.

RULES OF THE ROAD

Much can be gained from hangar talk before the flight starts. There are certain known areas that seem to produce thermals; experienced pilots or your instructor will point them out for you. Circling hawks or sailplanes are also good indicators. If you do see a plane working a thermal, you do have the right to join him, but as an inexperienced pilot you should be very cautious doing so. When you enter the thermal you must fly in the same direction he is flying. He knows you're inexperienced and will watch you carefully. Later you're going to have a lot of fun flying thermals with others. Use good judgment, think of the other guy, don't work too close to him until you're skilled; you'll have to earn your way with your fellow pilots.

To be successful at thermaling you can't depend on others. You're going to have to develop your own skills, which take much concentration. But the best variometer you can have is another sailplane in the air. Observing how it does it relation to how you are flying can tell you if the air is greener on his side of the fence. Move toward him if he's got lift.

While on tow, there are two techniques for discovering whether or not you're flying into lift or sink. By noting the variometer on climbout you can estimate the rate of climb of the tow plane. Let's assume it's 500 feet per minute. If the vario suddenly starts to read 800 feet up, you can be sure it's caused by a thermal, and not by a sudden increase of the tug's climbing rate. If you're at a good height, drop off, circle back, and find it.

By watching the tug you can make a similar observation. If he seems to float up in front of you and you have to make a corrective maneuver with back stick to stay in position, he's entered a thermal. In contrast to that, if the rate of climbout is 500 feet per minute and the sailplane releases in 300 feet of climb, it'll be in 200 feet of sink. Once the sailplane is released from tow and the climbing turn to the right is made, the plane should be flown at the best gliding angle speed so that valuable altitude won't be lost while searching for the thermal. A systematic search should be started upwind of the field. The search should consist of a cruise over the most likely areas to produce thermals: the sunny side of ridges, dry ground, towns, quarries, sand pits, etc.

Unless the inexperienced pilot blunders into a strong thermal, he doesn't have much chance of finding one. During his training, which consisted mainly of gliding flight, he learned to correct for any turbulence that upset level-wing flight. Now he should be looking for such turbulence.

SINK STREETS

There is a phenomenon called "cloud streets" that we will discuss shortly. On exceptionally good days the wind lines the thermals up in "streets" and makes excellent soaring. Many pilots have a theory that just as the up air of cloud streets line up, so does the sink air. Warm air goes up, cool air goes down. The warm air is concentrated, and in relatively small packages; the cool air covers a much broader area surrounding the thermals. The general rule is, the stronger the updrafts, the stronger the sink. Obviously, the task is to find the updrafts.

On the outer edge of a well-formed thermal is an area of vertical wind shear or turbulence; cool air is going down and warm going up. Sometimes this is hard to distinguish from gusty turbulence. The rule: When either wing is lifted, instead of leveling the plane (a protective reflex based on the beginner's earthbound experience), a quick turn should be made in the direction of the up-tipped wing. That's where the thermal is going to be.

It is not necessarily a sharp buffeting of the wing, it may only be a nudge. By flying level you'll find yourself flying the sink streets. A well-trimmed plane, flown hands off the controls, will fly the sink air between the thermals. As a wing is lifted it will turn the plane away from the lift and right itself into level flight; thus it'll fly between the thermals.

There are two theories about the direction to fly to get out of sink air. Some feel that straight flight should be maintained until the wing gives an indication of flying the outskirts of a thermal.

If left to its own devices, a sailplane will fly between thermals: as thermal lifts a wing, sailplane will be turned away.

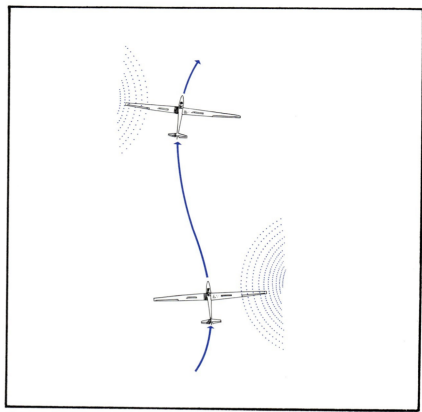

Others feel that a direction should be maintained for a descent of only 500 or 600 feet, and if no lift is encountered, a 45-degree, or up to a 90-degree, turn should be made so that if a sink street has formed you will get out of it fast. This latter technique seems to make more sense. Under no circumstances should you turn the sailplane in the direction it has a tendency to turn in, nor should you circle; 360-degree turns cost altitude and are a fast way down.

SEARCHING SPEED

The vario will give an indication of the speed to fly while searching. This is an important conservation matter. If the sink is only a few hundred feet a minute, the best glide angle speed should be used. If heavy sink is encountered, speed should be increased by about 10 mph over the best L/D speed. For the plane we are flying that will be 55 mph. The purpose of this is to get out of the heavy sink as soon as possible. Don't sustain the higher speed too long or you'll find yourself getting ready to enter a landing pattern. Don't lose heart over heavy sink; it indicates that when you do hit a thermal it'll be a good one, and that it's nearby.

There are two factors you have to keep in mind when deciding at what speed you should fly in a straight and level-wing glide. One is the stability of the air; are you in sinking air or lifting air? The other is the wind's velocity and its direction.

GLIDING IN SINK AND LIFT

In sink air you should increase your speed in order to get out of it faster. It's obvious that if you fly at the best glide angle, 45 mph, you'll be in this sink air a much longer period of time than if you fly at 60 mph. It's also obvious that at the end of that same period of time you will be getting low with the nose of the plane pointed down at that faster speed. You might be just as low flying slower in the sinking air, but by flying out of the sink, you've got a chance of finding more lift, whereas if you stay in the sink, you've had it.

The opposite is true in lift. The object of the game is to stay in it as long as possible.

To determine speeds to fly for maximum distance in different conditions, the rules are easy.

In still air, or zero sink: Fly the best L/D to cover the greatest distance.

In weak rising air: Reduce the speed and fly at minimum sink speed. Stay in that condition as long as possible.

In sinking air: Move out as soon as you can, but do so with the minimum loss of height. Increase the speed slightly above the best glide angle.

With the wind on your tail: Reduce the speed to slightly above the minimum sink and let the wind carry you with it without losing height.

With a tail wind in sinking air: L/D speed, your best angle of glide, will take you farthest.

Against the wind: Increase the speed. Add about one-third of the wind speed to your best gliding angle to penetrate the head wind.

Against the wind in sinking air: Increase the speed well over the head wind velocity, or best L/D speed plus one-third the wind speed plus another 5 or 10 mph for penetration.

Against the wind in rising air: If you don't need the height, trade the lift for forward speed; put the nose down and go. The maximum speed will be indicated by the altimeter. When it stays constant, you'll have the speed and descent in balance.

THERMALING SPEED

If your variometer starts to register lift, speed should be reduced immediately. You will want to stay in the lifting mass as long as possible. Remember the sailplane in flight is always descending. Speed is in direct relationship to your rate of descent. Flying too fast within the confines of a thermal is wasting a good part of its energy. Also, to stay within the invisible bounds of a thermal, especially if you are low, tight banking will be necessary. Turns at high speed require a greater radius than low-speed turns with the same amount of bank. This means that at high speed the best you can do is to fly in and out of the thermal's core, using only a fraction of the lift.

What should the thermaling speed be? Minimum sink speed would be best, but a very important factor will determine speed to fly: angle of bank. The greater the angle of bank, the higher the stalling speed of the wing due to loading. As the G force increases with the angle of bank, the stalling speed increases.

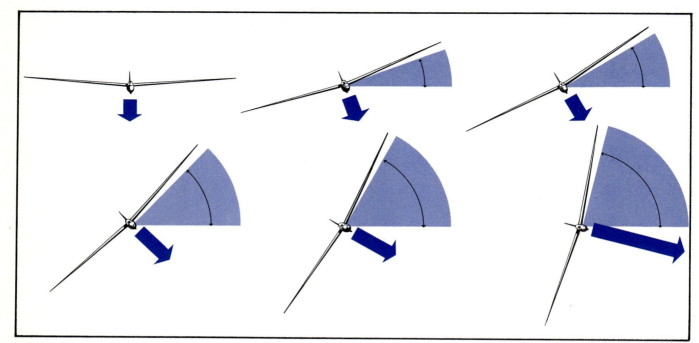

As the angle of bank increases, the G-load increases and the stall speed becomes higher. Fly faster to prevent a stall

Angle of Bank	G Load	% Increase in Stall Speed	Stall Speed of our Plane
0 degrees	+1	0%	30 mph
20 degrees	negligible increase	negligible	30 mph
30 degrees	+1.2	8%	32 mph
45 degrees	+1.4	18%	35 mph
60 degrees	+2.0	40%	42 mph
75 degrees	+4.0	100%	60 mph

By estimating your angle of bank you will be able to determine the safe speed to fly. Since the minimum sink speed is 36 mph for our plane for level flight, add about 5 mph to the *increased stall speed* for the best speed to fly; this will include the necessary safety margin.

The main problem the beginner has is overestimating his degree of bank. When banking at 20 degrees it feels like 30 degrees to him. Learning to rack the sailplane over to 30, 45, or more degrees is going to take some practice, but the beginner will have to do 30-degree turns to be successful in a thermal. Later he'll rack it over and learn to love the feeling.

Many planes today are equipped with an accelerometer. It's a rather inexpensive instrument that measures the G force. It's easy to learn to judge the degree of bank with an accelerometer to measure Gs. Bank the ship over to 45 degrees using the horizon as your guide. When you think you have it, glance at the instrument. It should read plus 1.4 Gs. There is another way to tell. At about 2 Gs you'll feel yourself being pressed into your seat, at 2½ Gs your face will start to sag, and you'll be able to sense it.

Steep banked turns are an unnatural state of affairs to the novice pilot. But when we discuss centering the thermal, this will become the decisive factor between success and failure. One of the best ways of learning this maneuver is to fly in a thermal in radio contact with a more experienced pilot. Not only will you see how far he is racked over in a steep bank, but he'll instruct you to steepen your bank until you'll feel as though you're going to fall out of the sky. You won't as long as your speed is increased to accommodate the higher stall speed. It really doesn't matter to the plane what its altitude is as long as it has flying speed and the controls are coordinated. Keeping the yaw string centered while making steep turns in the thermal is important. Compare slipping turns in a thermal to the man walking slowly down the up escalator; suddenly he starts to run down, negating the escalator's upward motion.

One last consideration before we discuss the all-important thermal-centering techniques. Although we were more interested in vertical air movements, we can't ignore the horizontal flow of the wind. If the thermal were rising in a controlled environment and we were only concerned with temperature and density differentials, the bubble would rise straight up. But this is not the case; even light winds alter the situation.

At ground level, a light wind favors the production of more frequent thermals, but the wind will distort them. Stronger winds tend to reduce the rate of rise of the ground temperature by distributing the heat up through the turbulent layer just above the surface. Moderate or strong winds, therefore, suppress the development of thermals from ground sources. But these warmer parcels that are in the turbulent level above the ground produce incipient thermals; their origins can't be related to any likely spot.

It's not important here where the thermals originated, but the effect the wind shear (wind speed change with height) has on thermals is worth noting. On good convection days if the wind increases by about 2 to 3 knots per 1,000 feet of ascent, the shear will give a turbulent distortion to the thermal and make it almost impossible to fly.

With less of a wind shear thermals retain some semblance to their bubble shape as they rise, but they will drift downwind. When they reach condensation level, the cu that develops could be miles downwind from the ground source. Once the sailplane is climbing in the thermal, it too will drift downwind at the same rate as the whole mass.

When you are searching and you see a sailplane circling in lift above you, flying directly under him will produce nothing. You will have to fly upwind of his position; the distance will depend on the velocity of the wind. Your best indicators of velocity at low level are such things as smoke, flags, and somebody's clean wash out on the line. In this case we're more interested in the upper wind velocity, which can be judged by the movement of cloud shadows. Watching them as you fly will give you their direction and an indication of their speed.

WIND AND WIND SHEAR

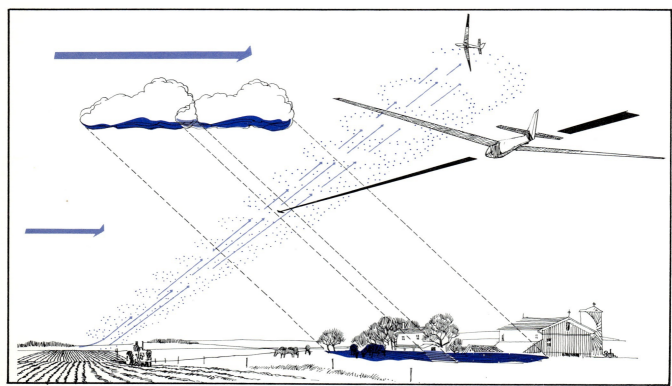

GHOSTS IN THE SKY

(Drawing above) Don't fly directly under a sailplane that has climbed in a thermal: that isn't where the lift will be. Watch cloud shadows to determine wind direction, and try to spot source of thermal. You'll find the thermal on the diagonal between its source and the plane that's climbing in it

Often a slight amount of turbulence will be encountered flying from sink air into rising air. One reason the beginner has problems finding thermals is that flying the plane is the focus of his powers of concentration. As flying becomes natural he'll become more sensitive to the slight turbulent signal, or a nudging up of a wing. But even more important is learning to ignore and then respond in a new way to a congenital reflex. Man reacts instinctively to regain his balance. The baby learns it quickly and soon walks; a man who slips walking down the street responds innately to maintain his footing. Put the same man in a sailplane, a new environment, and automatically his first reflex will be to level the plane since levelwing flight is more natural to him. He'll start to soar when he has gained confidence in the plane, can relax at the controls, and recognizes that he must change an old habit.

There is a supernatural aspect to the search for the elusive, invisible thermal; most of us deal in solid, substantial, tangible realities, except those of us who believe in ghosts. It is not difficult to understand why the novice pilot who wanders into the fringes of a thermal, and promptly loses it, skeptically abandons the search in the faint hope of blundering into a boomer elsewhere.

CENTERING THE THERMAL

There are three major clues that a thermal is nearby: First is a tipping of a wing as it sweeps into the outskirts of a thermal. Second, a buffeting and slight turbulence usually indicates a thermal is close at hand. The third clue is an upswing of the variometer needle as the whole plane enters the updraft. Or you may find a combination of all three.

It's important as a beginner to exploit any lift you encounter and not assume that something better will be found. Once you have gained height you can become more selective if you wish.

Ask half a dozen pilots how they center on a thermal and you might get half a dozen answers, but certain things are quite evident.

If your variometer starts to move up and record less sink, you can be sure that you are on the edge of a thermal or that a thermal is incipient or expiring. That's the signal to search. The thermal can be to either side or straight ahead.

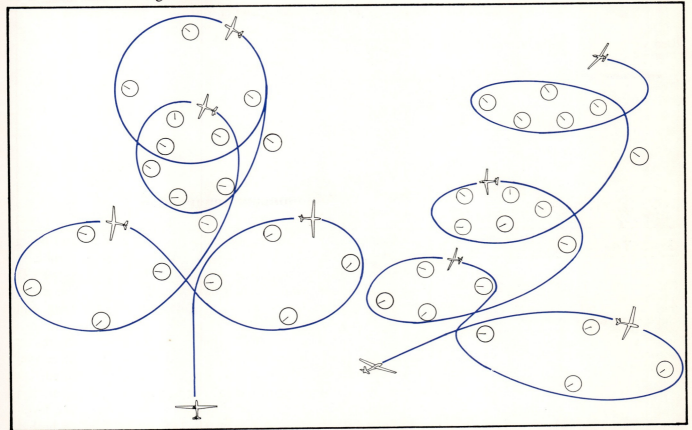

Unless a wing has tipped up, tipping you off to its location, the direction of your turn is immaterial. The important thing is to turn immediately. Don't wait for the vario to show a large plus reading before you make the turn. There is some lag in the instrument, and hesitation could cost you a thermal.

We'll assume the first turn is to the right. As you enter the turn take a ground reference and a direction heading. Make a tight 360 turn and slow up to the correct thermaling speed. Watch the vario. If it starts to fall, you have turned in the wrong direction. Continue the turn through the full circle; when it's completed, according to your headings, rack the plane over and circle to the left. If this circle brings no results you can be confident that the thermal is ahead of that starting point.

Fly ahead on original course and observe the variometer. Try to feel for the slight turbulence or a lifting sensation.

Searching out the thermal. Vario needle in nine o'clock position registers zero sink; needle goes up from there in rising air and down in sinking air. Trace the paths and see how the pilot flew to center the lift

Let's assume that the thermal is straight ahead, since we have eliminated the right and left sides. The question now, as the vario starts to indicate rise, is whether we should immediately turn one way or the other or fly straight ahead. This is where the experts seem to disagree.

Those that say fly straight ahead have this plan in mind. A specific path is flown that will record a history on the variometer of the exact position of the best lift. Here is the procedure. While flying the original straight ahead course, observe the vario needle. As soon as it indicates an upswing, start to count off seconds. If the lift persists for five seconds it will be large enough for thermaling.

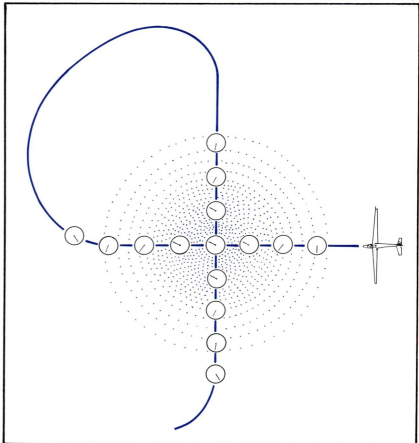

Continue to fly straight, counting all the way through the lift, and make a turn at the end of the lift. Now fly back through the area at 90 degrees to the original heading. As soon as you hit lift, start counting again and watch the vario. Once you have pinpointed the strongest lift, fly back into that area, circle tightly, and you should go up.

For the beginner this method leaves much to be desired. For one thing, since the whole mass is moving downwind, flying out of it and then back in could be a frustrating experience. This method also assumes that the thermal is symmetrical and a single unit. Experience will soon show the pilot that thermals can have more than one core.

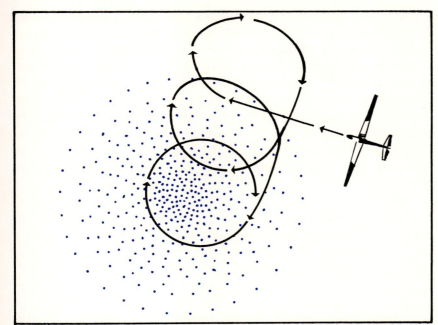

The experts that say turn as soon as you find lift offer the beginner a psychological advantage; staying within the lift, even if it's weak, gives the student's spirits a boost along with his ship.

In weak lift the turn should be gradually opened so that a broader area is searched. The moment the vario shows an increase, the turn should be tightened in an attempt to center the core.

If the rate of climb is good the angle of bank can be reduced after height is gained to improve that upward rate, since there is a direct correlation between the angle of bank and the rate of descent.

Although it may seem to the beginner to be an inconsistency, he has to learn to rack the plane over into a sharp bank even in weak cores. His inexperience leads him to think that a steep turn will increase his rate of descent and discount the effects of the thermal's upward movement. He can even explain his theory by using the man on the escalator as an example. A steep bank, he will say, is increasing his downward rate as he walks down the upgoing stairs; therefore a gentler bank will improve his condition, slow up the descent, and improve his chances for ascent.

This reasoning is fallacious because he won't core the thermal with wide-sweeping circles; he'll be slowing up the escalator or even stopping it.

The electric vario is a superior instrument for centering because of the short lag time. The variometer will indicate to the pilot which way to move the plane for centering. First he must make a landmark reading. We'll assume here a lake is straight ahead, and we'll call that position 12 o'clock on our flight circle. Now we'll be able to ascertain with the vario readings which way to move the sailplane. Here's a hypothetical case: As we pass the 12 o'clock point the vario is reading 200 feet per minute up. As we swing around to three o'clock it moves to minus 100 feet per minute. At six o'clock it reads zero; then it starts climbing as we approach the nine o'clock position. We'll assume the vario peaks to over 250 feet per minute at 10 o'clock. It will be obvious that the plane should be moved over to the left toward that 10 o'clock area. To do this, the direction of the circling must be continued, and another orbit started in almost the same path as the one just flown. If the pilot's skill is such that he can make excellent, smooth, controlled turns, he can start to tighten his turn as he comes up to the 12 o'clock lake heading. So now, when he arrives at the three o'clock position on this second time around he'll have moved his flight path out of the minus area and hopefully into zero sink. The tightly banked path should be continued.

Immediately after the lake appears off the lower wing (six o'clock position), that wing should be sharply rolled up into level flight and then immediately rolled down with coordinated movements to reinstate the previous angle of bank. This will move the plane into the desired stronger lift that was outside the original circle at the 10 o'clock position. In effect we have now moved the circle in the direction of the stronger lift. This procedure should be continued until the vario reading is constantly high through the whole circular path.

The question remains, is the rate of climb as high as possible? Experiment with slight adjustments in the angle of bank as the climbing proceeds to see if higher readings can be found. Less bank will be needed as the thermal widens, and in this way the sink rate will be reduced, and this gives you a larger search area.

Air speed should be held as constant as possible throughout all these maneuvers. The nose of the ship must be held at a specific spot on the horizon as you go around. Variations of speed will cause the ship to fly an elliptical flight path and the thermal will be lost. Fast speed will produce a high rate of sink, and slow speed will cause mushing descent.

It will be important to learn your individual variometer and its lag time. In strong updrafts when you feel the acceleration in the seat of your pants, immediately observe the length of time it takes for the vario to register the change. Of course, small amounts of acceleration up or down won't be felt.

By acquiring sensitivity for this lag time you will learn how to move the plane toward the desired quadrant of the circle.

One of the keys to thermaling is a developed sense of orientation in relationship to landmarks, and remembering your progress. Then if you fly out of the lift you'll be able to relocate it quickly. But don't become so engrossed with all these problems that you neglect to stay within easy reach of the field.

Don't be satisfied with just climbing. Search continually for better lift; that's the way experience is gained.

The trick to thermaling is opening and tightening your circles: testing until you have the core. However, a thermal can have more than one core, and these will have different intensities

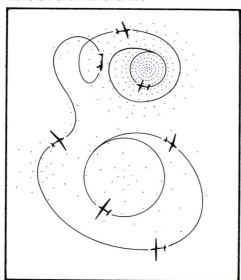

CLOUD STREETS

The day that thermals become organized into streets is a red-letter day in soaring. Long flights can be anticipated in the direction of the wind.

Specific wind and stability conditions that sandwich in the unstable layer produce street formations. First, good convection is needed to produce the thermals, and then this unstable layer must be capped by a layer of stable air to impose a firm lid on the thermals. The favorable wind condition is one that does not change direction up to the stable layer. Its velocity only increases up through part of the convection layer. Here is the way these conditions work together to form the streets. The temperature inversion producing the stable layer is the top of the container and limits the size of the thermal. As thermals reach their maximum height they will tend to spread out horizontally. The decrease of the wind velocity in the upper regions of the unstable layer helps this spreading action. The steadily increasing winds of the lower convection level line the thermals up into long streets.

Flights for many miles can be made in street formations, which are easily recognizable by long parallel lines of cumulus clouds. The distance between adjacent layers is usually two to three times the height of the convection layer. Lift, of course, will be found under the cloud formations, and considerable sink will be found between them. Flying with or against the wind will be relatively simple; flights across streets will be another matter because of the strong downdrafts.

FLYING CLOUD STREETS

If the flight path is across the prevailing direction of the cloud streets, the best procedure would be to climb high, just as you would in any thermal, then fly fast and get out of the sink air between the streets as quickly as possible; fly to the next street and climb.

Flying parallel to the streets is a thrill, no matter how much experience the pilot has. Straight, level-wing flight with the variometer reading "green air" is an incomparable experience. To get the most distance out of flying a street, use air speed to maintain a constant altimeter reading. Let's assume that you decide to fly 200 feet under cloud base. Note the altitude, and adjust your air speed so that you will stay at that altitude. If the altimeter starts to inch up, increase the speed, which will also increase the rate of sink. If the altimeter starts to fall, decrease the air speed, but of course never below minimum sink speed.

Cloud streets make the best condition for cross-country flying. Flying downwind you'll have the added advantage of tail wind speed for a maximum over-the-ground distance against time.

FLYING THE SEA BREEZE

Although we won't discuss flying the jet stream or large mass cold fronts, there is a local cold front condition that merits some discussion. The sea breeze presents a classic condition of convergence of a warm and cold front.

Temperature differential is the basis for convection.

During the day, the temperature of air over water is cooler and more constant than it is over land. When the general wind velocity is low and a temperature differential develops between the air over land and that over water, a local wind condition is produced. As the sun heats the land mass and raises the temperature of the air above it, the air becomes less dense and rises. The constantly cool air over the water rushes in to take the place of the rising warm air, and an onshore, or sea, breeze is created.

In temperate latitudes a sea breeze seldom penetrates more than 50 miles inland. It produces a narrow "wall" of convection that is similar to a cloud street. Coastline flights with the flight path well defined by the clouds are not uncommon.

The wedge-like cool sea air acts like a ridge. As warm inland air rises to get over it, its moisture is released and cumulus-type clouds form. The wedge moves inland. On occasion over island or peninsula land formations, stationary or lenticular clouds form over the area where the opposing sea breezes meet. Lift will be found under the lenticulars.

Sea fronts are often accompanied by thin, fleecy, curtain-like clouds that stand vertically. Flying on the land side of such formations will give long lines of lift, but in most cases the width of the lift area is so narrow that circling flight can't be sustained.

Unfortunately, sea breeze conditions are not always linked with the curtain cloud formation, and as a result many opportunities for this kind of soaring go unnoticed. Since the wall, which is a result of this miniature cold front, may not show itself by cloud formation, the variometer becomes necessary for the search. If the vario shows a sudden upsweep, chances are you've flown into the narrow corridor of convection. If you do circle, thinking it's a thermal, you'll fall out of it. To find it again, fly perpendicular to the direction of the wind and make short sweeps to each side and try to relocate the green air with the variometer.

If the clash of the sea breeze and offshore wind is not marked by cloud vapor or formation, it'll be difficult to find. As the day wears on, the sea breeze penetrates further and further inland if the offshore winds are light. So, the search will have to be adjusted for the time of day. If the offshore winds are strong, the junction of the sea breeze and the normal air mass could be on the coastline and the belt line of lift could be out over the sea. This is often observed when cu's do form.

The long line of sea breeze cumuli resembles the cloud street. On both sides of the belt of lift, you'll find heavy sink. Another interesting fact about the sea breeze lift is that rarely if ever will the sea breeze air warm sufficiently as it penetrates inland to produce thermals. You'll have to move inland to find them.

Because of a variation in pressure due to the invasion of the sea air over the land, the wind direction shifts. At noon the wind could be perpendicular to the coastline and by late afternoon it could be almost parallel to it. This should be remembered when preparing to land in a sea breeze area. Landing conditions after a flight of an hour or two could be entirely different from what they were on takeoff.

THE LEE WAVE

THE LEE WAVE

Of the three major sources of lift, the lee wave is by far the most spectacular. Hill soaring is fun and an excellent way for the beginner to learn to fly his ship. It's the oldest means of soaring, and impressive flights of over 400 miles, out to a predetermined destination and back, have been made flying the ridge. Thermal flights require a skill that results in exhilaration and great satisfaction for the pilot. Flights of over 700 miles have been recorded cross-country on convection currents. But man has always been fascinated by height. For a long time philosophers have suggested that the very beginnings of life on earth might have originated on some distant planet. They theorize that man has had an atavistic homing instinct that expresses itself historically by his fascination with the heavens. If the depth of the sea has always inspired fear in man and the height of the sky has inspired his poetry, it is small wonder that flying the lee wave is a celestial experience. Sailplanes have carried man to over 46,000 feet on a wave. When a pressurized cockpit is built, even that record height will be broken.

WHAT IS THE LEE WAVE?

Have you ever sat on the bank of a brook and watched the water flow over a submerged rock? If the current is rapid enough the water rises over the rock, then dips steeply behind it. Then it undulates, forming waves downstream, behind the rock. Superficially it appears that there must be a series of smaller rocks, each producing its own wave. Close examination reveals only the original rock. The illusory moving waves are in reality stationary, while the water flows through them.

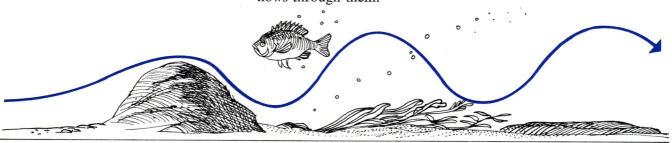

Water is a fluid; so is air. We can see wave action in water, but only feel it in air. The sailplane flies up on side of crest of the wave

There is a superficial similarity between this phenomenon and the lee wave. The upstream flow of the water, if compared to the wind, must be fast enough and steady enough to produce the wave. The boulder in the stream can be compared to a mountain range that stands perpendicular to the wind's path. The result of a steady wind striking the range is the "downstream waves" or the lee wave.

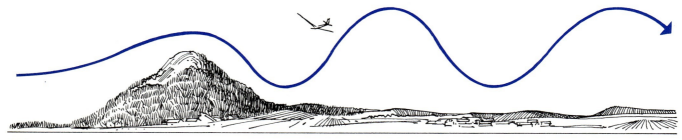

Studying the profile of the stream bed, it would seem obvious that the wave length (distance between crests of two succeeding waves) would be a function of the velocity of the water flow and the shape of the rock. The amplitude of each wave (height it reaches above the normal surface level) would be again a function of the shape of the boulder and the water velocity.

In the lee wave, wind velocity and the shape of the ridge are only part of the story. True, the wind does affect the wave length and its amplitude, and a ridge that's not too broad with relatively steep lee escarpment is best for setting off a good wave; but air temperature and stability are factors. A wind blowing over a range one day can produce little or no wave, while the same wind the next day can produce fantastic flying.

The temperature layers of the oncoming, upstream air will give an indication whether or not the wave will form. What is needed is a layer of unstable air at the low level. Temperature readings showing a high lapse rate will indicate this. Then above that, a stable layer is necessary. This layer is an inversion of the temperature readings. Above that, another unstable layer of decreasing temperatures is necessary again.

We will then have a condition of a stable layer sandwiched between two unstable layers. The unstable layers will act like springs that confine the stable layer in the middle of the sandwich.

When the whole airstream receives a jolt as it hits the mountain range, here's what happens. If all the air above the ridge were unstable, it would put up very little resistance to the jolt, since unstable air has a tendency toward vertical motion. If all the air above the ridge were stable, with no tendency toward vertical movement, it would absorb the shock and spring back as quickly as possible to its original shape. The condition we want is one that sets up an oscillation, and this occurs mainly in the stable, sluggish layer. The unstable layers are flexible enough to set up the vertical motion and are resilient enough to maintain this motion as a series of vertical oscillations. The stable air sandwiched between them acts like a heavy coilspring and dominates the leeward oscillations.

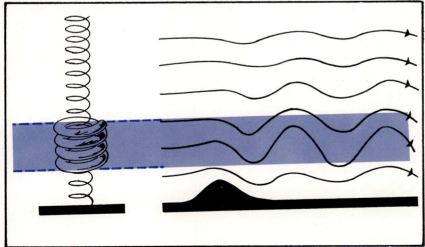

Stable air sandwiched between layers of unstable air is necessary to produce a wave

Waves almost always have their maximum vertical lift in the stable layer. It should be easy to see that the wave condition is as dependent on the lapse rate of the atmosphere as it is on a strong steady flow of wind and the ridge itself. The temperature variations and depth of the three layers set up the conditions for wave length and amplitude, and the wind velocity determines their magnitude.

By taking temperature soundings in the tow plane upwind of the mountain ridge, valuable data could be gathered for making daily predictions. Experience indicates that a shallow layer of very stable air will produce a better wave than a deep layer of only moderately stable air, and when the upper winds are strong the waves are long.

WAVE CLOUDS

There can be three kinds of clouds associated with a lee wave. If the condensation level is near the top of the mountain range, a cap cloud will form over the crest. The cap cloud needs no further explanation; it's of little use to the pilot.

The lenticular cloud is the kind that starts the blood pounding. It indicates that the wave phenomenon is in progress. It hangs motionless at the condensation level in the wave. The moisture content of the air responds to the temperature variations at different altitudes as it flows through the wave. A downward motion of the air causes evaporation of its water content, and then when it swings up into cooler air, condensation takes place. Obviously, as the wet air sweeps up on the wave it will leave its mark, a cloud. The dried air will continue to rise to the crest of the flow, then start descending on the down side of the wave. As it comes back to the cloud or condensation level again, it will pick up and carry the moisture with it down into the warmer layer. It evaporates the water which is then carried on into the next wave. This continuous process of condensation at the cloud's leading edge and evaporation at the trailing edge makes the whole cloud appear stationary in the sky.

The cap cloud sits over the mountaintop; the lenticular appears to stand still in the sky, and the rotor is a tumbling, puffy ball. Vario readings show where lift and sink will be found in relationship to the lenticulars

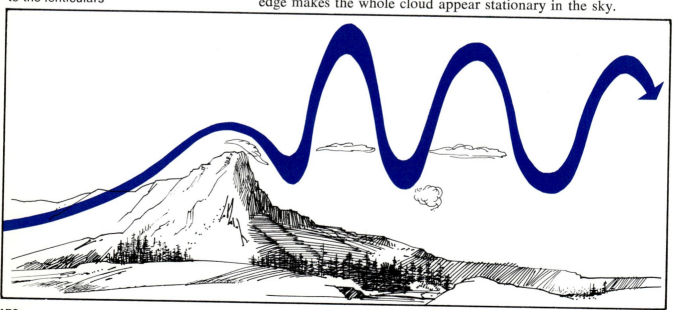

The almond-shaped lenticular is the classic cloud of the wave, but its shape can take many forms. The only certainty about the lennie is that it has sharp edges and appears stationary in the sky. Its shape really depends on the humidity of the different layers. If moist air is sandwiched between two layers of dry air the resulting cloud will be the traditional almond shape. If all layers are moist the sky could have a complete overcast look. The wave will be functioning, but it won't be readily apparent. If the air is all dry, no clouds will form but the wave can still be there and working.

A lenticular can show a pilot the location of the wave and how to fly it, but not much about its strength. The vertical currents of the wave are dependent upon the amplitude, wave length, and wind speed, not the humidity content of the air. The lennie is not an infallible sign of strong updrafts, nor does it indicate the level where the wave is most pronounced.

THE WINDOW

The window is from the trailing edge of one lenticular to the leading edge of the next lennie downwind. This is the area of evaporation and is very important to the pilot. As long as it stays clear he'll have a clear visual flight back to the ground. Quite often the streamlines of the wave reach their lowest level in this stationary gap, and the shape of this window is often a better indicator of the wave flow than the shape of the cloud itself. We'll have more to say about the window in the section on flying the wave.

ROTORS: CLOUD OR NO CLOUD

The third cloud formation of the wave is the rotor. This cloud signals the presence of turbulence. Flights in a lee wave are as smooth as silk, but—and this is a very important but—there are certain wind shear conditions that can cause violent turbulence. When there is moisture in the air, rotor clouds appear like tumbling cumulus clouds; airmen avoid them, they've learned about their force. It was the sailplane that discovered this phenomenon. At their slower speeds sailplanes could safely fly into a rotor to make scientific observations for their powered brethren.

The rotor can form for different reasons. It could be a variation of the wave's amplitude, or a wind shear condition. A local thermal condition can upset the flow and cause rotors, or it can be a "spilling" of the bottom of the wave into the lower ground level.

A pilot will know it when he has inadvertently blundered into a dry rotor. The wave is like riding in a Rolls, the rotor is like busting a bronco. If possible, fly to the windward side of the rotor. The upwind side contains vertical currents that can help you either back into the wave or out of trouble. The word "possible" has been used because under certain conditions whole valleys have turned into rotors and there is no getting out of it. Landing under these conditions will take plenty of extra speed. For the low-performance ship we've been flying in this book, a landing circuit of 70 mph will do the job.

FLYING THE WAVE

Drop a matchstick into a brook and watch it float down over the obstructing rock and into the wave formations; it bobbles up as it strikes a wave, levels out, and then descends into the trough, and then up again into the next wave. The difference between the matchstick and a sailplane is that the match floats *on top* of its wave and the plane flies *in* its wave. The sailplane attempts to stay only in the upstream side of the wave. It accomplishes this by flying upstream, into the current, or in this case into the wind. To hold position it must fly at the same rate of speed as the wind has flowing down through the wave. By standing still in relationship to the ground the wind will carry the plane up through the wave on its vertical component. The final aim is to reach the "surface" at the crest as the matchstick did in the water.

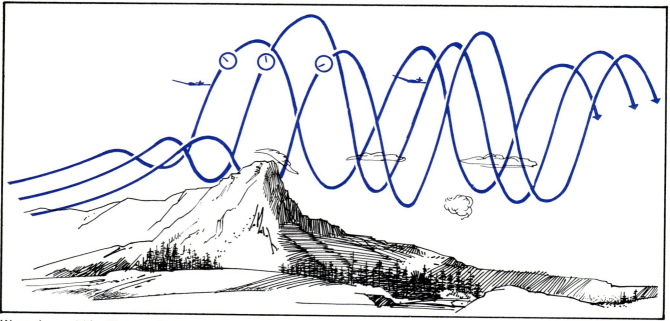

Wave has width. There will be strong and weak areas of lift along its crest. Pilot tacks along crest searching for the strongest portion

If the sailplane flies faster than the oncoming wind, it will move upstream and out of the vertical component and will start to descend into the forward trough. In like manner, if it flies too slowly, it will drift backward and out of the strong updraft. If it drifts backward far enough it will finally reach the strong downdraft that leads down into the trough of the next wave.

How do you get into this area of lift? The tow pilot, experienced with wave flying, will get you there with a minimum of turbulence. He usually knows the location of the rotor and will avoid these areas if he can. If he does misjudge the position of the rotor hang on, stay with him; he'll want out as badly as you do.

What he'll try to do is to fly around and into the trough, missing the rotor altogether; then he'll circle up. You'll know when you've struck paydirt. The tow plane will rise in front of you, and you'll follow him up like the curtain of a play on opening night. The noise and chatter of the audience before the curtain instantly subsides into a hushed eerie silence. You're alone . . . on stage.

The vario and the sudden quiet are your signal to release. Head the ship directly into the wind. The lift of the wave is a comparatively large area of rise, so there will be no need to circle to stay within its confines as you do in a thermal. The rising air will lie parallel to the range of mountains that is causing the wave. Since you will be in the lower region of the wave when you release, you should immediately assume a speed that will hold you stationary over a landmark such as a road. The air flow will be so smooth because of the stable and laminar flow of the air that if you trim your ship you can fly hands off for minutes at a time. Note the rate of climb on your vario and the altimeter reading. Calculate your actual rate of climb against your stop watch to see how you're progressing.

If you have good lift, hold your position. Since you are still low in the wave you could lose it by being impatient; the vertical lift will become much broader as you ascend. Then you can start looking for the strongest updraft.

As height is gained the wind speed usually increases, or a slight change in direction may be encountered. You will have to watch your drift and note the ground coordinates of the position that produces good lift so that you can return to that place if need be. If you start to lose height, you have either flown into the sinking air ahead of the wave or drifted back into the downward flow behind it. Your speed will have to be adjusted to get you back into the lift.

The stationary lenticular cloud will be of great help in orienting yourself in your position. Whether it's above you or below, you should stay out in front, upstream of it. How far in front will be a matter of judgment. Test it and see. Increase your speed and watch the variometer. Move forward until it starts to show descent. Then slow up and drift back. The vario will pinpoint the strongest lift. Once you have the best position facing directly into the wind you can start to search to either side to see if the air might be greener over yonder.

If you inadvertently drift downwind too far you will have to increase your speed to regain your original position. Penetrating against a strong wind, especially if you get into a down current in the back portion of the wave, will cost you considerable height.

In many ways, flying a wave is like rocking in a rocking chair. Not that it's so smooth and quiet that it will lull you to sleep, but your flight path in the wave is a rocking motion. You fly forward, testing, then drift back for the same purpose. You will get the best lift in the center of the arc while falling off slightly at the forward and back positions.

WATCH THE CLOUDS

Clouds, like fire, can be your friend or foe.

When the lenticular cloud is sandwiched between dry air, it's well defined and becomes an extremely useful navigation aid to the pilot. Excess humidity is really the foe; sudden changes are not uncommon, and if the pilot is not careful he could find himself trapped above a blanket of solid cloud cover. Without instrument-flying experience this could become a serious matter, since it only takes seconds of blind flying for the untrained pilot to become disoriented. The rule for wave flying: Don't get caught over solid overcast. Wait until you've had plenty of experience before you add this one to your log book.

Watch the cloud formations continually. If things start to over-develop, go down. The wave, as we have said, runs parallel to the ridge, and windows will be observed all along the line of the wave. When you have climbed a few thousand feet above the cloud layer and are flying headed into the wind, you will be able to see the lenticular formations and their windows off to both sides. If conditions start to thicken, you should keep all the windows under close surveillance. If you see the one under you start to close, you can move to another one and go down through it. Be prepared to go down through any one of them.

Although the lennie and its window appear to be stationary, actually they aren't. This can best be observed on a bright moonlit night when the wave is working. You will be able to clearly see the undulations of the leading and trailing edge of the clouds as condensation and evaporation take place. It's a most thrilling sight, and dangerous. Soaring pilots meet in ski regions to fly the wave. It has been recorded that this magnificent nocturnal event has caused such excitement among pilots that at least one has been known to fall over the chalet's porch railing making such nightly observations.

WAVE UPJUMPING

Wave upjumping, which is a sudden change in the wave length and amplitude, has been observed by pilots, but meteorologists have little explanation for this happening. One minute the sailplane can be flying at the same altitude as and ahead of the lenticular cloud, and the next thing the pilot knows he's in the middle of the cloud. The sudden change in wave length has more than likely been caused by an erratic turbulence. The lennie and the window have moved upwind, so the obvious pilot reaction should be to increase speed and penetrate forward to get out in the clear.

WAVE INTERFERENCE

The wind necessary to initiate the wave must have a velocity of at least 25 knots and a steady uniform character. This means that the terrain on the upwind side of the barrier should be flat, or even better, a large body of water.

Since a broad air flow is necessary to form a wave, it can be assumed that all barriers in the area will produce waves. This makes excellent conditions for long cross-country flights downwind. Theoretically, good height could be achieved starting at the first barrier and then on down to the second and third wave in the series. Between waves, fast runs downwind occur because of the tail wind and, more important, the necessity of high-speed flight in order to get out of the downdraft areas quickly. By careful planning, another series of waves could be picked up off a second barrier and the flight downwind would continue through that wave. Long daylight flights can be planned since the wave will work night or day if the conditions are right.

One of the problems is that the second barrier might not be far enough downwind and cause wave interference. To understand this, use the rock and stream analogy: if a second rock lay directly behind the first one, the wave it produced might be out of phase and cancel out the effect of the first one. The same thing can happen in the atmosphere, but wave interference won't usually take place if the terrain behind the original mountain barrier is a broad flat valley. If the wind runs its course in the first wave, flattens out before it strikes the second barrier, no interference will occur.

Flights to 30,000 feet in the eastern U.S. and to over 50,000 in the West could be attained at this writing. The 50,000-foot record is dangerously close to man's limits for sustaining life on oxygen alone, making a pressure suit or pressurized cabin necessary.

WAVE MAGNITUDE

Flying waves of this magnitude should not be attempted in planes designed for ordinary ridge or thermal soaring. Both positive and negative gust loads of high intensity could be encountered in such flights. High-speed performance and terminal-velocity-limiting dive brakes are very desirable. High speed with relatively low sink rate will be necessary for penetration in order to stay within the vertical component as the wind races through its wave pattern. The limiting dive brakes are important in the event that a high-speed descent is required.

At the other end of the scale, wave flights in a secondary or tertiary wave can produce zero sink conditions. Often there is no rotor encountered; the pilot suddenly finds himself in this minor wave. The only signal he receives is the abrupt lowering of the noise level, which will set his eyes scurrying to the air speed indicator to see if he has inadvertently slowed up to a prestall condition. This low-altitude wave can produce delightful flying.

The important thing to remember in wave flying is that the pilot has to be alert for sudden changes. At certain soaring locations the primary wave can be reached by flying the ridge and then jumping off, flying to the lee of the barrier and picking up the wave on its first ascent. This will take precision flying, since the lee of the ridge has its own downdrafts and turbulence that are not associated with the wave. This should not be attempted unless there are available landing areas close at hand. If the wave is missed, a fast landing might be called for. If the wave has been contacted, you will find yourself in smooth air, the vario will read up, and an 180-degree turn must be made immediately, or you could fly into more downdraft or even the rotor. All wave situations call for caution on the first approach, and it's especially important to have shoulder and seat harnesses fastened tightly. If the wave is approached by air tow from downwind, sudden changes in turbulence will be encountered from the rotor, and this is not the time and place to have the extra problem of loose safety belts.

THE COLD

High-altitude flights sometimes present temperature problems even in the summer. Readings of below zero are common, and on extremely high flights —50 degrees can be encountered. Comfort and safety become intertwined. Warm clothing will be required, with special attention to the hands and feet. Electric socks and surplus military gear are the answer to these problems. Insulation under the seat cushion is very helpful. If the sailplane is drafty—and some are—drafts could be sealed with plastic tape. But if the canopy is to be sealed this should be done in a manner so the seal can be broken easily from the inside.

Most modern planes are equipped with adequate ventilation systems so that the canopy will not fog up and freeze. The body gives off a surprising amount of moisture, and frost can cause serious visual problems. Although it can be scraped off, it will quickly form again. The compromise is cold air from the outside which will keep the canopy clear but make the pilot cold. Manufacturers are finally learning not only that ventilation is important, but that a means of directing the flow of cold air is essential. At low altitudes the warmly dressed pilot needs the air on his face; at altitude he needs it only on the canopy.

The extreme cold can congeal lubricants and affect the controls. There are many lubricants on the market today that solve this difficulty. There is one control, the dive brakes, that requires your particular attention. On certain planes there is a tendency for them to freeze in place if the moisture content of the air is sufficient and the temperature is low enough. This can be remedied by cracking the dive brakes every so often during flight. Needless to say, when descending from a wave flight, the dive brakes should be tested before the landing pattern is entered. This is a must. Although frozen brakes are rare, if the possibility is recognized before the landing pattern is entered, an alternate landing procedure can be used. The plane can be slipped down and/or a longer glide landing pattern can be used.

Attention to the electrical system should be considered for high-altitude flights. Batteries should be insulated. Some pilots who fly the giant waves in the West have a small extra battery that they wear under their clothing and can plug in in case of emergency.

OXYGEN . . . HIGH FLYING

The wave-soaring pilot should have a complete understanding of his need for oxygen and the equipment that delivers it. Stories about high flying without oxygen should be filed in the same pigeonhole as those about Russian roulette.

In the early days of soaring, in the open cockpit of a primary glider, all a pilot had to know about his breathing was to throw his scarf over his nose if the wind made inhaling difficult. The new dimension that wave flying has introduced to the sport calls for technical understanding of his new environment.

Our atmosphere consists of oxygen and nitrogen and a few rare gases that need no comment here. The mixture of the two main components is constant at all levels: four-fifths is nitrogen, one-fifth is oxygen. Our atmosphere, therefore, is virtually nothing more than layers of these two gases, some water vapor, and, unfortunately, man's pollution. The top layer is very thin with the molecules spread out, and its own weight makes the bottom layer denser.

The purpose of breathing is to get oxygen into the bloodstream and carbon dioxide out. Since the mixture of oxygen and nitrogen is constant throughout the whole atmosphere, a breath of air at 18,000 or 20,000 feet contains only half as much oxygen as it does on the ground.

The seriousness of the effects of an insufficient oxygen supply cannot be overstressed. It might seem logical that a deliberate increase in the breathing rate would satisfy the body's oxygen needs; double intake at 18,000 feet would equal one breath at sea level. Unfortunately, it doesn't work that way. The increased breathing rate removes too much carbon dioxide from the blood. The effects of this can be experienced by blowing excessively on a fire; you start to see spots before your eyes and get dizzy, and if you keep it up your fingers and toes will start to tingle. The next phase could be unconsciousness. The way to correct this is to hold one's breath and allow the carbon dioxide to return into the bloodstream, but holding one's breath at altitude while waiting for the chemical exchange can also induce unconsciousness.

Breathing at altitude must be at a normal rate.

The rule is this: any pilot who expects to fly over 10,000 feet should have supplemental oxygen and use it. This will give a 2,000-foot cushion for most people. The tolerance to hypoxia (oxygen starvation) for an individual will depend on his physical condition, not just in a general sense but for that particular day. The dangers of a lack of oxygen are deceptive. A feeling of well-being, elation, and a desire to chatter are accompanied by a self-assurance that the plane is being flown with a fine light-handed skill, when in reality the sailplane could be skidding and slipping all over the sky. This debonair response gradually changes to a dullness and confusion. The brain is the first part of the body to be affected by the lack of oxygen: drowsiness, faulty reasoning, blurred vision, poor memory, and failure of one's sense of time occur. It can all end in unconsciousness. The reason the first insidious symptoms are difficult to detect in wave soaring is that even with a sufficient supply of oxygen the climb in a wave is truly an exhilarating and exciting experience and the pilot may really not know to which sensation he is responding.

THE EQUIPMENT

There are three different types of oxygen systems: constant flow, diluter demand, and pressure demand. Each system has the same three components: storage tank, regulator, or pressure-reducing valve, and mask.

The most common type is constant flow, and it's good up to 25,000 feet. The diluter demand is satisfactory to approximately

35,000, and the pressure demand unit should always be used when flights over 35,000 feet are anticipated. Above 38,000 feet the atmospheric pressure is so low that even pure oxygen is insufficient unless it is forced into the lungs under pressure. The pressure system is adequate to approximately 45,000 feet; above that a pressurized suit or cabin is necessary.

THINGS TO KNOW ABOUT OXYGEN

Loss of efficiency occurs at even 10,000 feet if the duration of the flight is an hour or more.

Grease and oil should not be used on any part of the oxygen equipment, since fire or explosion can result when they come in contact with oxygen. Grease or lipstick can be used on the lips without any fear of fire. This will prevent skin irritation caused by the pure oxygen. Special pipe sealer should be used for oxygen connections.

Never smoke while using oxygen unless you enjoy fireworks. An ordinary cigarette will turn into a Roman candle in pure oxygen.

Only use aviator's oxygen when having the tank refilled. The moisture in other grades will freeze and interrupt the flow.

Check the system before every flight; make sure there are no leaks.

While using the system watch continually to see that the flow indicator is functioning and that all connections are tight. You won't be aware of it if the system fails and all you are breathing is thin outside air.

Storage tanks should be handled with care. If a tank is dropped and the valve broken it can become a deadly rocket. The tank should be mounted in the plane securely. A jerry rig could break loose in turbulence or on a hard landing and foul up controls or hit the pilot.

The fitting of the mask is most important. Leaks above 25,000 feet could be disastrous.

If turbulence is expected at altitude, the system should be turned on and the mask worn. It's hard to fly in rough air and put a mask on at the same time.

Get experience with your system; the rate at which one uses oxygen has many variables. It's important on any altitude flight to plan the descent time with a good supply in excess. Descents are sometimes more difficult than just pulling the plug.

Oxygen is very helpful even in normal flying if nausea occurs. A good practice after a long flight to high altitude is to use the oxygen all the way to the touchdown, just to ensure staying alert.

If a radio is to be used during high flights, the microphone should be built into the mask. Over 20,000 feet never take the mask off.

Don't buy surplus oxygen equipment unless you know what you are doing. Better to pay the full price to a reputable dealer than to save a few bucks toward a better casket.

While we're on the subject of high flights, don't eat gas-producing foods before such a flight; it can be rather painful. Sinus problems and colds are sufficient cause to postpone high flights. In rapid descents, clogged ears can be cleared by holding the nose closed with the fingers and blowing. Some people can accomplish this by swallowing.

If the moisture from breathing freezes in the mask, flex the mask between your fingers to dislodge the ice.

Check all systems before and after, and in between flights. When the tank valve is turned on in preparation for a flight make sure it is all the way on and not just cracked open.

The FAA, in cooperation with the Air Force, has a civilian training program that is the best $5 investment a serious-minded wave pilot could make. You'll learn from this training what your capacity or lack of capacity is. It'll take the guess out of high-altitude flying. For additional information about centers in your area, contact the Physiological Operations and Training Section, AC-143, Box 25082, Oklahoma City, Oklahoma 73125.

INSTRUMENT FLYING

The novice or non-instrument-rated pilot should not fly the wave on a heavily overcast day. The wave will function, but the only open area will be the window. If it closes suddenly, the pilot could be trapped above the cloud cover.

Most pilots who fly the wave have a turn and bank indicator in their panel for just such a rare emergency. Coupled with the air speed indicator it can get the plane down through heavy cloud cover, but this is not something one can learn from a book. The principles can be written, but they can only be learned by experience in a Link trainer and actual flying instruction with an instructor.

A straight descent in cloud cover is a relatively simple instrument-flying problem. The needle, ball, air speed method of controlled descent without disorientation is a matter of just a few hours of practice in the trainer.

The problem with blind flying is that the body comes to wrong conclusions when its only source of information is sensations. The turn and bank becomes your eyes, and the air speed substitutes for your ears. You'll learn to believe the instruments even though your brain tells you they are wrong. Even experienced instrument-rated pilots become disoriented within a few moments without instruments.

It has been said that you can get about as much out of a self-taught course in instrument flying as you can get out of a home-study course in brain surgery. A Link trainer is fun and good insurance.

PARACHUTE KNOW-HOW

Many soaring pilots wear parachutes, especially in wave flying. "But why?" asks the newcomer, with dismay in his voice. "I thought it was such a safe sport."

Wearing seat belts in a car doesn't necessarily mean you have entered the 500 at Indianapolis; it's a precautionary measure. And so it is in a sailplane; a chute is only mandatory in competition flying. In some planes the cockpit is built so that a parachute can be worn. Without it, or a cushion the size of a chute, the seat would be uncomfortable; so in many cases it's worn more for comfort than out of necessity.

Structural failures are extremely rare, but collision during thermal flying with two or three other planes can occur if somebody's eyes are glued to the instrument panel instead of the traffic.

Hangar talk on the subject would give one the impression that most soaring pilots would rather ride a plane down than jump. The argument is that there is no power plant to drive the sailplane into the ground or fuel to burn, and if some semblance of a wheel touchdown can be made, the pilot will walk away.

If you have determined that control of the craft has been lost and you are spinning in, get out and don't argue with yourself.

MAKE YOUR PLAN AND GO

Get rid of the canopy. Each plane has its specific procedure; know it beforehand.

Determine the attitude of the plane. If you are in a spin or spiral dive, the jump should be to the *inside* of the turn, so if you're spinning to the right go out the right side. If you're inverted, disconnect the oxygen or earphones, unfasten the safety buckle, and fall out.

If you're at high altitude and on oxygen, plan a delayed jump to get out of the upper air as quickly as possible to prevent anoxia, from lack of oxygen, and frostbite. Before you go over the side take deep drags on the oxygen, make disconnecting it the last thing you do.

You should always plan to go out head first; it's the simplest and fastest way to clear your head and shoulders. Don't release the safety belt until you're ready to go. Never stand up and pull the rip cord, relying on the chute to whip you off into space; it can foul on the tail surfaces. Dive slightly forward to help clear the ship.

Think out how you're going over the side. Glance at the rip cord just to make sure you know where it is.

You may have to draw your legs up to get out of a single-seater; straighten them as you go out, and *before* you pull the cord.

The Navy tells its pilots to get out and pull the rip cord by 1,000 feet to be on the safe side. If you don't have that much altitude, have your hand on the rip cord as you jump because you have no time to waste. You won't have time to jump under 600 feet. Above 600 feet your hand should be near the rip cord, you should look and see if you are clear of the plane, then pull. If you have height to spare, wait until your fall is vertical before you pull the cord.

It only takes seconds for the chute to open. The shock is less than you might think. Your body will always be too far forward in the harness. Readjust your position. Put your thumbs inside the straps under your seat and push down. Settle yourself back into the seat and relax. Note your situation. If you are oscillating, stop it by pulling the lines down on the opposite side of the swing; a few inches will do it.

You can slip a chute, to land at the best site, by reaching up and pulling the shroud lines on the side of the chute that corresponds to the direction in which you want to move. You can pull them down as much as 3 or 4 feet, but don't do it too close to the ground because spilling out the chute increases the rate of descent.

Land facing the direction of your drift. You can change your direction by pulling on two opposite lift webs; your left hand pulls the right web above and behind you, the right hand pulls the left web in front of you. Pull them simultaneously and you'll turn; check your rotation and hold that position for landing.

Stay in your seated position with your knees slightly bent as you touch down. Pull down on the lift webs as you touch. This will prevent going over on your head. Don't fight to stay upright. Relax and roll, enjoy the dirt. Once on the ground grab the bottom group of lines and yank them as soon as you can. This will collapse the canopy.

FINAL WORD ON THE WAVE

Rotor clouds, oxygen, instrument flying, and parachutes all have an ominous tone, but they should not deter the pilot from the lee wave. It is magnificent flying. It's a challenge because new knowledge is required; that shouldn't be frightening. Wave soaring can be just as safe as a Sunday game of golf if the beginner goes step by step and doesn't overextend himself. Much can be learned from the experienced pilots, but that goes for all types of soaring. The first wave experiences should be good-weather flights. Get the feel of the lee wave, then go for gold altitude.

IT'S GOING TO BE LIKE THIS

You sink down to 100 feet above the ridge after a three-hour flight. The heat of the summer day is over; the cool air spreads out across the valley and touches off smooth updrafts. The last heat of the valleys from Maine to Tennessee goes skyward. The sailplane floats along to the top of the ridge on an invisible sea. Time now to think of that cool drink. It will all be over very shortly, and you'll glide to the airport in the valley. The steady last flow of the day is a cushion—soft and easy to fly. The hawks have settled, and the sailplane's wing dips close to their nests, riding the last bubbles as they trickle up the ridge. As the day ebbs, the silence, the colors of the approaching evening flow over the land like a tide. The quiet is rich in treasures. The peace is welcome after a long day's struggle to stay aloft. The mind refuses more calculations—no more plans, no more decisions, no more assumptions, just the last few minutes to float before rejoining your earthbound species. The feeling of accomplishment has been satisfyingly attained; it stems from your own knowledge.

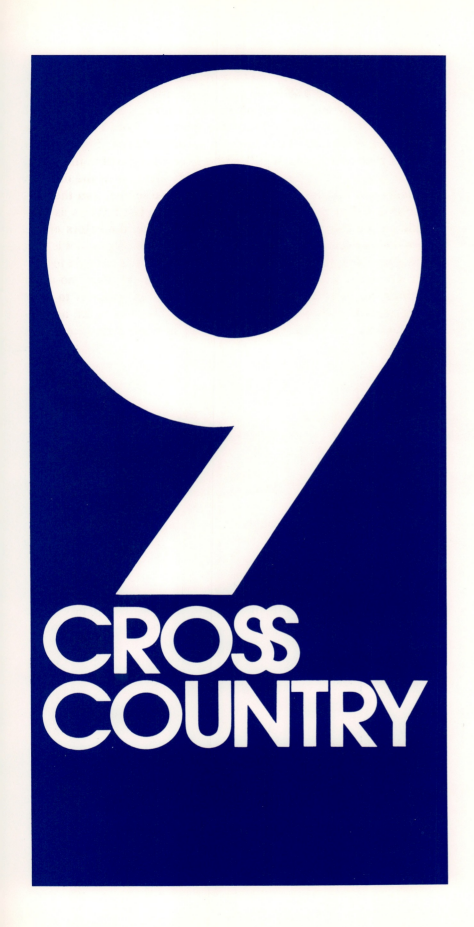

9
CROSS COUNTRY

CROSS COUNTRY

Now for the final phase. All the pieces of knowledge are ready for assembly of the final product, cross-country flight. Many soaring pilots never put the pieces together; they get their kicks flying locally. Apprehension and lack of confidence prevent many of them from breaking the umbilical cord that ties them to the local field. It's so much easier for the power pilot who gets his glider ticket to go off. His familiarity with the air gives him a distinct advantage over the student who has gone directly into sailplanes. The student should attempt his first cross-country when he personally feels ready, avoiding being pushed into it. Unfortunately, in this country too many instructors are not cross-country pilots themselves, so they can't be too helpful.

There is one piece of knowledge that will definitely help; it's knowing that you are not alone. Every pilot who has ever ventured off on his first cross-country has gone through the agony, the indecision . . . to go or not to go.

The neophyte pilot will have to argue this out with himself. He'll know when he has the skill and knowledge to go. When the decision is finally made, the first cross-country flight will be a highlight in the pilot's life. He'll be opening up a new world in which he'll have the satisfaction of knowing that he did it himself. No matter how much experience a pilot gets after that, he'll always be able to close his eyes and relive that whole first cross-country venture. There is much in common between the pilot about to go off and a young boxer sitting in his corner waiting for the bell for round 1: both are scared, but when the action starts they go to work.

There is more to this sport than the graceful beauty of the plane as it silently soars with invisible support. The accomplishment, the achievement, the feeling of a job well done is the real beauty and the reward. In cross-country flying the reward seldom comes while the flight is in progress; you're too busy working. Popular writing on this sport gives the prospective pilot the feeling that he is lord of the skies while he's up there. If he does acquire that feeling, it will be when he's on the ground. Cross-country flying is so completely absorbing that constant concentration is necessary, and you will literally leave the ground and all its problems below. The poetry of soaring flight is not composed in the cockpit. It's written in the study. In the cockpit, the pilot flies his machine, which is poetry in itself.

Granted, the apprehension of the first off-field landing for the inexperienced pilot is understandable. Essential for the venture is the pilot's confidence and psychological cool. Any off-field landing must be considered an emergency landing. The way to prepare yourself is on your home field. Spot landings should be practiced until the pilot and plane are coordinated and landings can be made within a hundred feet past a designated spot. The landing spot should be moved to different parts of the airstrip to simulate short field landings and extended final glide landings. Practice dropping in just over the fence, for getting into short fields, and slipping in with full dive brakes.

The fellow who gets his first off-field experience by being shot down may brag about it later, but he shows poor flight planning. The technique is like throwing a kid into the water to sink or swim. By the time you have gone through your training and have 50 to 70 hours, your air work will be automatic. Just thinking, the night before the planned flight, about the last 700 feet down to a strange farmer's field will give you indigestion. You just hope he's a good farmer and has his fields cleared of rocks.

Overconfidence can result from exceptionally good soaring days, rather than piloting skill. Good thermaling technique has to become second nature; staying up in marginal weather is the real test. Weather forecasting, to select the right day, is a major contributor to success or failure. When boring holes in the sky over your local airport bores you, you should be ready.

Approach cross-country tasks in a gradual step-by-step manner. When the pilot has gained confidence with his abilities and is familiar with the airport locale, it's time to start concentrating on chart reading, in-flight weather evaluation, and flying a compass course. Then the local flights can be extended. When he reaches a distance of 5 miles from the landing field he should note his altitude and head for home. Figuring the altitude loss in given wind and weather, he'll develop a sensitivity for his plane's performance.

Most beginners have little or no faith in the existence of thermals away from their home field. A pilot's conversion to a true believer will occur when he's lifted heavenward by a thermal while turning back to the home field 8 miles away. When he can stay aloft for two or three hours, fly a compass course to the next town 10 miles away, and is proficient in short field landings, he's ready.

Leaving "Mother" is never easy.

Next build your confidence by planning a triangular course with each leg 10 miles long, practicing chart reading, finding thermals, estimating altitude loss, noting new landing spots in the enlarged perimeter, and observing wind and weather changes. The beginner must learn the necessity of speeding up in heavy sink and changing course to get out of it. All the techniques of cross-country flying can be practiced in local flying within range of your home airport.

SECTIONAL AERONAUTICAL CHART

Every area of the U.S. is covered by one of the sectional charts scaled 1:250,000. They can be obtained at local airports, map stores, or by writing to the Director, Coast and Geodetic Survey, U.S. Department of Commerce, Washington, D.C. 20230. These local charts are scheduled for reprinting every six months in order to keep the information updated. The inexperienced pilot must acquire confidence in the charts; they're accurate.

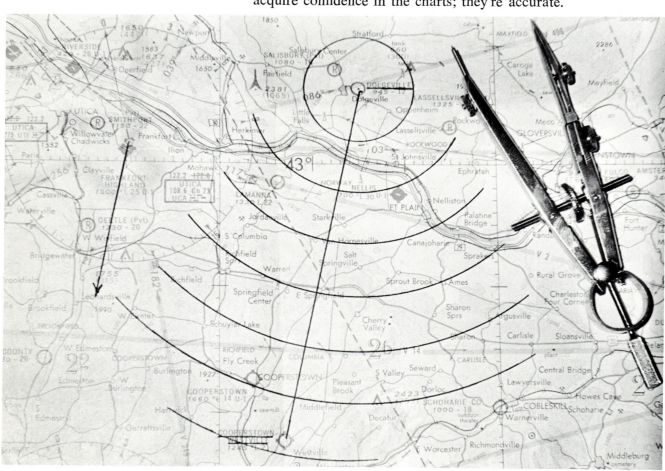

An hour's study of the symbols should make you a proficient chart reader. The chart shows all features that can be seen from the air: cities, highways, relief features, hydrography, airports, Air Traffic Control areas, railroads, high-tension lines, high points, race tracks, quarries, large buildings, etc., etc. Ground elevations are shown in color along with a legend, and scale is given in kilometers and nautical and statute miles.

Plan a trip. Draw a line between the takeoff and destination. Using a draftsman's compass, measure off 5 statute miles and draw a circle around the takeoff point. With the point of the compass held at the takeoff airport, scribe arcs through the planned flight line, at intervals of 5 miles along the way until the destination is reached.

"Travel" along the line reading landmarks below you, to either side and ahead. In actual flight you will mark off each 5-mile circle as you pass it. If you also mark off important landmarks as you go, you will always have an idea of where you are and any two landmarks will pinpoint your position. Isolated landmarks, such as mountains or lakes, are excellent reference points. It's important to know the chart and symbols before you go cross-country. You can't spend your time poring over a chart and fly at the same time. Consider wind drift and be familiar with areas downwind of your course. If possible, terrain permitting, in a crosswind, plan to fly on the upwind side of the flight plan line so that wind drift will help you.

Plot the same course on a good road map. Draw the circle and arcs. Many a soaring pilot who has gotten lost on the chart has reoriented himself with the help of his friendly Esso dealer.

Chart reading is a matter of not allowing yourself to become flustered; experience helps but so does logic. One of the best ways to get experience fast is to practice navigation from the copilot's seat in a small plane. The most important part of this game is to learn to recognize familiar things from a new perspective. One of the major problems beginners have is that they see everything and recognize nothing. The eye has to learn to be selective and pick out details. This should be practiced during local flying at the home airport.

THE COMPASS

It would seem obvious that the compass is essential for cross-country flying. You're going to be surprised to discover that it's not as important as you might think.

The magnetic compass is not as simple as it appears. But its complexities are problems more for the power pilot than the soaring pilot. There is no need to clutter up the brain with compass variation and solving the problems of magnetic north and true north, turning errors of the compass, rules such as "ands," "Yankee," etc. This material can be found in any power-flying manual if your curiosity is aroused.

There is a simple way for the soaring pilot to use his compass and figure his magnetic heading. Simply draw a line between the two points, takeoff and destination. Keep the ruler parallel to that line and slide it over the map to the nearest VOR compass rose. These roses are radio directional stations, and are marked as magnetic bearings. By placing your ruler at the center point and having it parallel to the flight path, a direct magnetic reading will be shown on the outer rim of the printed compass circle.

This might seem to be a rather inaccurate method, but for the soaring pilot it is fast and will do the job. A cross-country flight in a sailplane and one in an airplane are two different things. In an airplane, once you make a few simple calculations, you fly straight as an arrow on an exact magnetic heading, and after the prescribed time at so many miles an hour, you land at your planned destination. In a sailplane you're going to be all over the sky searching for lift, circling in thermals, drifting with the wind, flying to a ridge-soaring area to save you from being shot down, climbing again in a thermal, etc., so your magnetic heading is more a reference and a hope than a course.

There are pilots, including some world champions, who do not even carry a compass in their plane. They do all their navigation by pilotage; they observe the ground features and then locate their position on their chart, then select a landmark ahead on their course and go for it. This is the basic cross-country method, but the compass will help those who haven't spent half their lifetime in the air.

COMPASS DEVIATION

Compass deviation is an important matter for the soaring pilot. Deviation errors are caused by metal parts of his plane or the effect electric instruments have on the compass. Even if the compass is considered only a reference tool, it should be correct. The compass should be "swung." This is done on the ground by taking a careful reading at every 45 degrees and comparing it against accurate compass bearings taken outside the plane. Most large airports have a compass rose painted someplace on the runway for just such purposes. Small adjustments can be made, but if a compass is far out of adjustment it usually takes a professional to make the corrections.

The panel-mounted compass presents a problem for the soaring pilot; changes of speed or bank cause temporary errors. Steady, straight flight gives accurate readings, so the compass is only useful while flying straight between thermals or during very shallow turns.

TURNING ERROR

The turning error is another bad habit of the compass, but for visual flying the soaring pilot doesn't have to worry about it too much. This error can be demonstrated by flying a shallow 360-degree turn. The compass will move faster on some headings than on others. This turning error is at a maximum on southerly and northerly headings. When turning onto a northerly heading the compass is in advance of the turn, and it lags in a southerly direction.

This is not too important for the soaring pilot because before he goes into a thermal he should take a direction bearing from a landmark, a cloud, or the sun. Then when he flies out of the turn he goes onto his visual heading and only uses the compass to make the necessary minor corrections. This visual method will also take care of wind drift. For example, if his chart shows a lake 20 miles away on his flight path, he'll fly for it. On the way he enters a thermal and circles. When he leaves the thermal he heads back on course by heading for the lake. It's just that simple.

In competition flying the trailer and crew are just as important as the pilot and his plane. No matter how well the pilot does, his crew must retrieve him and get him back to the starting gate in time for the next day's event or he's as good as out of the contest. The problem is similar in cross-country flying. A pilot can get mighty hungry waiting for a crew that gets its signals mixed up.

The classic story starts with Eric Himmel radioing to his crew after release.

"Greta, I'm in a vunderful lift. Hook up der trailer, vill leave der vield on course."

"Vait, Eric. Ve can't find der car keys!"

"Ach. Dumkopf! . . . Hast du looked in der glove compartment?"

"Eric, vhat about der pocket in your lederhosen?"

Silence.

"Greta, I have die keys. Vait. I'll tie dem to der handkerchief, fly over dos vield, und drop dem."

Silence.

"Greta. Here ich come. Der dey go. Do you see dem? Greta! Do you see der handkerchief mit der keys?"

"Nein, Eric."

Obviously, a well-planned check list should be made for the pilot and his plane and the crew and its tow car and trailer.

A double set of charts and road maps should be made. Predetermined checkpoints should be indicated so that the simple code names will replace long descriptions in verbal communications.

If the sailplane and the tow car are equipped with two-way VHF radio, channels 123.3 and 123.5 may be used for air-to-ground and ground-to-air communications. This is line-of-sight communication and can easily be lost. When the crew leaves the field, it should head for high ground for best transmission and reception and wait for instructions. These points should be determined before the flight starts.

A back-up telephone system is essential. If radio contact is lost the telephone will become the means of communication. The pilot and crew will carry a prearranged telephone number. When radio contact is lost, the crew should call person-to-person to the phone contact. If the pilot has not landed and called in, the answering phone contact will not accept the call from the crew. The crew should continue its trip and plan to call in every half hour. When the pilot does land he should call station-to-station to the telephone contact and give precise details of his exact location and a phone number where he can be reached. When that information is received by the phone ground station, it can then accept the next person-to-person call from the crew. The crew will then have the pilot's landing location; the retrieve can be made.

For radio operations both the plane and the tow car will require Federal Communications Commission station licenses, and the operators of these stations will need a restricted radio telephone operator's permit. No tests are required, and forms can be obtained from any local FCC office.

If radio contact is maintained during the flight, all that will be required from the pilot is his position in relation to the nearest 5-mile arc drawn along the course. If each arc has its own number or letter, the ground crew will translate it from the air chart and onto the road map. The crew should try to stay under the pilot if possible, and acknowledge his transmissions with as few words as possible. For example, a typical radio transmission would start with the plane's registration number: "N1894 to ground. One mile east of C climbing 300. Move to D one." The ground would acknowledge the transmission with one word: "94 received."

The crew would locate the plane's position on the chart and find it on the road map. It would also know from the transmission that the flight was going well. The sailplane at the time of transmission was climbing in a thermal at 300 feet per minute and had enough height to go on because the crew was instructed to go to "D one," the high point near the next 5-mile arc on course.

It's more important for the pilot to fly his plane than to do a lot of unnecessary talking.

PILOT COMFORT

Sitting in one position for many hours can become a painful experience if the pilot doesn't have his cushions worked out properly. One pilot continually complained about his leg going to sleep on long flights. He tried every cushion arrangement possible, to no avail. Finally, a fellow pilot suggested that he remove his wallet from his back pocket, and that did it.

Clothing is important. It's not uncommon to swelter on takeoff and shiver after 20 minutes of the flight. Layers of clothing are better than one single heavy garment. Front zippers are desirable so that body warmth can be controlled. For winter flying, electric socks are very useful. Good judgment has to be used in all these matters, and much depends on the country and the time of the year. An extra sweater stowed away for the evening will be very comforting while waiting in a farmer's field after the sun goes down.

Many pilots wear a tennis hat to fly in. The brim is short, so visibility above is not obstructed, and the green underside of the brim cuts down glare. Sunburn oil should be included on the check list with sun glasses and reading glasses, if necessary. Picture yourself trying to fly a plane and reaching into an inside pocket while harnessed in both a chute and seat straps. Next time you'll remember the reading glasses or handkerchief, and have them within easy reach.

Sun glasses are an important item and should receive serious consideration. Optical glass is the best; plastic scratches. Personal preference does enter into the selection of color, but once a person gets used to the brilliance of yellow flying or shooting glasses he won't use anything else. The yellow does brighten everything, but they filter out the objectionable wave lengths that cause eye strain and squinting problems. They give better penetration in haze conditions by increasing contrast of objects. The bird shooter uses them because his eyes must make split-second decisions about dark birds flying against dark foliage. Yellow glasses actually improve visibility late in the day; they improve contrast in shadow areas, expanding the pilot's ability to observe.

Now that we've looked at the head, let's consider the feet. If the cross-country flight is traversing rough country, the pilot might be called upon to do some rather arduous hiking to get to a telephone. Zippered flight boots make excellent footwear. They'll keep you warm at altitude, and they're light and flexible, allowing for feel of the rudder pedals. They afford foot and ankle protection for walking in all kinds of country. Another consideration should be a simple first-aid kit. Special tools for taking the glider apart should be carried on the flight, but stowed securely. Should a sudden storm arise it would be inadvisable to wait for your crew to come to disassemble the plane. Getting the wings off can spell the difference between damage and no damage. Tie-downs are a must. You should never leave a plane unattended without them. Face the plane into the wind, dive brakes extended and tied down. If you lack a hammer, a rock will serve to drive the pegs.

Some pilots who fly over rough country carry aluminum sleeping bags that fold to the size of a paperback book. Food must be considered. A sandwich after five hours in the air will taste like a good steak, and water carried in a collapsible container will taste like vintage wine. Once again, the amount will depend on the character of the country.

The food should be a variety that will keep well. Small packets of raisins are a source of fast energy.

Water produces another problem: bladder care for the male pilot. There are plastic "human element range extenders" that can be bought at any aircraft supply house. Just what the ladies do is beyond this author. In either case, consider this need before the flight starts.

Don't forget money, credit cards, and plenty of dimes for the pay phone. Be sure to carry an ample supply of singles; a farm boy can do a lot of work for a small bill.

Organize the stowing of all this gear before the day of the flight. A vital must: don't stow anything loose behind your head. Many a pilot has been seriously hurt by flying objects in the cockpit. Make sure that gear will not slip to where it can't be reached or where it will jam controls. If for any reason you have to loosen the shoulder harness in flight, remember to tightly refasten it before you forget. Pilots have been hurt on hard landings because they forgot this rule.

Make a check list for the trailer and tow car to assure their readiness to roll at a moment's notice, complete with essential tools and gadgets. The list should be checked again after the retrieve to avoid leaving anything behind in the farmer's yard.

THE TASK

The first cross-country flights should be over easy country, not too ambitious. Several different flights should be planned and marked out on a sectional chart well in advance of the day of the flight; triangle flights, out and returns, and out and land for silver distance should all be considered. You should become familiar with each course, traveling over it, if possible, by car or airplane. Mark off the mileage, note compass headings, and "fly" it with your pencil right on the chart.

It's not too realistic to choose the flight that you would like to do and hope the weather will conform. Gather all the weather data you can on the day of the flight, then make your decision. For example: if the wind is strong and the thermals are weak, only going to 2,500 feet, you'll have a difficult time going against the wind. On such a day triangles are going to be difficult to complete, but outs or out and returns going parallel to the wind will make sense.

If the day looks good and the triangular course is selected, the upwind leg should be flown during the part of the day that will produce the best lift. If the day looks as though it's going to start feebly but have improving conditions later, the first leg should be downwind. The first flights should be short so you won't have to contend with fading conditions during the late part of the day. Plan to be in the air during the best thermaling time.

Fly over topographical areas that will help you. Hills and mountains are good lift regions. Low marsh ground and areas downwind of industrial areas should be avoided since they'll be poor producers.

Once you assess the situation and make your decision, take off and fly around. Test the thermals and the wind, and be ready to reevaluate the situation, a preflight decision. Weathermen have been known to be wrong. If the decision is to go cross-country, keep assessing the conditions. If they deteriorate it'll make more sense to change the task and get back home than to blithely go on to an off-field landing.

If there is a marked inversion below where the clouds top out, they'll spread out and cover the sky. This overdevelopment will cut off the sun and stop the production of thermals. As the clouds evaporate or burn off, thermals will start again. Many a contest has been won by the smart pilot who recognized this as overdevelopment, not general deterioration, and deviated from the course to find a ridge on which to sit it out, waiting for the recycling to take place. The tasks should be thought out on the ground; make up conditions and "fly" the pencil courses on your chart. But also be ready to do some thinking in the cockpit.

All is ready. Weather has been checked and is ideal; a cold front passed through the area the night before. A steady northwesterly flow that spells good soaring in the area has been predicted.

At noon the ground heating will have taken effect, and the moisture content of the ground is just right. This gives plenty of time for the planned 40-mile Silver Badge distance flight. The flight plan will be downwind to take advantage of wind drift.

At release from tow the immediate objective is to gain altitude and ascertain weather and wind conditions aloft. Radio to the crew, set your plane to the compass heading, and go out on course. Expect to feel uneasy until you have reached a point of no return. This feeling will not be a new one, except for you. Every pilot has had it. But then an interesting thing happens: the feeling disappears as you get busy making decisions one by one as they're needed.

The first 5 miles will go quickly. You'll be familiar with the terrain; then towns, railroads, major highways, reservoirs, etc., will appear just as the chart says. Major landmarks should be checked off as you go, so if the chart reading does become confusing you will be looking for landmarks ahead and not behind. There will be periods when you are not absolutely sure of your position. Fly on, it'll work itself out if you don't panic, and there is no need for that. The worst you'll have to do is land when the time comes and ask the farmer where you are.

ALTITUDE CHECK LIST

There are three altitude checkpoints to remember, and each should initiate certain decisions.

Three thousand feet. Even in poor conditions you would still have a half hour of flying time left, but in our simulated flight, conditions are good. This altitude checkpoint is a terrain check. For example, if there were miles and miles of wooded area ahead on the course it would be advisable to search for lift before you flew over the area. This would be playing it safe, but in general at 3,000 feet you can afford to remain on course.

The 2,000 marker will call for another decision. Fly to good potential landing terrain. Fly off course if necessary and then search for lift. If you do deviate, do not fly into blue sky if it can be avoided. Go in the direction of cumulus or patchy cloud cover. Ridges become an important part of cross-country flying at this juncture. Check the wind direction; see if a nearby ridge lies perpendicular to it for potential ridge lift. The ridge could save you from landing; remember its sunny side is a good source for thermals and could get you up and off again. Make a mental note of all the good landing areas.

By time you have reached the 1,000-foot altitude checkpoint, a landing site should have been selected. We'll discuss this further when we're about to land in this simulated flight.

When you acquire more skill it will be feasible to continue the search for lift at this altitude. As a beginner you should not enter the landing pattern at an altitude lower than 800 feet.

Fix these altitude checkpoints firmly in mind, and we'll continue cross-country flight.

SPEED TO FLY

In contest flying, ground distance and speed are of equal importance. In cross-country flying, the object is to get there. Since the distance is covered by a series of climbs and glides, the speed of the glide to obtain maximum performance must be considered. The climb speed will be slightly over minimum sink speed. The

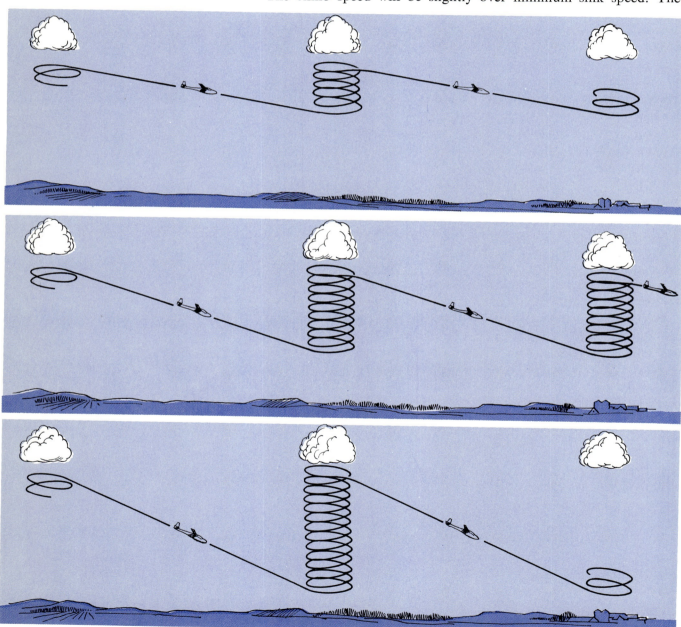

glide between thermals is the cross-country component, and is the subject of much discussion among soaring pilots. In general most planes will fly as far or farther by cruising at a relatively slow speed, approximately 10 miles faster than the maximum glide ratio, especially in low-performance planes similar to the one in our simulated flight.

Visualize the flight path. We will assume that the thermals are equidistant. Flying between them at 80 mph will make the ground coverage excellent, but it will necessitate climbing longer in the next thermal to get back to altitude. Fast flying costs altitude and thermals are smaller and harder to find at low level.

It's evident that altitude loss will be lessened by flying slowly, and you will be catching the thermals higher. This will require a shorter climbing time, but there won't be much over-the-ground coverage. The optimum flying speed will be somewhere between the two.

Obviously, cruising speed is never below the best glide-angle speed, and the maximum speed should not have a sink rate that is so high that you'll be on the ground before the next thermal is reached.

When the conditions are strong, faster cruising speeds are in order because with more and stronger thermals on your flight path you'll be able to regain altitude quickly and without wasting altitude in the search. If conditions are weak, cruising speed should be slowed to just above the best L/D speed.

Sometimes the mathematics of this game lead our thinking astray. For example, if we were flying at 40 mph into a 20-mph head wind, our over-the-ground coverage would be 20 miles in an hour's flight. But if we increased the speed to as much as 70 mph,

Opposite page, three examples of flying speed are shown. The time interval in all three cases is the same. Slow flight, top drawing, took us as far as fast flight, bottom drawing, and left us at a higher altitude in order to go on. Too much time must be consumed climbing in fast flight (bottom drawing). Middle drawing, which shows compromise between slow and very fast flying, proves to be fastest cross-country technique

If you fly too fast against the wind between thermals, you will have to spend a longer time climbing; and all the time you are climbing, you are being drifted backward. By flying slower and catching the thermals higher, you save time

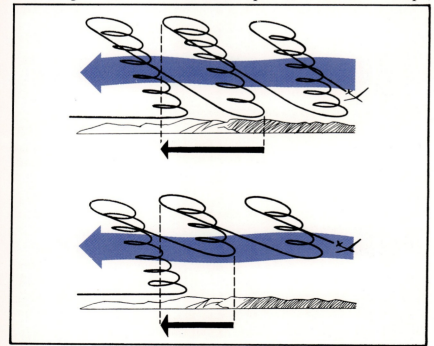

the numbers say we'd more than double the ground coverage to 50 miles. True, the ground speed against the wind is increased with an increase of air speed, but the increased rate of sink will cause loss of altitude. Now since the plane has gotten so low, it must climb longer in the thermal, consuming more time to regain altitude. Also, because of the longer climbing time the head wind has a longer time to drift the thermal and the plane backward. Although the numbers say over-the-ground coverage would be 50 mph, it won't work out that way. Against the wind, increasing the speed 5 to 10 mph should be about right for a low-performance sailplane.

STOPPING FOR FUEL

The weather conditions should indicate to the pilot how to determine his height bands. These bands relate to the strength of the thermal he will select while cruising at a given altitude. For example, if cloud base is 5,500 feet, he should arbitrarily decide that above 4,000 feet he won't stop for a thermal that won't produce at least 500 feet per minute of lift. At 3,000 feet he should only consider stopping for thermals that can produce lift of 300 feet per minute. At 2,000 feet he's no longer choosy; any lift will do. Differing conditions will elicit band strata determinations.

ACTUAL CLIMB

Certain assumptions can be made. In the area of your flight, providing conditions do not change, all the thermals will be of the same strength if you catch them at the time of their greatest output. That means while in flight that your next thermal could be as strong as your last one. Just how strong was the last one? There are two ways to measure it. One is by rule of thumb. Experienced pilots assume that one-half to three-quarters of the vario reading is the actual rate of climb. A more accurate means of calculating it is by a stop watch. As the pilot enters a thermal he starts the stop watch and notes his altitude. At the end of a minute the difference on the altimeter will be his actual rate of climb.

A direct correlation can be made between rate of climb and speed to fly between thermals. The stronger the lift, the faster flight can be made between thermals, but this will depend on the flight performance of any given plane.

A speed ring can be used with a linear scale variometer (constant spacing on the dial between the 100 feet per unit markings) such as the 1,000 feet per minute PZL, or Winter. Once calculated, the vario will give the pilot a direct reading of the speed to fly for any given rate of climb.

Making the speed ring is an involved mathematical procedure and is only essential for serious competition in high-performance planes. There are variometer–air speed combination instruments, factory-calibrated for any design plane, that show the correct speed to fly between thermals. A dial is set for the average amount of lift obtained in the thermals. Then the instrument indicates the speed to fly in the varying amounts of sink that are encountered between thermals. This takes the guesswork out of figuring the most efficient cruising speed, but it doesn't figure in wind speed and direction.

A high-performance sailplane has a low rate of sink while thermaling and a flat glide ratio at high speeds. A low-performance plane usually has a very low rate of sink while thermaling, but at high speeds its sink rate increases rapidly. It usually does not pay to use a speed ring in a low-performance plane; it's simpler to just apply the rule of thumb: use 10 mph above the best L/D speed between thermals as a base. In heavy sink that speed should be increased by 5 mph to get out of the down air fast. In extremely strong lift, an extra 5- to 10-mile increase can be used in order to take advantage of the excellent conditions.

THE SPEED TO FLY, BY RULE OF THUMB

A LOOK AT THE NUMBERS

Soaring is not a precise sport, and that's why it's so fascinating. There are many mathematical formulas for determining speed to fly. To arrive at them, assumptions have had to be introduced into the equations, and then the precision part of it all goes up in hot air. For example, the mathematics of the speed ring, which we spared you, assumes that the strength of all thermals at a given time is equal, that you fly into them when they are building at an equal rate, and that you can find them in the first place.

A book could be produced by interviewing the 150 top competition pilots and analyzing their speed-to-fly system. Their subjective judgments about their mathematics would make interesting reading. More could be learned from the judgments than the mathematics. Some use complicated mathematical systems and some use none at all. But there is one thing they will all agree upon when they are discussing the beginner. The beginner flies too slowly. He has a tendency to fly slow in order to conserve altitude. The accompanying table will show you the price paid for speed. These figures are for a 1-26, which is the Schweizer low-performance single-seater.

SPEED TO FLY

COLUMN 1	COLUMN 2 Cost in feet per minute	COLUMN 3 Minutes for 1 mile	COLUMN 4 Cost in feet per mile	COLUMN 5
mph				L/D
35	159	1.73	275	19.2
40	162	1.5	243	21.7
45	174	1.33	231	22.8
50	192	1.2	230	22.9
55	216	1.09	235	22.4
60	246	1	246	21.4
65	282	0.923	259	20.4
70	327	0.857	278	18.9
75	378	0.8	302	17.4
80	435	0.75	325	16.2
85	498	0.706	348	15.1
90	570	0.666	379	13.9

DATA: still air

Mull these figures over. They will give you a mathematical "feel" of a sailplane's performance.

First, here is how they were derived, so you can work them out for any sailplane. Each manufacturer supplies with his ship a polar curve which demonstrates the sailplane's performance, feet per minute lost at flying speeds in increments of 5 mph. This is Column 2 in the table. Multiplying feet lost per minute by the time required to fly a mile, Column 3, gives feet lost per mile, Column 4. Dividing Column 4 figures into 5,280 (feet per mile) will give you the L/D of the ship at each speed increment, Column 5.

Unfortunately, it's Column 2 that the beginner becomes familiar with first. He gets these figures with the sailplane, and the talk is always about L/D even before he gets to know its real significance. Scan Column 2. These figures indicate that the slower you fly, the longer you will stay up. For example, the beginner will see from Column 2 that if he flies at 65 mph, he'll lose 282 feet a minute. Common sense tells him that if he flies at 50 mph—the best L/D (22.9 in Column 5)—he'll only lose 192 feet per minute. This will be a saving of 90 feet; sounds like it makes sense. Now look up the loss in feet per mile for 50 mph and 65 mph in Column 4. The difference between 230 feet at 50 mph and 259 feet at 65 mph is only 29 feet per mile. For the extra speed, that's not much of a loss. Try another one. Flying at 45 mph will cost you 231 feet per mile, Column 4; flying at 55 mph will cost 235 feet, only a 4-foot loss per mile, but you'll go 10 miles farther in the hour. An extra gain of 240 feet in one good thermal will make up that difference, and that'll only cost you a few minutes.

The culprit in all this is Column 2, the one everybody sees. It inhibits the beginner. Psychologically, it would be better if the student pilot never saw these figures from the polar curve. Loss in feet per minute demonstrates a sailplane's performance and is a way of making comparisons between designs. Loss per mile tells a different story and will help the pilot fly his plane better.

A pilot should always be more interested in how far he can go than how long he can stay up. What Column 2 will show is that above 65 mph the performance of the sailplane falls off rapidly.

Take out your pencil and pad and play with these numbers, and they'll give you a feel for the relationship of speed, miles to go, and altitude loss. It'll pay off in your cross-country flying.

THE FLIGHT CONTINUES

It's important to keep a constant check on the strength of the thermals and how well you are doing in them. Let's assume the vario reads 600 feet per minute up. As you enter a thermal, start the sweep hand on the stop watch and check the initial altitude. After a minute, if your calculations show you are actually averaging 500 feet a minute lift, you can anticipate the strength of the next thermal and you can ignore anything less by flying through it. If you note the thermals getting weaker you'll have to adjust your thinking, accept less, and fly slower. If they are getting stronger you can afford to fly faster.

If your speed is fast, take advantage of it when you enter the thermal. Don't slow up and bank the plane into it. Instead, pull back on the stick and zoom up into it. Trade off your speed for altitude. Then as the speed is reduced, rack the plane over to thermaling speed. This way you stay in the thermal by going up its core. A bank at high speed might fly you right out the other side, and you'll waste valuable time relocating it.

In like manner, there is a trick to leaving a thermal. When you have decided that you want to leave it because it's petered out or you've reached the top or cloud base, don't just bank away and head on course. Remember, on the outer extremities of the thermal there is heavy down air. Go to the far side of the thermal, away from the course direction. When you are on this opposite side, bank the plane very sharply and increase your speed as you fly right through the center of it. Then fly off on course. It's better to gain the necessary speed in lift than in down. In this way you are getting one more useful thrust from the lift.

THE ALTIMETER

The altimeter should be set for the elevation of the takeoff field above sea level (ASL) for cross-country flying. For a beginner, during local flying the altimeter is usually set for zero, so that when it reads 900 feet the pilot should be starting to think landing pattern. Since the landing will now be at a different site and elevation from takeoff, it will be necessary to set the altimeter at the takeoff altitude above sea level. This will add a constant to the altitude readings. Under the name of every airport on the chart is a series of numbers printed in brown. The first number is the elevation above sea level and the second is the length of the longest runway, in hundreds of feet. If it is followed by a "U" the airport has Unicom radio, 122.8 VHF frequency.

If your flight is terminated at an airport, you will know its altitude above sea level from the chart. By subtracting the field height from your altimeter reading you'll learn approximately how high you are above the ground. This will make the starting point of the landing pattern easy. There will be a small error if the barometric pressure is different than it is in the area of takeoff, but in sailplane navigation this isn't too important. All during the cross-country flight altitude should be computed by subtracting chart elevations from the altimeter readings.

It's important to have a general idea of land elevation on the planned flight. For example: At Wurtsboro Airport, a very active soaring center in the eastern part of New York, the field elevation is 560 feet above sea level. If you fly east or southeast the elevations of the surrounding fields vary from 520 to 350. But if you fly west only a matter of 10 miles or so the field elevations are 1,440, 1,560 and 1,685 feet above sea level. Flying at 3,200 feet is fine if you're flying east, but to the west at the same altitude you'd better have a landing site available. If your altimeter reads 3,200 you could only be 1,515 feet above a landing field. Don't let the altimeter give you a false sense of security.

From the navigation chart's color key, contour markings, and the altitude notations of specific locations, it's possible to make a quick calculation of ground elevation above sea level. Using what you find on the chart and what you see from the cockpit will enable you to estimate it within a few hundred feet. By subtracting that guesstimate from your altimeter reading, you'll get a good idea how high you are above the ground. As you gain experience you won't go through the calculations, you'll eyeball it and come rather close. This all becomes important for cross-country off-field landings and estimating how far you can still go.

TO GO OR NOT TO GO?

That is the question. How far can the pilot go cross-country and still make either a safe return or continue on course toward his next landing area? The problem the beginner has is his lack of assurance about how far he can go if he runs into prolonged sink or has wind problems. It's not a blind decision, and here is how it is made. Airports and good landing areas should be figured out and marked on the chart. (This might require making the planned trip by car or airplane to see the off-field landing areas.) The distances between landing sites should be measured in miles and marked on the chart. The pilot will then always know how far he is from a landing area. For the beginner the arrival over any landing area must be at least 1,000 feet above the ground to provide for a normal landing pattern.

We know from the manufacturer what the L/D of the sailplane is. Let's assume that it's 26 to 1. That means in still air the plane will go 26,000 feet cross-country for every 1,000 feet of altitude lost. That's almost 5 miles, but remember it's flying under optimum conditions in still air. How do we figure a head wind, tail wind, or flying through sinking air? By adjusting the L/D figure to a safe margin, a table can be made that will show at a glance in flight what altitude is necessary to reach a specific destination. For the beginner, cut the plane's rated L/D in half. Instead of 26 it'll now be 13 to 1, or 13,000 feet cross-country for every 1,000 feet lost. That will take care of the sink problems, since we're only calculating the performance at half.

By dividing 13 into 5,280, you come up with a figure in feet that represents the altitude lost for every mile covered. For one-half this particular ship's L/D it costs you 406 feet of altitude to make a mile. Add to that 1,000 feet for landing, plus the altitude the landing area is above sea level. The figure you get will represent the altimeter reading necessary to fly 1 mile. Now, for every remaining mile add 406 feet to that figure.

Here is the way you'd go about making and using the table for a typical flight. We'll assume a 10-mile-an-hour wind.

On a 3-by-5 card make four columns. The first column represents miles to go; the second, no wind; third, 10-mph head wind; the fourth, 10-mph tail wind.

Calibrate the first column from 1 to 15 miles.

The second column, no wind, will be the total loss in feet for every mile up to 15 using L/D of 13 to 1, plus the 1,000 feet for landing.

The third column, bucking a head wind, should be figures for each mile at lower L/D, for instance 10 to 1. Add 1,000 feet for landing.

The fourth column, tail wind, should be figured for each mile at a higher L/D since a tail wind will help you; use 15 to 1, plus 1,000 feet for landing.

The card would then be used in conjunction with the navigation chart. Compute how many miles you have to go to the next safe landing area. Find out the altitude above sea level of this landing area. Decide which wind condition on the card fits your flying conditions. The no-wind column should be used when flying crosswind, since it will not significantly help or hinder.

The figure in feet from the correct column, plus the altitude of the landing area above sea level, will enable you to make your decision on whether or not to go. The chart will tell you the altitude necessary, and your altimeter will tell you the altitude you have.

It will take a little time to check the card out and see if your L/D assumptions are correct. This can be done flying locally around your airport under different conditions. At first, it's best to underestimate your performance. With more experience, you'll find you can assume a higher L/D for your calculations.

The table assumes the worst . . . no more lift will be encountered.

Miles to go	Altitude needed AGL flying crosswind or in no wind	Altitude AGL; assume 10-mph head wind	Altitude AGL; assume 10-mph tail wind
1	1,406	1,528	1,352
2	1,812	2,056	1,704
3	2,218	2,584	2,056
4	2,624	3,112	2,408
5	3,030	3,640	2,760
6	3,436	4,168	3,112
7	3,842	4,696	3,464
8	4,248	5,224	3,816
9	4,654	5,752	4,168
10	5,060	6,280	4,520
11	5,466	6,808	4,872
12	5,872	7,336	5,224
13	6,278	7,864	5,576
14	6,684	8,392	5,928
15	7,090	8,920	6,280

"GLANCE" THINKING

Glance reading of the panel is an important technique to learn. The idea is to not concentrate on any one instrument and neglect another. In like manner, no one problem in cross-country flying should become more important than another. Beginners have a tendency to work over their chart too much.

It's important to develop a scanning technique for all the problems that have to be considered. It's a matter of practicing rotation, allowing the situation or an instrument to determine the order of consideration. For example, if you're getting low, it's more important to concentrate on finding lift than on locating your position on the chart. Once you are above 4,000 feet and on course you can stop and take time to enjoy the grand perspective below. But usually your mind will be busy . . .

Centering on the thermal . . . keeping it centered . . . reducing the amount of bank and then racking over hard to stay in its strongest lift . . .

Deciding whether to take a thermal or to let it go by . . . where the next thermal will be . . . watching the ground to ascertain what areas might be the best producers . . . deciding what's directly ahead on course . . . which way to deviate to find the best conditions . . . remembering to try the heat off a highway and figuring the angle necessary to catch it . . . keeping in mind that planes often kick thermals off of small airports or trucks can do the same off of roads . . . shopping centers with large areas of blacktop are good producers . . . using a ridge and waiting for conditions to improve . . .

Starting the stop watch and calculating actual climb . . . deciding what is happening to the strength of the lift . . . whether conditions call for faster or slower speeds between thermals . . .

Watching the yaw string . . . feeling the ship . . . a lifting of a wing . . . the buffeting of the wind that should warn you not to get too slow . . . listening to air speed as well as watching the air speed indicator . . .

Navigating . . . keeping a running account on the chart to show the progress . . . watching the amount of wind drift and making the corrections . . . keeping track of the winds aloft . . . deciding the best air speed to fly for given winds . . . recognizing landmarks and establishing the course by a series of them . . . being ready to change the course if conditions warrant it . . .

Constantly checking surface wind direction . . . watching the altitude . . . height above the ground . . . observing the terrain . . . keeping a sharp eye out for areas that are good potential landing sites . . . deciding whether to divert to good landing areas or stay on course . . .

Calling the crew and giving instructions . . . constantly watching for general weather deterioration or improvement . . . watching for the development of cloud streets . . . deciding if cumulus clouds are active or dead . . . noting wisps and seeing if they are growing or dissolving . . .

Eating and drinking . . . moving around to keep from getting too stiff . . . adjusting the ventilation. . . .

There are a hundred and one things that will be thought about on a cross-country flight. Changing one's thinking and keeping the flight plan flexible is one of the most important. Flying into an area that has deteriorated because it's on one's course will only lead to an early landing. If you're low you will need certain facts; if high you'll need others. Certain problems will take constant attention in one sort of condition and not even come to mind in other circumstances.

The correct attitude is to take nothing for granted until you have the answer; then don't let that become an assumption for a decision later in the flight. There will be very few minutes in a cross-country flight when some sort of a decision is not being made about some phase of the flight. The point is that cross-country flying is not an idle sport. The pilot must be constantly alert and direct his attention to his next problem. But he must always know what his next problem is going to be.

Up to this point, we have used many skills in our cross-country flight: soaring ability, navigation, meteorology, and some in-flight logic. The major concern of beginners is the landing away from the home base.

If the destination is another airport and it is reached, there is little one has to know over and above what we have already discussed. Give yourself plenty of time before you enter the pattern to check your chart and find out the elevation of the field, for example 560 ASL. Add 1,000 feet to that field elevation. Now when your altimeter reads 1,560 you should be maneuvering into the start of the landing pattern. Prior to reaching the pattern altitude, crack the dive breaks open to check them out; it's a good precaution. Lock them closed and proceed with the pattern.

The new airport will have a wind sock or landing "T" which will show the landing direction in use at the time. The sock will not only show wind direction, it will also give a general idea of wind velocity. A sock that stands straight out indicates a wind velocity of at least 25 mph. If it is standing only halfway out it indicates 10 to 15 mph, and a flopping sock tells you there's no appreciable wind. The rule is to fly "into the tail of the sock" on the final leg of the landing pattern. Then you'll be landing into the wind. The rule for the "T" is to fly with its "wings" in the same direction as the wings of the plane. The stem of the "T" indicates the fuselage of the plane.

CROSS-COUNTRY LANDINGS

Rocks or markers indicate the pattern called for. Drawing on left indicates a left-hand pattern in either direction; that on right calls for a right-hand pattern. At some airports, because of an obstruction, a left-hand pattern will be indicated in one direction, and a right-hand pattern in the other

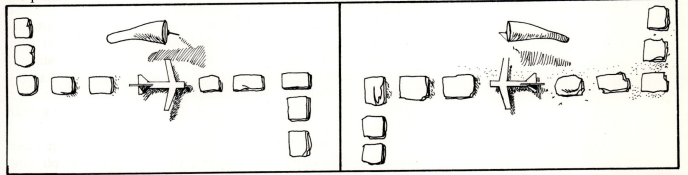

A left-hand landing pattern is standing procedure. Look for pattern indicators around the wind sock for special landing instructions. If an orange light is lit on top of the operations tower it indicates a right-hand pattern. And if you have no radio and see a plane in the landing pattern ahead of you, use the same landing direction he is using, no matter what you think the pattern should be.

Many of the fields you'll be using have Unicom; switch to channel 122.8 and call for landing instructions. Identify your plane by its N number and tell them you're a sailplane. Also ask for surface wind velocity and direction.

They will reply, identifying the runway to use by the first two numbers of the compass reading. For example, if they reply "Use runway 33," you will set up your pattern so that the final leg will be on a compass reading of 330 degrees. If they tell you 5, the final will be on a 50-degree heading. The runways are usually marked with large numbers. An "X" means the runway is closed. It's not necessary to use the hardtop. You can use the grass strip parallel to it. Remember, once you have touched down apply rudder to steer and taxi out of the way.

Landing rules at an airport where you are not under tower control give the lowest plane in the pattern the right of way. Sailplanes are so maneuverable that they can easily drop in ahead of a power plane . . . don't, take your turn. Never cut ahead of another plane.

The rule book says that balloons have the right of way over sailplanes. It is doubtful that you'll ever be vying with a balloon in your landing patterns, but sailplanes do have the right of way over powered craft. Put no faith in this rule; never argue the point.

The landing pattern is the "roadway" for all craft in the area. You should always assume when you are in a pattern that another plane is behind you.

LANDING SITE . . . FARMER'S PASTURE

Every off-field landing must be considered an emergency landing. That doesn't mean it *is* an emergency, it means that the pilot must make certain determinations and decisions as though it were.

If there is any one factor that causes landing problems it's that the landing decision was made too late. Hasty decisions affect judgment and cause panic.

There are a few problems that beginners often encounter. Once they select a field they tend to set up the landing pattern too close to it. Flying over the field to observe the conditions, they are reluctant to fly back far enough to set up a good pattern. This shortens the pattern legs and thereby shortens the flying time on each leg. Now things are going to be happening faster. The extra few seconds on each leg will give you just that much more time to take matters one at a time. Make the pattern the same as the one you used at the home base.

All through the cross-country flight the pilot experiences an atmosphere of relative silence. When the dive brakes are extended there is a new feel to the ship, but even more important a loud rushing sound. The sound itself can be rather exhilarating and can heighten the excitement for the inexperienced pilot. Relax and stay alert, that's the best way to fly a pattern.

SURFACE WIND

The direction and velocity of the surface wind is an important thing to know when planning a landing in a farmer's field. Its direction might be completely different from what it was at the takeoff site. Smoke is the best indicator. Flags are good. Trees will show wind direction, so will crops such as corn. Large bodies of water will show wind direction; the windward side will be calm. They will also show gustiness by surface ripples and swirls. Clouds can give an indication by their moving shadows, but this can be deceptive. Winds aloft are often different from surface winds.

If the wind is strong, search for a landing field by flying downwind if possible; you will have a longer glide downwind than against a head wind. Once you locate it, observe it from the upwind side to avoid drifting.

All landings should be made as close as possible into the wind. The advantage gained is the ability to make steeper descents on the final leg into a short field, and the roll-out ground speed will be slower. Sloping terrain is the only exception. A sailplane should always be landed up the slope no matter what the wind direction may be. If you attempt to land down the slope and the slope falls off at the same angle as the plane's glide angle, it will never touch down.

When the pilot ascertains the wind direction he should scan the adjacent area to judge whether or not a ridge, trees, or buildings might cause turbulence, eddies, and wind gradient effects. This will help him determine landing speed.

SELECTION OF THE FIELD

Fields near main highways usually have power and telephone wires that are often hard to see from 1,500 feet. Roadways leading to farm houses usually have utility wires going up the driveway or cutting across the field. Keep a sharp eye out for them. Fields with ponds will have a slope toward the water. Very often a farmer will keep livestock in a field that has a pond. Land there only as a last resort, especially if you have a fabric plane. Cattle can do a lot of damage to a sailplane. A good fact to remember about cattle is that they will stand in a field with their back to the wind; some pilots refer to them as leather-covered wind socks.

Pick a field 5 or 6 miles out of towns and villages if possible. If you land near a small town the word spreads quickly that a plane has just crashed and every kid and his brother will assemble to view the corpse. The fire department, police, and anyone else who has nothing better to do will be out tramping over the poor farmer's field. The amount of damage your plane will do is minimal; a hundred pairs of feet is another matter.

The size of the field you can use depends on its direction in relation to the wind and obstructions. High trees present a problem since plenty of clearance will be necessary. A tree-lined field will have to be longer than one where you could just skim over the fence and touch down. If you have a choice of two fields, one with trees and one without, in a moderate wind it would be better to take the longer crosswind final without trees than a shorter run into the wind with trees.

Get used to seeing your home field from different altitudes and keep the image in mind. This will help you determine length, which is very difficult to ascertain from the air. Telegraph poles can be used as a yardstick.

In different parts of the country the poles are spaced differently. Get to know what the spacing is in your locale. Poles can be used to measure off fields. If they are 300 feet apart and you see a landing field that looks good but are not sure of its length, lay your finger up at arm's length as an artist does and measure off six poles. Then measure off the field; six poles and you have a whole airport at your disposal.

COLOR

Color becomes an important part of field selection. Get to know the crops in your locale as you drive your car through the countryside. Dry plowed fields are light brown, dark when wet. Peas and short crops are brownish green; corn is dark green and can be destructive to a sailplane. Tall hay is greenish brown, short hay is brown. A worked field is better than one that is fallow. A worked field usually has a uniform color. A farmer will plow and plant around rock areas, and they can easily be seen by the color difference. Dried-up streams are visible against the uniform color of a worked field, and so are ditches. A green line across a field could mean a single strand barbed-wire fence or ground moisture; stay away. Circles of green or any other irregularities could mean that the farmer's machinery couldn't get to a place. There could be rocks or a stump there, and the place should be avoided.

If you have a choice, take a plowed field; it will present no surprises. Some plowed fields are very hard, but the most they will do is scratch the nose of the ship. You will stop fast and that's good. Long roll-outs on an unknown field present unknown problems. Freshly mowed fields make excellent landing areas, except for woodchuck holes. Many pilots prefer them, but from the air it's hard to decide if the grass is 2 inches or 2 feet high. High grass will catch a wing and cause a ground loop.

The roll of the land is crucial to the final touchdown. There are many signs to help you discern the contours of the surface. The tops of a line of woods, railroad and road cuts, late-afternoon shadows, work roads will all show ground roll. Again color can be used. Crops are sometimes deeper-colored in low areas that retain moisture. Color will show ditches, and land often rolls toward the ditch. Fence posts are good last-minute indicators. If there is any uncertainty, you should always carry a little extra speed so you can hold off the ground and avoid some of the rough spots that were not discernible earlier.

Once the pattern is established, land. Ignore any lift you encounter. Land!

If there is a question about a field and you have a choice of two that are next to each other, set up the pattern so a decision can be made while you are in the pattern. Plan the pattern as a compromise between the two fields. By the time you are on the base leg the decision should have been made. Stick to it! There is an old adage among soaring pilots. If you touch the wheel to the ground, you'll walk away from the landing. The fellow who delays too long gets into trouble. If he slows up to get a better look, it could be his last. While that close to the ground, there are more important things to do than see if there are a few rocks in the field.

Some good tips can be gleaned from hangar talk about off-field landings. Some pilots include some other factors in their final decision. They'll pick a farm that has a good house, possibly a swimming pool, TV, and electricity, conjecturing that the inhabitants will be a little more worldly and less apt to be upset by this happening. Pick a spot that is easier on the ship than on the crew. Of course, if you have a choice and can land near a gate, take it.

COMMITTED TO LAND

If you must come in over an obstacle on the final leg on a very short field, make the obstacle the primary consideration. Dive for the base of the obstacle. That guarantees adequate speed. Watch the obstacle fall lower and lower on the canopy until you know you are going to pass over it; then open spoilers and dive brakes fully as you pass it. Start the flairout and you'll slow up and be in a position for a short glide to touchdown. As you settle on the ground apply the wheel brake to stop the roll.

OBSTACLES

When the flight is over and the wing is touched down, take care of the plane immediately. Face the sailplane so that the lowered wing is toward the wind, put your parachute on that wing to hold it down, and extend the dive brakes. Tie it down with the tie-down equipment you've brought along. If there is any danger of a real storm coming up, get the wings off as soon as possible. When the sailplane is secured go off and seek a phone to call the crew. Be sure to pinpoint your location with absolute accuracy before you call. Also remember to give the crew your phone number.

Be friendly, no matter what the farmer's first words are. After all, he didn't invite you to use his field. Pilots report that most farmers are fascinated by the whole thing, and are not only interested but will give a helping hand. The farmer will like it too if you show interest in his farm. Most farmers are tolerant of minor crop damage, but if the damage is extensive your insurance will cover it. Don't try to settle such a matter; it might prejudice a claim if the pilot makes the admission of liability. Of course, an offer of $5 or

ON THE GROUND

$10 for the use of the field as a landing area might settle the whole matter. It's rare that there will be trouble. What you usually get is an invitation to supper. Try to keep onlookers away. If a swarm of kids invades the scene, hire the biggest kid for a buck to fend off the smaller ones. Rubbernecks can be more destructive to the farmer's field than the landing of the sailplane.

You're going to enjoy the success of the first cross-country flights and find that from here on even your local flying will be oriented toward cross-country tasks. By continually testing the weather and your plane and getting the feel of both, extended cross-countries can be made.

As you gain experience you'll naturally wonder how you would do in a sailplane of higher performance. There is no question that the beginner should fly low-performance gliders. Just when should the beginner step up to a higher-performance ship of over 30 to 1 glide ratio? The transfer can be made after some cross-country flying, and when the pilot has at least 100 hours. It does not have to be made in gradual steps by going into higher- and higher-performance planes. There is a mistaken notion that high-performance planes are difficult to fly. They are not, except for the very exotic ones. High-performance standard-class planes will produce no problems that a 100-hour pilot can't handle. Flying speeds will be relatively faster, and the controls will be more sensitive, but even

AND NOW WHAT?

This is a game. If you were flying right-to-left in this picture, which field would you pick for an off-field landing? Some considerations: Which way is the wind blowing? What are the obstructions? A has surface problems. B looks good; but are you too close for a right-hand pattern? Should you fly past B, then make a full left-hand pattern? C is rough. D has livestock. E is crosswind. So is F, and its too close, besides. G has corn. H is in cultivation and has strong crosswind. K and I look good from here, but have you enough altitude to get a better look? Conclusion: the planning was bad. Now visualize this as if you were flying from left to right. Should you ever allow yourself to get into this situation? One more question: Shouldn't you be over to the left trying to find the thermal that fire is generating?

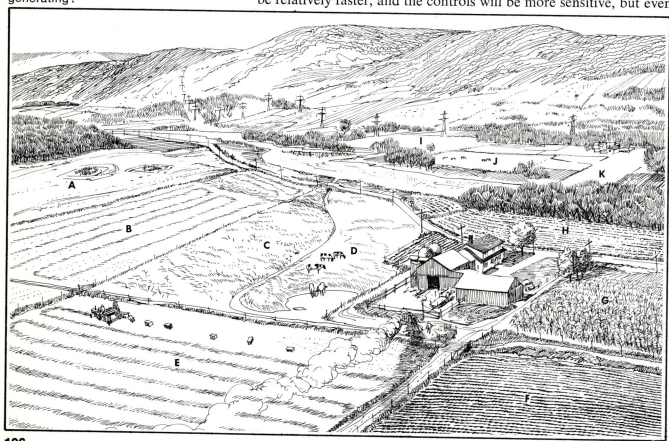

in the latest, cleanest fiberglass ships this feel is grasped immediately. There is one area that should be given special attention. Low-performance sailplanes are very forgiving; they'll practically fly themselves. You'll have to fly a high-performance sailplane more carefully in each maneuver, but all that means is that turns must be coordinated. This will be a different feel for the average beginner. To keep the turn coordinated, some high-performance planes require more rudder or the rudder initiated a fraction of a second before the bank is initiated with the stick. But the yaw string is going to tell you immediately what will be required if you are alerted to this difference of handling; otherwise, you'll skid and slip around and not understand why.

A most satisfactory method of making the transfer to high performance is to have an experienced pilot talk you through the flight by radio from the ground, just to remind you of your new problems. You should not acknowledge any of the radio transmissions from the ground unless told to do so. You should fly the plane. You'll be told when off tow to make a few gentle turns. Then you'll be advised to do a straight-ahead stall to get the feel of the higher stall speed, and you should make a mental note of that speed. Then you'll be told to make steep S turns and to watch the yaw string to sense the amount of rudder needed. That's about all there is to it. The rest of the air work will come naturally, but the voice from the ground will be very comforting. Before you get into the pattern for landing you'll be told to test the dive brakes. Pattern speed will be increased to about 65 to 70 mph. You'll be reminded of that, and also to put the landing gear down if it's retractable. If the plane uses flaps instead of dive brakes or/and spoilers, special landing instruction should be taken. Even good pilots say it takes about 100 hours to learn the characteristics of a new sailplane.

Cross-country flights should not be attempted in a high-performance ship until at least 25 to 30 landings have been made at the home air field, where the landing pattern is known as well as the back of your hand.

Think of going into a high-performance plane this way. If your only driving experience was in a VW and you then were put behind the wheel of a Cadillac, there would be certain things you'd have to learn. The seat position might have to be changed so you could reach the pedals. You'd study the dashboard to get familiar with the instruments, etc., etc. Step by step you'd go through all the controls. Do the same in the cockpit. Take all the time you want. Ask questions, and then dry-fly it on the ground. Hook it up and go.

There will be a lot to learn about high-performance flight, but that's the beauty of this sport—you never stop learning, and new worlds keep opening up.

Whether it's high performance or low, the mechanics of soaring are only one aspect. The big job is acquiring a soaring sense. It's almost magical, and the only way it's acquired is by experience.